# GAIL PORTER
## Laid Bare

EBURY
PRESS

1 3 5 7 9 10 8 6 4 2

Published in 2007 by Ebury Press, an imprint of Ebury Publishing
A Random House Group Company

The Random House Group Limited Reg. No. 954009

Addresses for companies within the Random House Group can be found at
www.randomhouse.co.uk

A CIP catalogue record for this book is available from the British Library

Mixed Sources
Product group from well-managed
forests and other controlled sources
www.fsc.org  Cert no. TT-COC-2139
© 1996 Forest Stewardship Council

Printed and bound in Great Britain by Clays Ltd, St Ives PLC

Hardback ISBN 9780091920401
Export trade paperback ISBN 9780091923082

To buy books by your favourite authors and
register for offers visit www.rbooks.co.uk

*For Honey*
*and my mum*

# Contents

# Prologue
# Crunch Time

I opened my eyes. A harsh white light burned into them and I squeezed them tight shut again. My whole body was tense, lying on a hard, unfamiliar mattress, partly covered with a sheet that felt cold and stiff. I tried to get my hazy thoughts together, to work out where I was. There were noises in the background – a murmur of voices, the sound of footsteps, a door banging, something making a clatter. Closer to me I could hear a regular beeping. My head was hurting, and the beeps seemed to drill into my brain. I became aware of a smell, a sharp, clean smell that made me think of antiseptics, of hospital. Hospital. Along with my senses, shreds of memory were coming back.

I opened my eyes again, blinking as they adjusted to the fluorescent light. I realised that wires were stuck on to my chest, leading to a monitor that was making that bleeping noise. And there was a drip attached to my right arm. I shifted my gaze round to the metal bars of the bedhead, and saw a white card attached to them. There was writing on it. As I squinted sideways at it, the words swam into focus: '24-hour suicide watch'.

Suicide? Me? Oh no...My heart thudded in my chest, my breath came quickly. I must have made a noise as a male nurse came up and touched me on the arm. He said something, but I couldn't make it out. I tried to speak but as I opened my mouth I felt a wave of nausea. The nurse must have realised I was about to throw up, and helped me to sit upright. He held a shiny metal dish to my chin as I vomited bitter bile. He wiped my face, and I had a close-up view of the nametag on his uniform. His name was Kieran, and he was speaking again but I still couldn't make out a word, though I could hear the noise he made when he sucked his teeth. My head was whirling, and I struggled to control the nausea. Every sound erupted in my head: the monitor beeping, the fluorescent light sizzling, Kieran's tooth-sucking. It was like a swarm of bees attacking me.

I tried to get a grip, lying back down on the bed and taking deep breaths. My heartbeat slowed and my breathing quietened down, but then something suddenly clicked in my mind and I jerked upright again, my hands gripping the sheet. Memory was rushing back with a vengeance. I remembered what I'd done, why I was here...

A lot of vodka and a lot of pills – a classic way to end it all. But what the hell had I been thinking? If I'd been thinking at all, that is. I hadn't exactly been doing much self-analysis recently. I was a bundle of confused feelings, anxious and miserable and dreading what each day would bring. I'd been diagnosed with depression, and had been duly prescribed antidepressants – not that I was keen on taking them. I was still working hard, on *Dead Famous*, a show that took me to the States every three weeks. I didn't want to spend so much time away from home, but work's work, and I couldn't pull out. Besides, I've always coped, that's what I do. I've always considered it a sign of failure to ask for help. But I'd never reached such a low point in my life. I had left my husband eight months earlier, and we were both dealing with what that meant. We had our stuff to sort out, our home, our finances, the legal side of things – and above all we had to think of our daughter, Honey, who was only two years old at the time.

Honey. My daughter was at nursery school and her mummy was attached to a drip and a monitor in some hospital. I grew cold as I thought, What if I hadn't made it? How could I have been so selfish, so pathetic, how could I have not been around for my daughter, the person I love most in the world? It didn't make sense. I didn't make sense. I lay on that hospital bed eaten up with guilt and anguish, but at the same time an overwhelming relief washed over me. Help had got to me in time, and I'd never been so grateful for anything in my life.

Lying there on the hospital bed, I had time to think. What would I do when I left hospital? Go back to the same old life and get hooked into the same old treadmill? I realised that no, I wouldn't. I couldn't. This was a wake-up call to end all wake-up calls. For my sake, and the sake of everybody I loved, something had to change, and only I could do that. I would try to work out what had brought me to this point, why my life had gone off the rails, and how I could get it back on track.

There's a saying I've always loved: 'Do one thing every day

that scares you.' That could be me talking, but Eleanor Roosevelt said it first. Canny woman. Those words had always struck a chord with me, kind of 'feel the fear but do it anyway'. Of course I had no way of knowing then that new trials and tribulations lay ahead – I just resolved to give life my best shot. As I'd always tried to do, ever since I was a kid.

# * 1 *

# feel the force!

My story begins a long time ago in a galaxy far, far away…oh, all right then, you got me. In the 1970s, Earth time. And in Edinburgh. Still, my part of the city has a very unScottish-sounding name: Joppa. Wouldn't look out of place among Alderaan, Tatooine and all the other fabulous places in the *Star Wars* universe. That first film in the sci-fi series has a special place in my memory. It burst into my young life with all the force of a dazzling meteor, grabbing my imagination and firing my ambition. I don't suppose that George Lucas was thinking of seven-year-old Scots lasses when he was working out his movie, but he couldn't have had a bigger fan of his imaginary cosmos than me.

I've always liked going to the pictures – they're a gateway into a wonderful, extraordinary world, full of excitement and adventure. But that day in 1978, as I stood in the queue outside the ABC cinema in the Lothian Road, I had no idea what an impact this particular film would make on me, how pivotal it would be. My little brother Keith and I had been vaguely aware of the publicity surrounding it, but we hadn't been that interested to find out much about it in advance. We were just happy that our mum was taking us out as a treat.

The queue was unusually long, and pretty mixed, I remember. Lots of spotty adolescent teenagers, a heavy quota of nerdy sci-fi types, older people and kids like me and Keith. Once we got into the foyer, we saw a stall set up with all kinds of merchandise: badges, posters, little plastic figures and other stuff. This was interesting, and quite a novelty in those days, before the really hard merchandising industry kicked in. Still, Keith and I spared it hardly a glance – the characters didn't mean anything to us then, so we didn't have any kind of allegiance to them. Not yet, anyway.

At last we were settled in our seats, clutching our bags of Revels. The lights went down, the curtain swished away, and after the obligatory boring adverts the main feature came on. The stirring music swelled, and against the infinity of star-spangled space, those immortal words scrolled over the screen: 'It is a period of civil war...' I could figure out most of the back story, understanding that it was a battle between rebel freedom fighters (the good guys – hooray!) and the Galactic Empire (the bad guys – boo!). From the very first scene of a mighty spaceship pursuing a smaller one, we were hooked. For the next two hours we watched open-mouthed as the classic tale unfolded. Brave heroes and evil villains, mysterious Jedi Knights, menacing Darth Vader, cute robots, weird alien creatures, spaceships, epic battles, futuristic gizmos...magic!

What sealed the film for me was Princess Leia. Luke Skywalker may have been the young hero, Han Solo the wisecracking daredevil, Chewbacca his big hairy friend, and Obi Wan Kenobi the wise old mystic – but what thrilled me was Leia. Here was a girl who was heroic too, not just some dumb girl who couldn't do a thing on her own and was always screaming and tripping over a tree root just when she and the hero were being pursued by something nasty. This girl had guts – she was one of the chief freedom fighters, for goodness' sake. She was bright and sassy, and I thought her beautiful, with her long white robe and exotic hairstyle.

When the film ended, my brother and I trailed out into the foyer with our mum. We were stunned, speechless. We had just witnessed the future, I thought.

Then Keith broke the silence. 'Use the force, Gail,' he laughed, poking me in the ribs.

'Yeah,' I said. 'Let's use the force to get Mum to buy us stuff!'

Right, straight to the stall. Time to buy tie-in merchandise. I chose a Princess Leia badge, and a Luke Skywalker one to go with it. Keith went for Han Solo and Chewbacca. From that day onwards, our *Star Wars* collection grew and grew. In fact I recently purchased a replica light sabre from the States. Some things you just can't grow out of – not that I've tried.

Walking home that day, I realised that as well as showing us the future world, the film had decided my own future.

'I'm going to be Princess Leia,' I announced to Mum and Keith.

My brother just laughed. 'You! A princess!'

My mum, ever patient, simply replied, 'That's nice, dear.'

The image of Princess Leia stayed vividly in my mind. She was someone special, and that's what I wanted to be: special. I wanted to be extraordinary, to stand out from the crowd. I longed to be like her, but what could I do? Well, not much at the time. But at least I could copy her hairstyle. I combed out my long hair, parted it into two bunches, wound each one round and round and pinned it into a large bun. My small face must have looked like the filling in an oversized bread roll, seen sideways on. Now, it's not easy to carry off this style. Even Carrie Fisher doesn't hack it for some mean-minded critics. If you do try it at home, children, make sure you stay indoors and don't go out in public. Otherwise, as I discovered, people will point at you and laugh.

It was typical of our family that Mum was the one to take Keith and me to the pictures. Dad was always working long hours, running his own building business from an office in the city. He was out of the house most of the time. Mum was the guiding light in our young lives, the focus of our home. Though she later worked with Dad in the business, it was Mum who took us to school and back when we were little, made sure we were fed and watered and wore clean clothes, listened endlessly to us, who helped and encouraged us every way she could.

This is very much the traditional view of family life, isn't it? The husband and father is the breadwinner, the wife and mother the homemaker. Certainly my dad had a very traditional outlook on life. He'd had a strict upbringing himself, and had fixed ideas on how children should behave. Good children studied hard at school, always did their homework, duty before pleasure. His children would be a credit to him, they'd abide by the rules and never upset the apple cart. Eventually they'd join the Establishment as a lawyer or something equally respectable and professional, up the social scale. They'd be hard-headed: no namby-pamby wallowing in emotion. He himself took great pride in being staunchly Scottish, the hardest folk in the world. He might as well have announced, 'I'll have nae feelings expressed in this hoose.' He was convinced that he knew what was best for all of us. All of us wouldn't always agree…

But when we were kids his clear boundaries gave us a strong sense of security. We lived in the same house all our lives till we left home, and my mum lives there still. She and Dad had moved in soon after their wedding in 1970. It's a solidly built house in dark brick, and we had the ground floor and the basement. Miss Kerr, a teacher, had the top floor, reached by a flight of stairs on the side (I can hear her now – 'Turn that music down!'). Originally we had two bedrooms, a front room with a big bay window, a back room, a kitchen and bathroom, a utility room and a playroom, with a neat garden at the front and a bigger back garden with a swing. The house was in a cul-de-sac, one of just twenty-eight in a horseshoe-shaped road in Joppa. That odd name – it's in the Bible, and apparently it's an alternative name for the Israeli city and port of Jaffa. I don't know why a suburb of Edinburgh acquired that name. Perhaps because it's near the sea too. At least it gave my dad a chance to announce, on more than one occasion, 'We live in Joppa, so we are Joppanese.' Yes, thank you, Dad.

Anyhow, our neighbourhood felt more like a village than a city suburb – a really close-knit community, a safe place to grow up in. We knew everyone, and some of them meant more to me when I was young than others. Several families had young kids, so there were friends close at hand. My best friend when I was little was Carolyn, who lived at number 10. My parents and her parents were good friends too, and as Carolyn's dad fortuitously ran a coach company, we all went on many holidays together to Spain. They were always great fun, but we kids had our patience tested on those coach rides. It's not unknown for Scottish people to have a love of the fermented grape and grain, and some of those trips got pretty…well, I'll say raucous. And the drive was always bloody long, too.

For most of my young life, those trips were the only times I left Edinburgh, though for a long time I kept a photo that made me look like a real jetsetter. I was about two when it was taken. Mum's holding me, and in the background a big plane is taking off into the blue. Bit of a letdown, though. It was just a painted backdrop in a photo booth. In Asda. Well, it was more interesting than curtains.

Another friend, Lynne, lived at number 12 with her brother Paul and their parents. Lynne and I still keep in touch. All of us used to play together for hours on end, indoors and outdoors. The playroom at the side of our house was a great space, nearly all glass, and let the light flood in. I loved it. I often turned it into a mini-schoolroom with my own blackboard, the little local kids lined up for me to enlighten them about the alphabet and other fascinating lessons. Of course I had to be the teacher. It was my blackboard and my chalk, and from an early age I knew I wanted to be the boss, given half a chance. One time we had a more collaborative exercise – we were all fired up with getting into the *Guinness Book of Records* for making the longest daisy chain in the world. What a life-enhancing ambition! We scoured all the local gardens and the park for daisies, and we were at it for days, carefully slitting the little stalks with our thumbnails, and threading one to another, yards and yards of daisy chain coiling round the floor. Then we heard that some other bunch of nerds had got in before us, with some impossible great length we could never hope to match. Sad sight, hundreds of rejected, wilted daisies.

I remember we liked to play practical jokes, too – the same ones time and again, the novelty never wearing off. We had a special favourite concerning Lynne's dad. She used to call him 'Mr Fuzzy Head' as his hair was – well, you've guessed it – rather fuzzy. When Lynne and I were playing at our friend Erica's house, Lynne would phone home. When Lynne's father answered the phone, she would put on a funny voice and say, 'Can I speak to Mr Fuzzy Head?' And hang up.

We'd wet ourselves laughing. How could he possibly know it was us? But soon afterwards the doorbell would ring. There was Mr Fuzzy Head, come to take Lynne home. I guess he figured it out. It still didn't stop us doing it every week – oh, what fun we were!

Our other favourite practical joke was wrapping my little brother in a tartan rug and sticking a note to him saying 'To number 10'. We'd ring the doorbell of number 10, shout 'It's the postman!' then run away and hide behind the garden wall. Carolyn's mum would answer the door and unwrap the blanket. Whereupon my brother would jump up and shout, 'Surprise, it's me!' Carolyn's mum was a good sport. Every time she managed to look shocked and exclaim, 'I had no idea!'

We could usually play safely in the street as it was a cul-de-sac and traffic was pretty light – and there wasn't the all-pervading fear of paedophiles that seems to haunt parents nowadays. We spent hours kicking a ball around, or chasing each other all over the place, we were Starsky and Hutch when we weren't being Bodie and Doyle, yelling out the theme tune. And we didn't just have the street – there were a couple of patches of waste ground nearby, all humps and bumps and brambles, where we could ride our bikes as fast as we liked. But even at an early age I wasn't that happy with messy surroundings. I was always trying to clean the place up. Our gang hut, a ramshackle affair, had a tatty piece of old carpet on the floor, which I was always sweeping, much to the amusement of my friends. I must have had a sense of decorum instilled into me, as I insisted that people knocked on the door before they came in. Actually, there wasn't a door, so it was an imaginary knock on a non-existent door. The municipal park was more pleasing to me, in its manicured way – a great place to play rounders. To get there, we used to take a short cut through some broken fencing at the end of the street.

In fact, when I think about it now, Joppa was like a giant play-ground – us kids were really lucky to have so much open space, although now, sadly, much of it is built upon. And of course there was always the beach. Mind you, you'd be looking at it for a long time before you thought of golden sands and palm trees – more like grey sand and grey dirty sea – but it was a magnet for us whatever the weather. If it was boiling hot, we'd all run there in bare feet, never mind the scorching pavements. And if it was freezing cold – hey, we're Scottish. We might wear a T-shirt. It'd only take a peek of sunshine for us to wear shorts. We'd often be bare-legged even in the depths of winter, trudging home from school through thick snow, despite the danger of getting tartan skin. Any Scot can tell you about tartan skin. This is when you'd be freezing outside, and as soon as you sat by the fire at home, red blotches would mysteriously appear on your milk-white skin – instant tartan tights!

Just as I was good friends with a lot of the local kids, so my mum was on good terms with all the neighbours. If some people are the neighbours from hell, she's the neighbour from heaven. She'd do anything for anybody, especially the older people. Miss Oswald was a special favourite, a grand old lady, who had a great relationship with my mother. Mum always looked out for her, right until Miss Oswald died, at the suitably grand old age of 101. As I started to write this book, she was taking care of another neighbour, Margaret, a lovely lady I call my surrogate mum as we're so close. Margaret had a fall and couldn't manage the stairs, so of course she must come to Mum's house and get looked after.

Not that Mum ever makes a big deal of what she does, even if she's not that well herself. She's very down to earth and hates fuss – being stoic is an essential part of her nature, and she taught me to just get on with things, don't ask for help, be self-reliant. Which is all very well, but can be taken to extremes. I remember one time when Mum was unloading my dad's go-kart from the trailer attached to our car. (He was a great fan of go-karting.) Quite why she was doing that and he wasn't, I don't know. The rest of us were in the front room, glued to the telly. We were watching *Glen Michael's Cavalcade*, a Scottish cartoon show that was hugely popular at the time. It was hosted by Mr Glen Michael himself, along with his sidekick, Paladin (a talking paraffin lamp – what else?).

Mum came into the house and we could hear her making a cup of tea in the kitchen. She then came into the front room and we could see she was hobbling.

'I don't want to be a nuisance, but Craig,' she said to my dad, 'would you mind taking me to the hospital?'

We all looked up quizzically.

Mum had wrapped a tea towel round her foot. We thought the tea towel was a red one until we realised that it was soaked in blood. It turned out that as she was unhooking the trailer from the car, she dropped it and the trailer attachment thumped to the ground, via her foot. Any other woman would have screamed for help. Not my mum, mad Sandra. No, she struggles to wrench a trailer holding a go-kart off her foot, makes a cup of tea and then asks if anyone would mind helping her. Crazy as a haggis at times – but always with other people's welfare at heart.

Mum always encouraged this attitude in Keith and me. Be considerate and always think of others. That was her idea of being Good, in sharp contrast to Dad's more utilitarian attitude and conviction that he knew best.

The friction created by this fundamental difference in their natures coloured much of my childhood. It could be something as everyday as dinner. Mum might be cooking the meal, and Dad would stand over her, putting in his twopenn'orth. 'Not enough salt,' he'd say, or 'The potatoes need a bit more mashing.' By the time we sat down at the table, Mum would be quietly seething, while Dad was oblivious. We would eat mostly in silence, us kids watching Dad add even more salt to his salt-saturated meal. Keith and I had to be careful that we didn't raise our elbows too high while we were using our knife and fork. If we did, Dad would correct us.

'Flying a plane, are we, children? Where are you off to? Anywhere exciting?'

Relentless. Every bloody mealtime. I wish I had been flying somewhere. Preferably somewhere I'd seen on the telly, where people sat on the ground and ate with their fingers – then my elbows could do what they bloody well wanted to.

At the end of the meal, either my brother or I might make the mistake of saying we were full.

'You are a what?' replied my father.

Fell for it again. 'Full,' we sighed.

'Ha ha, you're saying you're a fool?'

Fool/full. Did he want us to grow up dyslexic? He used that 'joke' every time he could. The end of dinnertime was such a relief. Another one over, tomorrow's yet to come. To this day I can't abide sarcasm; I like a laugh as much as anyone, but draw the line at humiliation.

When I complain about my dad and the way he used to piss me off, I realise I must sound very petty. Every family has its own dynamic, its tensions, its squabbles. It's easy for me to look back on my childhood – a very happy one, in the main – and gripe about what my dad did or didn't do. I'd hate my daughter to slag me off in twenty years' time! I know that Dad meant well, was always a good provider – but that conviction that he was in the right, that he was the final arbiter, did not always make for a harmonious atmosphere, especially as my brother and I grew up. What I saw as Dad's control freakery could well have sown the seeds for my later rejection of a 'respectable' life and image. And as for repressing emotions – well, that was never gonna happen with me!

Mum, while always one for a laugh and a joke, could be strict in her own way. A particular bugbear of hers was swearing – as well as being polite and respectful, we kids should never ever swear. And here she backed up her ruling with one of the big guns. Jesus. Mum told me that if I ever swore, Jesus would tell her and she would know before I even got home. This statement truly confused my young mind. I understood the whole Jesus thing – though our family wasn't especially religious, we went to church on a Sunday and my mum was even a Sunday School teacher at one point. Not that this made her any more keen to put up with being visited by boring Church of Scotland elders who'd drop in on people and talk and talk for hours. If she saw them coming she'd shout, 'Kids! Down!' and we'd all dive behind the sofa, ignoring the doorbell and waiting till we heard them march away down the front path.

But Jesus and the swearing thing...since when did a dead person set up a hotline with my mum about my use of foul language? Surely Jesus was busy. He couldn't be watching me constantly. And was it the big Jesus with the beard and sandals or the baby one that accepted gifts from strangers? Oh well, one of life's mysteries to puzzle a young child.

On a more positive note, it was Mum who encouraged me and

my brother to join every possible after-school activity going. There's only one way to find out what you'd like and that's to go for it. I'm with Mum on that one. So I took up violin lessons, piano lessons, tap, ballet and highland dancing, netball, trampolining, badminton, Brownies and the Young Ornithologists' Club. Yup, even the Young Ornithologists' Club. I won a prize for being the best young ornithologist in my primary school. How did I achieve that accolade? Easy. I was the only kid in the club. While all the other kids were off snogging, hanging out round the chippy, drawing on walls and generally messing around I was carefully drawing bird feathers in my sketchbook.

I was really good at dancing, though I say so myself, and was actually considered for a ballet scholarship at one time. Not that I was sorry I didn't get it – I eventually found ballet too restricting, too formal, too controlled. Highland dancing was much more my cup of tea, and it took me on the competition circuit – nothing grand, usually community halls. I can remember many an occasion, us dancers wearing traditional highland kilt and plaid, waiting for the piper to get his act together. Most of the pipers seemed to be pissed half the time, staggering slightly as they blew down the pipe to inflate the bag, managing to produce a sound like a cow in labour before they got going properly. There'd be calls of 'Oh God, when's it gonna start? I canna take much more o' this.' The audience was mostly mums, who sat on the hard wooden chairs chatting amongst themselves, smoking fags or knitting (the more dextrous doing both). They'd call out encouragement to their children: 'All reet, Jessie, ma girl, you're gonna win this time.' At least once I heard my own mum calling to me, 'Come on, Gail, you can take 'em.' Her encouragement must have worked, as I managed to accumulate quite a few medals and trophies, which were all given pride of place by Mum at home. She's still at it – over the years I think she must have collected every article and photo of me ever published.

My brother Keith was up for most things, but he drew the line at dancing, highland or otherwise. He was sporty, and later we both took up one particular sport that we immediately loved: martial arts. We still practise it as much as we can to this day. Keith has six black belts, at the last count, and I've got one. We took up shoto kan karate when I was ten years old and Keith was eight. Our club, the Kasuga, was slightly bonkers and rather hard core, tucked away in a rather rundown backstreet in the city. On our first day there, I stared at a tatty banner pinned to the wall. On it was written in wonky letters: 'They can conquer who think they can'. It was the club motto. I had to think about it until the meaning sank in, then – cool! That was my kind of attitude. Gung ho or what?

We were taught hard and we fought as hard as our wee bodies would allow. We both advanced quite quickly, and were soon junior blackbelts. It made our brother-and-sister scuffles at home rather interesting – though to tell the truth we hardly ever fell out. We got on really well most of the time, and our shared hobby brought us closer together. When the other school kids were off to the cinema to watch something like *ET* or *Indiana Jones*, my brother was re-enacting every move from Jackie Chan movies. When everyone else went away at weekends to caravans, Keith and I were at 'Ninja Camp'.

Ninja Camp, I'm sure, was a concept created by our crazy karate club contemporaries. It involved driving to some random hill or mountain, walking miles, then pitching up our two-man tents, which would be home to at least four of us kids for the weekend. As we never strayed out of Scotland, at least we knew what to expect from the weather.

We were given tasks such as punching holes in the ground with thistles attached to each hand. We stopped only when we bled so much that we could punch no more. Then there was running backwards up fields, which of course resulted in a lot of landing in cow shit that you couldn't see in advance. There was lots of jumping into freezing lochs, various stances and exercises and almost anything that would push our pain thresholds to the limit. And you know what? We loved it; it was exhilarating. We thought we could conquer, all right – we were bloody sure of it!

Apart from the odd Ninja trip to the wilds and those coach trips to Spain, life for me was centred on Edinburgh. Mum and Dad had grown up in the city, and the wider family all lived there too. I was particularly close to Mum's parents. Grandma was Mary Twiddy. We used to spend hours poring over her collection of old film magazines, like *Photoplay*. She loved films, and together we'd admire all the glamorous actresses posing in their fabulous outfits, heavily made-up with their hair waved and curled. Such style! Those images made a deep impression on me, and I'd imagine myself dolled up to the nines and gazing at the camera...

Grandpa, who I'm happy to say is still with us, rejoices in the resoundingly heroic name of Horatio Walter Stanley Twiddy. I loved telling my friends his name. It sounded so important, like he'd won a battle or discovered time or something. His mother, my great-grandmother, was very long-lived – she died just a couple of years ago, at the age of 101, so for most of my life there were four generations of our family.

Dad's parents were Pappa and Lally (I don't know why everybody called her that – and still do, as she too is very much with us). Pappa was the first of my grandparents to die, when I was quite young. He was a big smoker and a bigger drinker. He used to go to the pub at lunchtime and have something called a nip and a dump – which sounds quite unsavoury, but was actually a nip of whisky poured into a pint. When I think of Pappa I think of Polo mints. He chomped them all the time to try and cover the smell of drink. When I visited him and Lally, he always asked me to do one of my singing and dancing acts (not that I needed much encouragement), and I always got some Polos as a reward from his never-ending supply.

Mum had a sister and a brother, and Dad had two brothers, so there were aunts and uncles and cousins too. While I was still at primary school, we saw a lot of one of my cousins, David. He was the son of Mum's brother, also called David. Uncle David had been left literally holding the baby when his wife left. It was hard for Uncle David, who's profoundly deaf and has certain related problems, so the baby often came and stayed with us. I loved helping to look after him.

But one day, I don't know exactly when, Baby David died. We children were just told the bare facts, that he'd caught measles and been taken to hospital where he died. Then it was as if he'd never existed. His name was never mentioned; he was airbrushed out of our lives.

I couldn't get my head round this. I was upset – were we all going to die? – and tried asking questions, but was met with a stone wall. I don't think this is peculiar to my family – a lot of people can cope with bereavement only by battening down the emotional hatches. I was left totally bewildered. In Bible class I'd say to the teacher, 'My little cousin died – why did God take him? He didn't do anything. It's not fair.'

Then I'd get the reply that gives no satisfaction to any child with the ability to think: 'That's the way God works.'

Oh, is it?

'Why?' I'd ask.

'That's just the way.'

'Why?'

'You don't question God's will.'

'Why?'

And so on and on, until one Sunday I said to Mum and Dad, 'I'm not going to church. I can't believe there's a God.'

They didn't kick up much of a fuss – sometimes it's useful that things aren't talked about. My young self rejected religion and all its works, and nothing I've seen or experienced since has given me any reason to change my mind.


All through my childhood we'd see our other relatives quite regularly – we'd visit them or they'd come to our house. There was only one time of the year when a lot of us would get together: Christmas. Fabulous time for kids, tense time for parents. When we were little, Keith and I would wake up practically every hour after midnight. At the time we shared a room, with bunk beds – me on the top, Keith on the bottom.

'Has Santa been?' we would ask plaintively.

'Go back to sleep, kids,' came my dad's grumpy voice from the bedroom next door.

Two a.m. 'Has Santa been?'

'For God's sake!' Mum yelled.

By six a.m., the parents relented. 'Yes, Santa has been.'

Rock'n'roll! We'd scramble to the sacks at the bottom of our beds. How did Santa do it? How did he make it down the chimney to land on top of the electric fire in the front room, dodge our vigil and quietly deposit our gifts at the bottom of our beds? To be honest, we didn't really care. He did it. End of story.

Dressed in our cosy tartan flannel pyjamas, Keith and I would drag our sacks into the front room and switch the fire on. If we needed any more proof that Santa had visited, there it was in the grate. An empty plate that had held a Wagon Wheel, and an empty glass we'd filled with milk, to help Santa on his way round the rest of the world.

Then it was time to tear open the festive wrapping as if our lives depended on it. Actually, Keith ripped. I tried to unwrap gently, neatly folding the paper and tidying up as I went along (yet another OCD alert – something that's stayed with me!). This meant that Keith was always way ahead of me in the unwrapping stakes. I was very much into Sindy, as well as Girl's World – a head that magically grew hair, which I hacked to death. Though we both loved *Star Wars*, it seemed to be Keith who got the merchandise, and I loved those toys. I did once get a red racing car, I remember, an ungirly pressie I found thrilling

One year I found a receipt in one of my presents.

'Look, Mum,' I said. 'Santa's been to Asda.'

'Oh well, right, erm, sometimes if the elves are too busy, Asda helps Santa out,' Mum stuttered. I wasn't convinced, but Christmas is too short to question Santa or my mum.

After the frenzied present attack, Mum would make us breakfast. By this hour, she and Dad had usually fallen out. Dad would have bought Mum a crap present, and, like clockwork, he'd open the gift from Mum and announce a bit too dismissively, 'That's nice, Sandra, but it really wasn't necessary.' Not a good thing to say to your wife, especially at the most family-loving, if stress-inducing, day in the calendar. It's probably not coincidental that a lot of divorce proceedings start in the new year…

After breakfast Mum and Dad and their frosty silence would retreat to the kitchen to prepare the festive lunch of traditional turkey and all the trimmings. Keith and I would visit the kids in our street. 'What did you get?' The ultimate Christmas question.

Our favourite house to visit was number 12, where Lynne and Paul lived. Lynne was always delighted with her gifts, though Paul often looked a bit grouchy. Their parents weren't too happy either – obviously we weren't the only family not to wholly embrace the festive spirit.

Then Keith and I would return to our house, play with our toys and wait for the arrival of the family for dinner. We usually had

Mum's mum and dad (Grandma Mary and Grandpa Horatio), Great-Grandmother (whose false teeth didn't fit her mouth), Dad's mum (Lally), Mum's sister Susan and her husband, and Uncle David. This made a total of eleven. Mum was always completely stressed.

Uncle David kept us kids in fits. He used to smother his Christmas dinner in HP sauce, getting a sharp look from his sister. He would comment on our table manners, his deafness preventing him knowing how loudly he was speaking. 'Look at Great-Grandma's teeth. It's disgusting. They're falling out. Grandma, sort your teeth out before they fall in the turkey.'

One time, when Uncle David was looking after us, we invited the local kids over, announcing that they could swear at him behind his back as he wouldn't be able to lip read what they were saying. We would all mumble rude words under our breath – what a thrill. One particular kid, who was not that bright, made a V sign in front of him and got a clout around the head. 'He's deaf, you idiot, not blind!' we laughed.

Although Christmas was stressful for our parents, we loved it. The only part we hated was when the grown-ups wanted to turn on the telly to watch the Queen's speech at three o'clock. Completely boring. Then it would be our turn to choose a programme. We would scream to watch the *Top of the Pops Christmas Special* set at the loudest possible volume, so as to drown out the noise of our elders shouting at one another. 'What is this claptrap? This isn't real music. Is that a man or a woman?'

I'd sit there in the front room, eyes glued to the latest singing sensation, never even imagining that years later I'd find myself in the heart of it all.

While Christmas may be the best time for presents, the real highlight of the year for us fun-loving Scots is Hogmanay. Party party party! Open house all round – every door in the street open from early evening on New Year's Eve, light streaming into the street. Keith and I would get out the pipe music album and dance round the front room, with an ever-changing audience as friends and neighbours came and went. Knocks on the door, visitors with the obligatory piece of coal for luck and bottle of whisky for – well, drinking. We'd dance out into the street and visit our neighbours, a mini-ceilidh in every house. For as far back as I can remember it was a fantastic night. We'd all count down to the chimes of midnight and a great shout would go up to welcome the new year – then it was back to the singing and dancing, laughing and joking, eating and drinking. Us kids would fall asleep exhausted, the sounds of celebration still ringing in our ears.

Beats me how Scots got a reputation for being stingy and straitlaced. Not in our neck of the woods.

As I'm looking back, trying to figure out what made me the way I am, I realise I'm as much a product of my childhood as everyone else. My mum's strong sense of duty, her care for others, went deep, and her try-anything-once attitude was right up my street, along with her love of a good laugh. I responded to Dad's work ethic by being diligent, conscientious and very aware of the need to earn my own living at all times. I'm haunted to this day by the thought of insolvency!

If there was anything in my young self that pointed to my later troubles, I wonder if it might have been my sleepwalking. It was taken for granted at the time, but now strikes me as, well, a little odd, maybe. I used to sleepwalk a lot. And I mean a lot. I guess most kids go through phases of walking in their sleep, when they're unusually agitated, but for me it was a regular occurrence. One time, Mum and Dad heard a loud thud. I'd flung myself off my top bunk and landed flat on the floor with arms outstretched – maybe I thought I was a plane. Another night, Mum and Dad were in bed and I just walked into their bedroom, and carried on walking straight ahead until I smacked whack bang into the wardrobe and fell backwards like a plank of wood and just lay there. Once I even made my way out of the house, at eleven o'clock at night, clutching my duvet which trailed behind me. Mum happened to notice the front door open, and there I was – in the middle of the street. She ran after me and apparently I said, 'I'm going to Erica's to stay the night.' She guided me back into the house, with me still insisting I was going to Erica's.

Even if I didn't go walkabout, I'd often sit bolt upright in bed and talk out loud, before lying back down again and going quiet. My brother used to think it was the funniest thing, and would tease me a lot.

I don't pretend to know exactly what this means, if anything. I suppose, if sleep is the time you recharge your batteries, then something was interfering with the normal process. Perhaps there was some underlying impetus, but I'm not sure what. In any case, even if I stayed quiet in my bed when I was asleep, I got little real rest. I've always had the most vivid dreams, so real, so lifelike, that sometimes when I wake up I have to really think about what is fact and what is fantasy. At least I didn't have that trouble with night-mares – I knew they weren't real. One recurring nightmare struck me most often, ironically, at one of my favourite times of year: Christmas. I'd dream that Santa Claus was trying to murder me. I'd hear sleigh bells tinkling down the chimney and get really excited, then I'd get up and find he'd murdered all my family – then he'd chase me out of the house and round and round the street, trying to murder me. I'd wake up drenched in sweat, my heart pounding.

It seemed that my brain was always maniacally working, work-ing, working. It wouldn't or couldn't switch off.

Mum and Dad were a bit worried about my sleepwalking, but really it became just part of what I was. I was never taken to the doctor about it. It makes me smile now to think what did prompt my mum to consult a doctor. It was to do with Keith. Apparently he was farting like mad, pumping out his own greenhouse gas on a grand malodorous scale. So, farting a lot: take to the doctor. Wandering round the house and beyond while fast asleep: take for granted. I suppose every family has its norm to get used to.

Talking of norms – another one for us kids of course was that other important component of life outside home: school.

# Learning Curves

The note was passed to me from the kid on my right. I opened it and read the contents: 'Ian is a FFF'. I closed the note and passed it on. That's what you do when you're at primary school and receive a classroom note. I had no idea what it meant, but to someone this note was extremely funny, extremely rude or extremely insulting – possibly all three.

Our teacher, Mrs Nisbit, had an eagle eye, an all-seeing power that could make us quiver with fright. Inevitably, she spotted this scrap of highly classified kids' info, and pounced. She grabbed the note from the hand of a trembling, though innocent, reader and opened it up. The class sat frozen.

'Hmm, "Ian is a FFF". Someone had better explain the meaning of this waste of paper,' said Mrs Nisbit in her well-modulated accent from the right side of Edinburgh.

I was rather pleased she said that, as the code in the note had me baffled too.

Silence.

Mrs Nisbit, tall and thin and towering over us, glared from under her neat grey fringe. 'Well?' she snapped. 'You will have ten more seconds to give me the author of this note and its meaning, or the entire class will receive the belt as punishment.'

She was very hot on discipline, Mrs Nisbit – and this was one of the things I actually loved about her. She was a brilliant, inspiring teacher, but she didn't take any crap. You knew where you were with her. Step out of line and you risked a swipe from the belt. Understandably, kids weren't so keen on this instrument of torture. If someone caused the entire class to be belted, that person would have a mini war on their hands in the battlefield that was our playground.

A hand rose slowly in the air. It was Darren's. He got the belt more than anyone at our primary school.

'Darren,' said Mrs Nisbit. 'Hardly a surprise, is it?' She went on, 'Well, enlighten us with your words of wisdom, Darren. Kindly tell us what "FFF" means.'

Darren shuffled his feet and grew red in the face. 'It's just that Ian is snogging loads of birds and well, like, you know...' he tailed off.

'We do not know, Darren,' Mrs Nisbit said icily, 'and we are all waiting.'

'You know...' Darren muttered. 'He felt a bird's fanny, so that makes him a Phantom Fanny Feeler – FFF, see?'

My hand shot up immediately.

'But please, Miss,' I begged. 'Phantom is spelt with a P, so Ian is actually a PFF.'

Immediate hissing from round the class: 'Shut yer face, Snobby Porter.'

That was me, Snobby Porter. Always got my hand in the air – 'Ask me, Miss.' And always eager to please – 'I will wash your car, Miss.' 'I will volunteer to clean the playground all weekend, Miss.'

To many of my fellow pupils at Brunstane Primary I was a bit of a freak. So well brought up, so ladylike, so keen on study and all those after-school activities too. I was a Good Girl all right, swotty as well as snobby – and it wasn't an act. Quite apart from the work ethic drilled into me, I genuinely enjoyed learning, especially English. My reports usually described me as well prepared, attentive and co-operative, which would have pleased my dad. I also had a tendency to chatter, I recall. No change there, then.

I had no trouble obeying rules; I hardly ever got into trouble. In fact the only time I'd ever actually been punished was in the first year, when one of the other kids made me laugh at an inopportune moment. 'Gail Porter, I said no giggling!' thundered the voice of doom, and I was smacked on the hand. I'd never been hit before, and I was mortified. I cried all the way home, and didn't get over it for ages. It wasn't the pain, which hardly registered – it was the shock, the affront. That set a pattern, all right. Emotional hurt: tears. No change there, either.

For most of my time at Brunstane, I'd hang around with the other 'nice' girls, quiet and studious like me. The tougher kids laughed at me, but at least they didn't beat me up. They'd stick to taking the mick, like the girl in my class who enjoyed teasing me about my non-swearing rule. As my mum had told me, Jesus would hear me if I swore, and report directly to her. In the days before I lost any faith I might have had, Jesus was a force to be reckoned with, a kind of holy bogeyman.

This girl would gradually take everything from my desk, starting with a ruler, telling me, 'Say a swear word or I'll keep your ruler.'

I'd ignore her, then it was the turn of another piece of stationery to go.

'Say a swear word or I'll keep your rubber...'

This would go on until my desk was empty. If the teacher was in class, she would demand the return of my school stuff and the 'Snobby Porter' whispers would start up.

One day, I caved in. My desk was empty, the girls were laughing and I just broke.

'Fuck,' I whispered. I'd heard other kids saying this word, and knew that it was Bad.

'What did you say?' said my tormentor. 'We can't hear you. Louder, Snobby!'

'Fuck!' If Jesus has heard me once, then why bother worrying any more? 'Fuck, fuck, fuck. Now give me my stuff back.'

My belongings were replaced, much laughter ensued and I had to sit till the end of class with the knowledge that Jesus had contacted my mother. But how had he done it? Special Jesus phone? Carrier pigeon? Telepathy? Could my mum be telepathic?

It was the first time that I dreaded hearing the final bell. It rang for what seemed like eternity. I packed my satchel and headed for the longest possible route home. Every step was a step closer to my mum and the wrath of Jesus.

I opened our front door, and tried to sneak as quickly as possible to my room.

'Is that you, Gail?'

Rumbled.

I walked to the kitchen. Mum was grinning her head off. She must be looking forward to berating me with the speech that she and the holy bloke had agreed on.

'How was school?'

Trick question?

'Fine, you know.'

'What did you do?'

Just tell me you know that I swore.

'You know, art, reading and stuff.'

'What did you make in art?'

'OK, just tell me. He spoke to you.'

'Who spoke to me?'

'Just get on with it.'

Mum was getting exasperated. 'I have no idea what you're talking about.'

Oh my God. It was all a cunning holy plan. Mum doesn't talk to Jesus. It was a grown-up trick of instilling fear into the mind of a poor innocent child. I was stunned as realisation dawned on me. Then excited – if Jesus wasn't watching after all, what else could I get up to? But you know what? I honestly was 'Snobby Porter'. I couldn't even think of being naughty. I didn't want to be naughty. But this new knowledge probably paved the way to my later suspicion that God and all his works weren't what they were cracked up to be.

It was in my last year in primary that I took up Ninja, along with Keith. It did give me a kind of cred, though not enough to shake off the 'Snobby' tag. One day, though, something happened that actually made me look dead cool in the other kids' eyes. I caused a scandal.

It was at lunchtime. Every day my mum would make me a packed lunch, usually a sandwich, crisps, a chocolate biscuit and a can of Coke. (Sorry, Jamie Oliver, it would be a good few years yet before you made any difference to school dinners.) This particular day, Keith and I had walked to school as usual, me with my satchel slung over one shoulder, my Young Ornithologist's notebook tucked under my arm. I worked through morning lessons with my usual keenness and diligence until the lunch bell sounded, and everybody headed for the school canteen.

We all sat down amid the lingering smell of cabbage, and said grace:

> *Thank you for the world so sweet,*
> *Thank you for the food we eat.*
> *Thank you for the birds that sing,*
> *Thank you, God, for everything.*
> *Amen.*

We usually raced through this as if we only had one breath in which to get it all out. Mr Manson, our headmaster, would make us repeat it and repeat it again until we sounded sincere enough.

On this particular day we managed to thank God with some semblance of sincerity and we could eat. I opened my Tupperware container. As usual, there was my sandwich (sandwich spread today), salt and vinegar Disco crisps, a Breakaway choc bar – and a can of McEwan's lager. The kids at the packed lunch table erupted. 'Snobby Porter has beer for lunch!'

I was instantly removed from the canteen and marched to the headmaster's office. I sat there, feeling like the world was falling about my ears, as Mr Manson made the phone call.

'Mrs Porter, I have your daughter with me. I am not sure if you are aware of her behaviour, but she has come to school with a can of lager in her bag.'

Beer, lager – how did he know the difference? I was ten. I thought they were the same.

I could hear my mother shrieking from the earpiece. 'Oh my God!' She spoke some more, and after he hung up Mr Manson turned to me.

'Your mother said she must have picked up the lager can by mistake, as it's the same colour as a Coca-Cola can.'

Of course, that's how it would have happened. There was always a beer or a lager in the fridge for Dad when he came home in the evening. In the morning, my harassed mother had to wake up two grumpy kids, sort us out, make our breakfasts, pack our lunches and get us to school. Mum must have been on auto pilot and just grabbed the first red can she saw.

So that let me off the hook – I wasn't a Secret Drinker. But I was the coolest kid in school! A mad snobby Ninja whose mother sent her to school at the age of ten with a can of lager. The novelty soon wore off, though, and I was back to just being Snobby again. Snobby with her ladylike airs and graces. And her own toilet paper. Well, I wasn't going to use the school's; I used to call it tracing paper as it was so thin. Talk about your fingers going through it.

It was scratchy too. Horrible. So Mum would give me a wad of quilted Andrex to take in every day. I was also too grand for the school milk. Disgusting stuff, left to get lukewarm and rancid by morning break. It put me off milk in any shape or form for life (except when heavily disguised as ice cream). I persuaded Mum to write me a note excusing me, so there was another thing to single me out.

But whatever hassles I might have had in my primary years, there was a bigger fear lurking on the horizon. A secondary school that had such a scary reputation it sounded like the natural home of Darth Vader.

Along with a lot of kids from Brunstane Primary, I was going to Portobello High, one of the largest comprehensives in Scotland. We'd heard all the rumours about the tough kids who picked on new arrivals. We had the impression that as soon as we set foot in the school, our new satchels would be snatched from us, along with our lunch money, and our heads would be shoved down the toilet as someone pulled the chain. Then we'd be forced to do other kids' homework on pain of death – or at least a beating-up. Grange Hill was a walk in the park compared to this school!

On our last day at primary, our headmaster prepared us for this brave new world. 'In your final year at primary school,' he announced, 'you have been the big fish. At high school, you will be the little fish.'

Right. I hadn't come across this analogy, and found his words confusing. Did he mean that the older kids were the big fish and would be like sharks preying on us tiddlers? Whatever it meant, I did know I shouldn't take this warning lightly. If I'd had a bumpy ride in primary school as Snobby/Swotty, then I'd be in for a kamikaze rollercoaster ride at Portobello, where I had a vision of hulking thugs and bullies roaming the corridors, looking for lady-like, studious little girls like me.

So it was with more than a touch of trepidation that I arrived on the first day of the autumn term. Portobello is in the town of the same name, in Duddingston Road, about a five-minute walk from the beach. After the relatively small, familiar world of primary school, this new world was bewildering. It seemed like thousands of kids were milling around, the older ones strutting confidently as if they owned the place. It was a mixed school, and the older boys and girls looked frighteningly grown-up. I was nervous, though at least I looked the part of a classic new girl, all tidy and clean in a brand-new uniform. My mum had combed my long hair into cute girl-next-door bunches (which stayed firmly where they were – no more cut-price Princess Leia). I wore a knee-length navy skirt, knee-high navy socks, white starched shirt and a multi-coloured tie, plus a blazer that had been a bone of contention between me and my mum.

'It's too big!' I'd wailed, looking at my reflection in the uniform shop. The shoulders projected way beyond my own, the sleeves were half over my hands, and it was far too long.

Mum was adamant. 'It's expensive and you'll grow into it,' she'd said, making it sound like an order.

On my first day, I slunk around trying to be as inconspicuous as possible, and was cheered up when I saw other kids comically dwarfed by their blazers. Obviously a common practice for mums.

By the end of that day, I felt totally knackered. So much to take in – getting allocated to my class, getting to grips with the timetable, meeting so many new people, and, not least of it, finding my way around this huge school. It's not the most beautiful structure ever built. Most of the buildings date back to the 1960s, and by my time it was getting pretty run down. Jumping ahead some twenty-five years, the school is overdue for replacement, and there are all kinds of wrangles going on. Still, it was something us new kids just took for granted back in the early eighties.

There were two main buildings: the Annexe, down by the golf course, where first and second years spent most of their time, and, a few minutes' walk away, an eight-storey block that contained the gymnasium, the swimming pool and the separate 'houses'. All the pupils were split into four houses: Abercorn, Brunstane, Creighton and Duddingston, named after local areas. I was glad to be in Brunstane House – at least the name was familiar after primary school, and I liked its colour: blue. It was cool. I couldn't really figure out the reason for the segregated houses. I suppose it broke us up into more manageable units and we could always be pitched against each other in sports and plays and other stuff, though unofficially for the kids it was just an excuse to pick fights with one another.

Still, amid all the confusion of that first day there was one positive thing – I hadn't been waylaid by any evil stormtroopers who pinched my new stuff and then up-ended me in the toilet. Perhaps there were grounds for optimism after all. I allowed myself to feel a kind of cautious anticipation. Things might not be so bad.

The first big difference from primary school was that lessons were held in different classrooms. At the start of every new period there'd be a tidal wave of kids surging along corridors – and, in the case of us newcomers, taking wrong corners and going round in circles till we got our bearings. You could almost find your way around by the different smells suffusing the place: gas and chemical stuff from the science lab, stale sweat and old trainers from the gym, chlorine from the pool, over-boiled cabbage (why is it always cabbage?) from the canteen, and rather more enticing cooking odours from the home economics section. Added to these was the nervous sweat from us newcomers – at least for a while. It didn't take long for us to get used to this olfactory stew, to the point where we didn't notice it – though the whiff of boiled cabbage always catapults me straight back to the school canteen.

The great big plus about high school was the fact that at last I didn't stick out like a snobby little thumb. There were others like me! Kids who liked learning and were happy not to run around like Rottweilers off the leash. There were rough types, sure, but there were eggheads too. I made some good friends, especially Nicky Fraser and Anna Wilson. They lived round the corner from me but had gone to different primary schools. They were both studious and had a fantastic sense of humour. We bonded almost straight away, meeting up to go to school in the morning and again to go home after the final bell. We usually walked. We'd cross over the local golf course, dodging the golf balls and jumping in the sandpits – or bunkers, as the annoyed golfers called them as they yelled at us to get out – then risked cutting through Jobby Lane (Dogshit Alley to English readers). Sometimes there was a whole bunch of us local kids – it was all very sociable and larky and made the half-hour walk pass quickly.

So, what with interesting subjects and friends, school was good. I fitted in. I was studying the usual subjects, like English, maths and science, but if it had been left to me I would have done nothing but English. I loved it in primary school and I loved it now. My favourite teacher in secondary school, Mrs Chapman, taught English. Years later I mentioned her in an article, 'My Favourite Teacher', and I gather she's still got the clipping. Perhaps she found me a good student just as I found her a good teacher. Like Mrs Nisbit in Brunstane Primary, she was strict – in fact I've got friends now whose kids go to Portobello and they say, 'We can't believe she was your favourite teacher, she's really strict.' But again that was what I liked. She took the subject seriously and you had to concentrate, had to work hard. And she encouraged you to read, read, read; for this bookworm, that was just great.

It wasn't all academic – we had craft lessons too, with no distinction between the sexes. Boys and girls alike did woodwork, metalwork, cookery and sewing. I was particularly terrible at sewing. It was so fiddly, so boring and I hated it so much. I'd say, 'I don't care what anyone says, I'm never gonna sew anything in my life, so what's the point?' I still don't sew or iron; I'll go out looking creased if necessary. That's a side of domestic life I can do without. I'm fine with cleaning and sorting, but not that kind of housey stuff. I think my mum was making a point recently when she gave me a plaque that read: 'I've only got a kitchen because it came with the house.' Of course I do everything for my daughter, and other people when they visit, but left to myself I'm no Domestic Goddess.

After school hours, there were even more activities to join in. I chose the choir, the hockey team, the athletics team, the music group and, especially, the drama group. Outside school, I was still keeping up the martial arts, along with my brother Keith. We'd regularly go along to the dingy little club and get put through our paces. We were getting really accomplished for youngsters. And it did me no harm at my new big school to be known for this. There was always physical bullying, but no one tried it on with me, small though I was.

Much as Keith and I loved the challenge – 'They can conquer who think they can', remember? – there was one time that nearly finished us off. It was so bizarre, such a contrast to our conventional life at home and school.

I was thirteen, and Keith was eleven. I think it was just before he himself started at Portobello. We were on one of our Ninja camps in the wilds of the Highlands somewhere. One late evening us kids were in our tents, trying to get to sleep but disturbed by sounds of revelry outside, singing and shouting. The grown-ups, the senior members, were evidently giving the home brew a good bashing. We suddenly made out a sort of hissing noise right by the tent. What? We suddenly realised what it was – 'They're pissing on our tent!' Then our door flap was yanked open. It must have been ten o'clock by now. One of the seniors was swaying in the entrance.

'Right, Gail and Keith, get up – we're playing Ninja,' he commanded.

We scrambled up, got dressed and timidly ventured out into the dark. There were four seniors, all dressed in black Ninja outfits. The only thing visible in the near dark was their rather bloodshot eyes – red spotlights homing in on us.

The Master Ninja addressed us. 'Gail and Keith,' he said solemnly (or as solemnly as he could in his condition), 'here is a stick each. You must protect these sticks with your life.'

So he was announcing our mission.

'No matter what, you must not let the Ninjas obtain those sticks. They need the entire stick – if it breaks and you have a partial stick in the palm of your hand, then you are the successful Ninja. If you return with nothing, you lose.'

You have got to be kidding me. It's ten o'clock at night, I'm thirteen and my brother's eleven and we're having to fight off four rather tipsy seniors – for a stick.

'OK, Master,' my brother and I answered in unison. Such good and yet rather stupid students.

We were given a five-minute start. I was practically shitting myself. We ran so fast that my lungs felt like they would explode. We searched for a hiding place in the forest up from the loch. Keith and I dived into a ditch and covered ourselves in mud, and lay there awaiting the unknown.

'I bet Mum thinks we're tucked up in bed, fast asleep,' whispered Keith.

'I bet she does,' I replied. 'We mustn't tell her until I'm sixteen.'

Sixteen – that magic age. When you're thirteen, you think everything'll be fine by then.

Suddenly we heard a rustling from above us somewhere. An overweight senior came flying out of a tree shouting some sort of unintelligible attempt at Japanese. The big bastard landed on me. My brother and I instantly tuned into battle mode. I wriggled free and we fought as a team. It is true what they say, the bigger they are, the harder they fall. The senior had hurt himself during his Ninja stunt. His boozing may have numbed his pain, but no amount of alcohol could disguise the fact he'd hurt his leg and couldn't walk.

Right. One down, three to go.

Keith and I had adrenaline pumping through our veins. This wasn't British bulldogs in the playground, hopping about and barging people with your folded arms – this was a full-blown Ninja war.

We ran around the trees as quietly as possible until we rumbled two of them together. We needed just to out-dodge them to get back to the camp. They caught sight of us, and came at us, screaming. Keith and I split up and tried to be as slippery as possible. Keith distracted one as I tried to avoid the other. The one chasing me caught my ankle and I came crashing on to the woodland floor. He jumped on top of me and we fought like cat and dog (but one dressed as a Ninja). He broke my stick, the bastard, and I panicked. I couldn't lose. If my brother returned to camp with his stick and I didn't, I would never hear the end of it. I could take a big Ninja-style beating, but I couldn't take ridicule from my little brother.

I managed to wriggle free, clutching my bit of broken stick, and ran with all my might towards the break in the trees that would take me back to camp. The final senior jumped in my path. We stood poised for a moment, eyeballing each other, then he ran at me. As he moved to grab me, I crouched down and he went flying over me. Tipsy Ninjas make good sparring partners!

I carried on running with the sound of the seniors catching up behind me. It was like a scene from a dream. I could feel that I was running but I didn't feel like I was getting anywhere. But my wee legs did me proud. I fell to the ground at the entrance to our camp. Keith had beaten me to it. He was back and exhausted. We both opened our hands to reveal the last remnants of our sticks. I was so proud of him and I think he was of me, but of course, he could never tell his sister that!

We went to our tent, black and blue, completely knackered but proud of our insane achievement and safe in the knowledge that our mum thought we had been tucked up in our beds hours ago with a nice hot chocolate. If she knew her adolescent daughter had been grappling with drunken grown men in the dark, she might just have got the wrong idea...

'We'll tell her when you're sixteen,' mumbled Keith.

'Yeah, sixteen,' I replied before drifting into a Bruce Lee-filled sleep.

Not that we ever did tell her. By the time I was sixteen I had other things to think about, including the world of work. Though I was still at school, and would be staying on into the sixth form, it wasn't too soon to learn about paid employment. In fact the moment I turned sixteen, my dad said, 'Right, time to get a job.' His point was that everybody should help pay their way as soon as they could. That's something I've held to all my life.

My first job was in Chelsea Girl, then a hip and happening clothes store, on Thursday nights and Saturday mornings. Then I switched to selling shoes in Peter Lord's. Finally I worked on Sundays, in a branch of B&Q for some months. I wore a badge that said, 'Hi. I'm Gail, I'm here to help'. Well, I tried filling those shelves to the best of my ability. Come to think of it, it was at B&Q

that I sort of stole something, completely not on purpose. One afternoon I picked up a can of car air freshener that someone had dropped on the floor, miles away from its proper shelf. So I put it in the pocket of my overall, thinking, I'll put it back on the shelf later. To my horror, when I reached home, it was still in my pocket! I felt so bad, I didn't sleep all night and I took it straight back the next day, crossing my fingers that no one would see me place it back on the shelf. Guilt is practically second nature with me.

Dad had always been hot on the work ethic where school was concerned – I had to keep up to the mark, and carefully ration my time off. O levels were looming, and I had to do the requisite amount of study and revision, cloistered in my room. I'd had my own room for quite a while now – the wonderful old playroom had been replaced by a new extension, giving the house an extra bedroom and a redesigned kitchen. Dad, being a builder, did the job himself, and it proved quite a bone of contention between my parents. You know when you have builders in and they come and go and never seem to finish anything on time? Well, we had a live-in version. The job took ages. The only light relief was when the playroom was knocked down. Any pang I might have had was assuaged when Dad said to me and Keith, 'Right, you two. You can come and give me a hand to break up the windows.' Cool! Armed with hammers and wearing gloves and goggles, we had a truly smashing time. There's something so liberating about letting rip and making a lot of noise…

Anyhow, all that revision paid off, and I passed all the nine O levels I sat. I got an A for English, which made me enormously proud. But after that scholastic hurdle came a greater challenge:

Highers – the Scottish equivalent of A levels. I chose English (but of course), politics, maths and (unaccountably, as it happens) accountancy. I really don't know why I took accountancy – must have been mad. It was so not me, so boring I wanted to die. I spent most of the lessons carving my name in my wooden desk with a compass point or the end of a ruler – I probably could have chewed through the whole desk. This was the naughtiest thing I ever did at school. When friends' kids tell me, 'I've sat at a desk with your name carved in it,' I nod knowledgeably. 'Right. That must have been an accountancy lesson then.'

Another bad choice was maths. I'd done quite well at O level, but now I was in pastures new and I couldn't get my head round anything. I hated maths, and maths, frankly, hated me. Confronted with it, my eyes would glaze and all I could hear was a beeping in my head, like that on a life-support machine. I even had a tutor to help me who'd come round to the house. He would get so exasperated, and so would I. Arithmetic was fine, I could do that – but what's all this other stuff? It was like the requisite part of my brain had closed down.

In the event, I found the English exam a breeze, politics OK, maths a bit of a predictable nightmare, and accountancy – well. I just sat and stared at the paper, the words swimming before me incomprehensibly. Then my mind cleared. I don't care, I thought, I really don't care. Soddit. I could sit here for the next however many hours and waste part of my life. Or I could just leave. I stayed for half an hour – we were obliged to do at least that – then I left the room and went straight to the beach, walking bare-footed on the sand for hours. When I got home, Mum noticed my sandy feet. 'Oh, I just thought I'd clear my head after the exam on the beach,' I said airily.

I got my results – good in English and politics, and, God knows how, a C for maths.

'Where's the accountancy result?' asked my mum and dad. 'It's not on this sheet.'

'Oh, it'll be coming separately,' I assured them.

Of course, after a couple of weeks it was quite clear that no result was coming, and Mum and Dad just had to accept it. I must say the whole fiasco left me with a burning desire never to waste any of my life again – plus, not so positively, only a feeble grasp of my own financial affairs.

Of course, school is about more than just exams – or ought to be. You learn to get along with a huge variety of other people, or at least tolerate them. And you're growing up, physically, mentally and emotionally. Those school years see you turning from a little child into a young adult, old enough to vote. Most people find the transition awkward. Easier to cope with at home, where you can skulk in your room, but at school, in public, every difficulty is magnified. At least, that's what I found.

# * 3 *

# Growing Up

When you're a little kid, you think nothing's going to change. This is the world as you know it, and that's the way it'll always be. This is how you are, and you won't change either. But there's no getting away from it – time, tide and puberty wait for no one…

For girls, it starts with bras and periods. I'd heard a rumour that you couldn't have a period till you were wearing a bra. Or it might have been the other way round – you couldn't wear a bra until you'd had a period. Whatever, I was a bit hazy about the whole thing. Mum didn't have that 'chat' with me beforehand, so when one day in my last term at primary school I found myself bleeding into my knickers, I was taken aback, to put it mildly. Of course, I must be ill, I was probably bleeding to death. Or could it have been one of our playground chase games? We used to play Kiss, Cuddle Or Torture. When a boy caught you, you had to choose one of those three options. I always opted for Torture (Chinese burns, rabbit punch, kick up the arse, that sort of thing), as I was a Ninja and could take it, and I didn't like the thought of getting cosy with boys, strange creatures that they were. Maybe one of the punches had broken something?

After an anxious walk home, I confided in Mum and she hurriedly and rather self-consciously put me straight. Or tried to. It still seemed very odd, and I couldn't pretend I understood much of it, if anything.

I gathered that it was the sign of a girl turning into a woman (not that I'd thought I'd turn into anything else). After a brief account of the biology, which only left me more confused, Mum put her own particular spin on the phenomenon.

'It's a challenge women are given as we are stronger than men,' she announced. 'We can endure the greater suffering.'

I had to think about this.

'So we suffer because we are stronger?' I quizzed.

'Yes.'

'So the stronger you are, the more you have to pay for it?'

'Kind of.' Then Mum evidently gave up and said, 'Let's eat ice cream and talk about shoes.'

OK. I was none the wiser, but hey...I'd work it out. And in fact Mum was right, as I was to learn years later, the hard way. The stronger you are, the more you have to fight.

But back in my new pubertal phase, there was soon the bra question. Mysteriously I seemed to have grown boobs overnight and nobody had thought to send me the memo in advance. What do I do with these things? Are they going to grow any bigger? Will they explode? What, in my face? Little did I know then that my rather large assets would serve me well in the future when I became a lads' pin-up. At the time, though, they were nothing but a severe embarrassment. Not that I was the only girl to suffer. My friend Nicky's father always joked that it was the sea air that made us Edinburgh lasses grow humungous boobs. I wondered if there was a grain of truth in it. Did the salt from the sea make our boobs thirsty? Were they storing water in case the sea air dehydrated them? Were we like camels and their humps – tits of the desert? Whatever, all I knew was that they had to be hidden under huge unflattering tops and that my back hurt. And I attracted unwelcome attention from boys in the school playground: 'Porter's got boobs! Porter's got boobs!'

I remember getting my first bra – it was one of the most humiliating days of my life. Mum went with me to Tammy Girl, and I secretly think she was just as embarrassed as me. Once inside, she hurriedly held some random bra up against my chest. There was no trying it on! And we shot straight home as if that outing had never happened. My first bra was a white one, size 28B. I had zoomed straight to a B cup. As soon as we reached home, I could hear mum having a word with Keith and Dad: 'Do not mention the word bra. She is not happy about it.' But it was only minutes before my dad sneaked up behind me and pinged my bra strap. I was mortified – and furious.

Looking back, I wonder if Dad's thoughtless joke didn't help to plant the seeds of my insecurities. The way my young mind reasoned was this: my dad was supposed to love me, support me, look after me. If he made fun of me, how was I supposed to cope when kids at school – who most certainly didn't love me – made fun of me?

Then again, a pubertal girl with raging hormones isn't the most balanced judge of anything. No doubt my dad thought I was just being prickly over no hing, while to me it was a really big deal. At least I was spared the curse of acne.

My periods were proving troublesome, though. Even after I'd been at secondary school for a couple of years, they showed no sign of settling down and becoming regular. Sometimes I'd bleed for two weeks, and then not have another period for two or three months. I never knew what to expect. I think this was around the time that I started feeling what you might call moody. I couldn't put a date to it, it was a gradual process, but I realised that at some times I felt dragged down, for no particular reason. I'd had ups and downs as a little kid, of course, but as far as I can remember there was always an obvious reason for this. If I was doing something exciting I was on an up, and if my dad had shouted at me I was on a down. That was understandable – life was simple then.

Now I found myself feeling low and tearful when nothing noticeably bad had happened. And to even things up, so to speak, sometimes I felt ridiculously happy, even if nothing especially good had happened. Not that I was complaining, especially about feeling happy. I took my state of mind for granted, accepting that I was confused by it all. If somebody had said 'premenstrual tension to me', I'd have just gone, 'Pre- what?' Things like that weren't talked about.

I suppose most teenagers think they're depressed at times, sitting alone in their rooms feeling sorry for themselves and angry with an unfeeling world. I'd sit for hours in my new bedroom, doing schoolwork, listening to The Smiths, feeling awkward and lumpy, lamenting the fact that my fair hair was getting darker – and was that the start of a moustache? I just knew the rest of the world was out enjoying itself. I now had a window facing the street, and sometimes I'd stand there and watch my mates going off out somewhere. Sometimes they'd see me and wave, 'Gail, come down!' With a mental image of my dad looking over my shoulder, I'd mime, 'Can't – got to work.'

On top of whatever was going on in my mind, I developed a craving for ice cream. Unusually for me, I started to eat huge amounts of it, literally half a bucket at a time. Not surprisingly, I put on weight. My boobs of course had always been big – now the rest of me was catching up. One day in class, someone called to me – 'Oy! Big Bum!' I was crushed. Oh God, I thought, I'm getting really fat.

It wasn't just the ice cream, though. My mum had finally twigged that when I got a period it seemed to go on for ever. The fact I was getting through packets of Tampax at a rate of knots might have given her a clue.

'There's something here not right, Gail,' she informed me.

No kidding. For once she encouraged me to go to the doctor, whose solution was to put me on the Pill.

'That'll make your periods settle down,' he said.

Well, I stuck at it for about six months and sure enough the periods did get a bit more predictable, and not so heavy. The bad news was it made me feel awful, really low, and I put on even more weight. I'm sure it was the Pill that did this – no one could eat that much ice cream.

So there I was, feeling even more miserable and even fatter – all of nine and a half stone, which for someone small-boned and short like me was pretty heavy.

In his inimitable way, my dad had a suggestion. 'When you're not wearing uniform,' he said, 'wear black. It's slimming.'

God knows where he'd picked up that nugget of information, but I believed it. I'd also heard a variant on the same principle. When God created the butterfly, he made it bright and colourful, but when he created the elephant, he made it grey. Ah – so that's the message:

(a) *It's bad to be fat.*
(b) *If you are fat, be as inconspicuous as possible.*

I reckon this was the time I started to have an uneasy relationship with food. I didn't go mad on crash diets, but I definitely had the idea I had to lose weight. Every compulsion has to start somewhere!

Periods and moods aside, the other effect of sex hormones was kicking in. At secondary school I became acutely aware of boys, not just as boys to play games with, but as the opposite sex. In primary school the closest I'd ever come to having a boyfriend was holding hands with Ian Bristo. I'd fantasise about kissing him one day after school, and practised snogging on my hand when no one was looking. Not that I had any confidence where boys were concerned – I used to feel butterflies in my tummy if a boy even looked my way.

Now, with the huge number of boys around, I was spoilt for choice. I had a crush on a different boy each week. Justin, Kieron, Derek...the list went on. When I was older, I picked up on the school grapevine who fancied who, who were the hottest boys, and all the usual nonsense. Like most of the girls, I did have a quick snog with boys at the school disco, but that was all.

Opportunely, this was the time we had sex education lessons, of a sort, during biology classes. In one question-and-answer session, the teacher asked: 'Can you get pregnant if you don't have sex?' Before she'd even finished her sentence, my hand shot straight up and I said with all the confidence of the dead ignorant, 'Yes, Miss, you can.' Kieron, the boy I had a crush on that week, had kindly informed me if I got sperm on my tights, I could get pregnant. So there I am, proudly explaining this to the whole class: 'If you get sperm on your tights, you get pregnant.' I was their light entertainment for that lesson, all right.

My first real snog (with tongues) was when I was fifteen. It was at the school disco, and we were slow dancing to a Jim Diamond song. The boy's name was Elliot, he was blond and I bit his top lip. Afterwards, I rushed home and never breathed a word to Mum. Actual sex wasn't on the agenda at this time. I knew some other girls were sleeping around, some as young as fourteen. Call me old-fashioned, but it shocked me. Snogs were fine – but all-the-way shagging? Not a chance. I just couldn't understand how girls could go from one boy to another – yuk!

I was still a very good kid. As well as never even being tempted to lose my virginity (though I did allow myself to speculate on this mysterious milestone in life), I didn't smoke, didn't drink or sniff glue, I never swore and stealing was just not in my psyche – no wonder I was so horrified when I accidentally lifted that aerosol from B&Q! A lot of the kids at my school would steal things from shops – bubblegum, the *Beano*, anything really – just for the thrill of it. Not me.

I fell in love for the first time as I was starting to work for

Highers. Andrew was at my school, two years older than me and the brother of one of my friends. I started carving his name on desks as well as my own. I thought he was wonderful, if somewhat mad. He was always getting into trouble, fighting and ending up damaged and scarred in hospital. Once he fell down a flight of stairs at school while he was mucking around with a coat hanger, which somehow managed to get stuck in his eye socket. All in all, quite a terror – but there was something about him that really appealed to me. I probably couldn't have put it into words at the time, but now I realise it must have been his unconventional edge, his refusal to accept norms, his liking for risks – and a great capacity for laughs. Irresistible. Deep down I think I knew even then that I was just a bit of a laugh for him – a quick snog every so often.

I thought of him as my boyfriend, luxuriating in my romantic yearning. In truth we didn't have a relationship as such. I trailed after him, all dewy-eyed, like an adoring puppy dog, much to his embarrassment. To him I was just his kid sister's little friend. He usually snubbed me at school, but I could take it – in the name of love. At least he would talk to me on the phone, when his mates couldn't see him. It'd usually be me who'd call, burbling on, and calling him again the minute he hung up. That's me, a fledgling stalker.

Mum would get very exasperated with all this carrying-on.

'For God's sake!' she'd snap. 'He only lives five minutes up the road – why do you have to spend so long on the phone?'

'Oh, Mum,' I'd whine. 'I'm being a stroppy teenager, let me be annoying.'

Poor Mum. Must have driven her mad.

'I lurve him!' I'd say.

Mum would roll her eyes and say, 'You *will* get over this.'

She was right, of course, but for a while I thought he was the coolest thing on the planet. Even if the nearest thing he got to an endearment was 'All right then, Fattie?' I think he meant it affectionately…

Eventually I did lose my virginity, the summer after I left school. And believe me, it was a case of, 'Hang on, I've lost my virginity. I had it a minute ago.' Or rather, two minutes.

The boy, who shall be nameless to spare mutual blushes, was visiting me in my room at home. Mum and Dad were out. First it was just 'Hi, how are you?' which rapidly progressed to 'OK, let's give it a go.' We'd known each other for quite a while, and it just seemed the right time and the right thing to do.

It was terrible. Then we heard a noise downstairs, and it was trousers yanked up in a panic before he made a quick getaway out the window, hissing, 'See you later.' How he didn't break anything jumping from the first floor, I don't know.

So he came and went, so to speak, in a flash. I was stunned. You've got to be winding me up! I'd been looking forward to that for weeks, months, even years. Is that all there is to it?

Well, no, as I was to happily find out some while later. Meanwhile, as I'd been growing up, I'd been thinking about what I was going to do after school. I'd always had my ambitions, among them one I'd been nursing since I was a kid…

# * 4 *

# Acting Up

When I'd had my Princess Leia moment at the age of seven, it wasn't just the fact that here was a stunning, beautiful girl doing amazing things and fighting the forces of evil. I could tell fact from fiction! I knew Carrie Fisher was acting. I'd always loved performing myself, happy to sing and dance at the drop of a hat, incorrigible show-off that I was. But here was drama – what a fantastic world of adventure and make-believe. My young self was very impressed. That's what I'd do. I'd be an actress too. Though as far as my dad was concerned I'd have as much chance of being an actress as I would of becoming a real princess. According to him, acting's no job for a well-brought-up Scottish girl. But I was young. I could bide my time, and Dad couldn't object to me joining the school drama club at Portobello and getting my first taste of the stage. I loved it.

And I wanted more. I started going to the Edinburgh Acting School, along with my friends Nicky and Anna. It was run by a lovely lady called Anna Tinline. She was petite, cute and totally passionate about amateur dramatics – but had professional standards. The school gave people from all walks of life a chance to get to grips with the performing arts, and actually work on stage in front of a paying audience. I can't remember now who first suggested it, but Nicky, Anna and I all applied (there was no audition) and joined the weekly classes. We must have been getting on for fourteen at the time, and it was one of the best things we ever did.

The classes were held in the Pleasance Theatre, in the eastern end of Edinburgh's Old Town. Since it was opened in the mid-eighties as a venue for the Edinburgh Festival, it's gone from strength to strength, a fabulous place. In fact, I was now old enough to appreciate the Festival. For four weeks in August, Edinburgh bursts into vibrant life with culture of all kinds from all places, a love for all things colourful and wonderful. Comedy, theatre, art, song, dance, music, mime – you name it, the Festival and its Fringe have it. My young self was hooked, and I've made a yearly pilgrimage ever since.

Along with this dawning cultural awareness came an appreciation of the city itself. Edinburgh was a magical place to grow up in. As little kids we didn't appreciate its beauty and history, but the older we got and the more places we visited, its uniqueness shone through. We didn't realise that no other city was fortunate enough to house a castle, a palace and an extinct volcano in its centre.

Edinburgh felt theatrical. It felt right to be attending my acting classes in the heart of this vibrant city. We would sit in a circle and discuss improvisation, characterisation, plays and actors, before attempting to act out anything ourselves. Of course, 'being a tree' always cropped up in the improvising workshop. It makes me smile: be a convincing tree and that's great; be a wooden actor – not so great.

I really got on with everyone at drama. Everyone had that thirst for knowledge that I had often been ridiculed for. Everyone was polite and attentive. No talking back in class, no disrespecting our elders. It was my parents' dream class. I never seemed to suffer from nerves here. Perhaps because I didn't fancy any of the boys who attended the class. Potential snogs would always be a cause for embarrassment. Also, there was a distinct shortage of boys at our workshops. I suppose it was not the kind of after-school activity that the boys in my neighbourhood were looking for.

We performed our productions in public at the Traverse Theatre in Edinburgh's Cambridge Street. This has been going since the early sixties, and concentrates on new writing. I'm sure our efforts were an interesting change to the usual fare! We gave a performance every evening for a week, just like a professional company, and it all gave me a tremendous buzz. I loved the whole set-up, from first read-throughs to final curtain. I was realising what it was I liked so much. I'd always wanted attention, of course, ever since I was a little kid. If my acting could make people laugh or smile or think – raise any sort of reaction – then fine. But more than that, I liked the fact of being in a group, being part of a bigger whole. Even now, if I do a job entirely by myself I feel lonely, and I've always found it difficult being alone. I can do it – let's face it, I tend to think I can do anything – but I'm happiest working in a team. I love the camaraderie.

Mind you, I scuppered some of that camaraderie during our first public production: a play written by our teacher about a feminist. I can't remember the premise of the play – just that I was the feminist, and on the opening night I managed to miss out a whole page of dialogue. This may not seem like such an awful thing to do except for the fact that the page of dialogue I omitted was the only page that my friend appeared in. OK, a bit bad…and it got worse. Her parents were in London and had travelled up especially for that evening's performance to see their daughter's debut. Yes, I was a total screw-up, to say the least. There were many tears backstage. I apologised a lot but also wanted to point out that because I missed out her page, it had turned into virtually a one-woman play and I was quite tired actually. Not a point that would have gone down too well.

Our second, and final, effort was *The Dracula Spectacular*, some kind of gruesome musical extravaganza. My audition for a part didn't go as well as I hoped. I got the part of a one-eyed, deformed coachman, and my Transylvanian accent left a lot to be desired. But then again, did you see Keanu Reeves in the Dracula movie that he annihilated? At least I pulled off the one-eyed, deformed bit all right!

We had further fuel for our acting ambitions one day when a bunch of us went to London to see a play performed by real actors. London! My first glimpse of Leicester Square as we came up out of the underground hooked me for life. I just went, 'Oh my God!' It was magical – the crowds, the lights, a sense of excitement in the air. We wandered around, getting our bearings and taking in the heady atmosphere. We were heading for the Strand, and the Vaudeville Theatre, which was showing *Blithe Spirit*, by Noël Coward. I'd never seen a professional play performed before, and this was a cracker to start with. For anybody who hasn't had the pleasure to know it it's a comedy about a posh bloke, Charles, who's haunted by the ghost of his first wife, Elvira, after an eccentric medium conjures her up. Elvira promptly tries to put a spanner in the works of Charles's second marriage (being visible only to him), and much comic dialogue and funny business ensues.

It was wonderful – I was caught up in it and laughed like a drain. If I hadn't already been drawn to live theatre, this would have done it for me.

And there was icing on the cake. We had an invitation to go backstage and meet the actress who played Elvira, none other than Joanna Lumley. She was brilliant in the play, really beautiful and with perfect timing. So there we were, four or five of us squeezed in her gorgeous little dressing room, which was adorned with all the requisite flowers and telegrams and photographs you'd expect for a proper actress.

Joanna gave us tea and biscuits, and chatted in a very friendly way. I was just sitting there gobsmacked. Wow, it's like a dream – I've just seen this fantastic actress on stage in the funniest play and here she is talking to us! Signing our programmes! Towards the end of our visit, she leaned forward and gazed at us earnestly. In that posh, breathy voice she said, 'Now, if any one of you ever becomes an actress, or famous, promise me you won't forget me.' My immediate thought was: 'I will never forget you, Joanna Lumley.' And I haven't. Apart from following her career with some interest (especially in *AbFab*), the very first time I got a job on TV, my first thought was: 'I do still remember Joanna Lumley!'

I've never actually met her again, but you can tell what an impression she made on my young self all of twenty years ago.

After *The Dracula Spectacular*, drama school started to quieten down a lot. By now we were getting a little older, sixteen or so, and other things were becoming more interesting to a lot of the teens. Playing make-believe wasn't on their activity agenda. Eventually, the class became too small and we were too old for the other classes available, so the end of our drama time had arrived. I moved on with a wealth of knowledge. I could mess up a friend's debut, I could play a one-eyed deformed coachman with a bad accent, and I could mimic a tree. Watch out, world, I'm coming to get you!

Seriously, though, it was a fantastic experience, with dedicated teachers. I really did learn a lot.

I suppose us kids were dreaming of a career on the stage, or on film or telly. Meanwhile we'd take every opportunity to practise our routines. Nicky and Anna used to come round to my house after school as often as possible, and I'd dig out our old VHS camera and set it up on a tripod. In my room we'd put on music and we'd mime to it, sing songs, dance, act out mini-dramas – generally ham it up for the camera. We had hours of video footage. When we showed it to Nicky's mum and dad, Sheila and Bruce (curiously, not Australian), I remember their reaction. They looked at us almost sorrowfully, shaking their heads. 'Girls, girls, you're like fifteen, sixteen – why are you staying indoors making videos? Why are you not out enjoying yourselves?' But we were! We thought it was the best fun, even if other people thought we were weird.

\*

We were going to finish our school careers with a dramatic bang too. Every year the sixth form put on a show, and this year it was *Grease*, probably the best musical ever for kids to join in. The school had done the old Rodgers and Hammerstein classics before, like *Oklahoma!*, and they were fine in their own way, but *Grease* pressed all the right buttons for us. We had auditions, amid much excitement, and I was thrilled to get the part of Sandy (well, I already had the ponytail). Most of my friends had parts too.

There was a great bunch of people in the sixth year: bright, funny, dynamic. I was in a regular posse – Joanne, Lesley, Danielle, Anna, Nicky – along with some great blokes, especially Rajan, one of the nicest people in the world. He was playing Danny in the show. By now, a lot of kids had left school to get jobs, or go on schemes, or just laze about – or, in some cases, have babies. The ones who were left were the ones who actively wanted to stay on, and we had quite a bond. We took the show seriously and worked hard at rehearsals, singing and dancing and perfecting our American accents. Though we were so busy with schoolwork and revision for the upcoming Highers, we managed to fit it all in – in fact the excitement of preparing for the show balanced the grind of the work. When I was at school, busy and actively enjoying myself, I felt a different person from the misery guts that was often me at home. I'd leave school on a high, and by the time I was sitting in my own room that bubble would break, and I'd feel negative thoughts crowding in, fears and panic. All the more reason to make the most of school then!

It was funny that my part in *Grease* mirrored my own life in a way. Sandy, the little earnest innocent with her tidy clothes and ponytail, the others kids taking the mickey out of her – that's me all right. But then she funks up and stuns everybody, not least heart-throb Danny. Right, I thought, perhaps in real life I'll one day get to strut my stuff in skintight black leather pants and stilettos and slay 'em in the aisles. This girl was starting to change, all right. Little Princess Leia was finding herself drawn to – well, if not the Dark Side, then to something not squeaky clean and regimented.

Rajan and I had to snog on stage, and, in a bit of life imitating art, we actually went out together briefly (Andrew, at this time, was being more than usually elusive). Us girls in the show had Pink Lady nights in my house, where we'd drink wine, eat nuts, and talk about boys. It was just part of the whole build-up to a fantastic experience.

We gave five performances in the big school hall. It was open to everybody and we had about three hundred people a night, and each time we were rewarded by a standing ovation. And afterwards little kids were waiting for the cast's autographs. Star treatment! I'd never set out to be one of the cool kids – how could I? – but now I found myself part of the coolest gang, looked up to by the rest of the school.

Our production became a hot talking point, part of the school's mythology. In fact I had proof of this recently when I went back to the school, nearly twenty years later. A young friend of mine at the school – she was born in my street, I've known her all her life – was giving a talk on me and how I was coping with the various crises in my life that had been heavily publicised. I went in and sat in the class. The first thing the kids said was, 'We've seen *Grease*, Gail – Miss MacRoberts shows it every week!'

Miss MacRoberts was the music teacher who'd done a great job producing the show, along with another teacher, Mr Leslie.

'Every week?' I said.

'Yeah – she loves it so much, she says it's the best thing she ever did.'

Then someone had the idea of playing the tape and I cringed.

'I'm thirty-six! Please, Miss, turn it off!'

The kids were blasé. 'It's OK, Gail, we've seen it about a million times already.'

Well, it's nice to think I made a lasting impression. What was more important was what it did to us as a group – we really were brought together; we bonded. Again, I simply loved being part of a dynamic team.

The fact we all got on so well made it harder to leave school, in a way. We were quite upset – something good was breaking up. So we made many promises of keeping in touch, and some of the promises have lasted.

To take away the sting, there were parties. I felt I was off the leash now. I'd worked and studied for years and years, and Dad couldn't confine me to my room any longer. He couldn't now legislate who'd be my friend and who wouldn't.

One party, memorable for entirely the wrong reasons, was given by Kieron and Niall, two handsome brothers I'd got to know very well. I'd gone through the snogging stage with both of them and we were all good friends now. Their mum and dad were going away on holiday, and the boys were planning a big party in their house.

I knew their mum, Vivien. Before she went away she said to me, 'Gail, whatever you do, make sure they don't ruin my table.' (I still had the reputation of being very sensible.)

She had a huge, beautiful oak table, which dominated the dining room. It was her pride and joy, so I promised I'd look after it, and the house generally.

As soon as the parents were gone, Kieron and Niall were on the phone, organising the party. I went along, but with Vivien's plea ringing in my ears I was on tenterhooks, watching out for damage. I was picking up fag ends, wiping spilled drinks, but when I came back from clearing vomit out of a sink, it was to find a bunch of guys sitting round the table, passing a huge joint to each other. Hot bits kept falling off and making burn marks on the table.

I freaked out. 'You can't do this!' I shrieked. But all my jumping up and down made no impression, and by the end of the night the table was covered in scorch marks. The enormity of what had happened was dawning on Niall and Kieron. I said to them, 'Look, I'll come round tomorrow and help you clean up.'

'That's grand, thanks,' they said.

'And you're gonna have to think about what to do with the table.'

With that, I left them to it.

I came back next morning, entering the garden through the back gate as usual. I saw a sight that initially horrified me, then made me laugh out loud. It looked like some kind of alien android, human-shaped but sandy-coloured with a rough, flaking skin. It was Niall, the elder brother. He was dressed just in shorts, and covered from top to toe in sawdust. He'd taken it upon himself to start sanding down the table with an electric sander to try and get rid of the burn marks.

When I saw the table I realised he was shrinking it! Grinding away whole layers.

'You're gonna have to get this done properly,' I said.

And this is where we turn into an advert for Yellow Pages.

Niall looked through the directory and booked a french polisher, then we all went through the house cleaning it from top to bottom, restoring it to its usual immaculate state. And I wish to put on record that people should never ever be sick at a party anywhere but in the toilet.

The french polisher took the table away and brought it back next day, a nail-biting half an hour before the parents were due back. 'You'd better watch it, though,' he said. 'The surface isn't quite dry – don't put anything on it.'

So then the parents came back and it was all 'Hi! Great to see you! Did you have a good time?'

'Us? Oh, just had a few people round, takeaways, watched a few videos, chilled out…Would you like a cup of tea?'

Vivien was delighted by the state of the house. 'It's as if we've never been away,' she said. 'I'm impressed, you've really looked after everything,' she added, putting her hot mug down on the table. Without a mat.

The rest of us stared at the mug. Oh my God. She lifted it up and a chunk of the surface came away with it, stuck to the bottom of the mug.

A sudden silence.

'Well, I'm just gonna go home now,' I cried cheerily.

As I hurried out the door I heard a loud 'Niall!'

Just like the advert. We thought we'd done so well, but we were caught out.


Before leaving school, those of us planning to go on to further education had made our choices of college and courses, filled in our forms, waited for interviews. I had no doubt of what I wanted to do. I'd applied to Edinburgh's Napier University for a drama course, the stepping-stone to a career as a professional actress. Dad had made predictable grumbling noises. 'Why not study law?' he'd say, evidently seeing me as a hotshot Edinburgh lawyer. To humour him, I did work experience in a lawyer's office, and was bored out of my mind. I'd thought that at least the criminal side might be interesting, but it was all divorce stuff. No, acting was my path; I knew it, and so did Mum.

I was thrilled to be called to an audition – but once in the bare rehearsal room, standing in front of a panel of judges staring at me behind a long table, I found myself intimidated. I had to do a cold reading, a passage from Shakespeare, and I felt no affinity with Juliet or the verse. I stumbled and made a hash of it. I was aware of the judges glancing at each other and making notes.

Later I heard, 'Thank you, but you're not what we're looking for.'

Rejection. Not even the chance of a waiting list.

I'd never felt so gutted. I'd pinned all my hopes on that course, and now they were shattered, dust and ashes. I'd been rejected. My confidence was shot, and I didn't have the heart to try anywhere else.

What could I do now?

# * 5 *

# Kicking Out

I'd set my heart on that drama course at Napier. I hadn't thought of options, so I had nothing up my sleeve. One option definitely not open to me would be just hanging around, kicking my heels, watching my friends start their college courses or their good jobs with prospects. I'd have to do something. But with my fledgling acting career nipped in the bud, it was easier to say what I didn't want than what I did want.

I've always known that I didn't want to do any old job for the sake of it. Every time I happened to be on a bus or a train at commuting time, I'd look at all the people going into work, at their grim faces, and make instant value judgements. There they were, dressed in their drab suits, men and women alike, on their way to a dreary office where they'd be caged all day doing boring, routine work. Banks. Insurance offices. Civil servants. Paper-shuffling, pen-pushing. Same old stuff day after day.

I'd say to myself, 'I'm getting up and learning something

every day at school – what are these people learning? They can't be learning that much if they're sitting in the same job every day.'

Dullness, regularity – my idea of hell. I wanted a job that would be stimulating, ever-changing, one where I could meet new people all the time, not the same old faces day in, day out. I've always loved meeting new people – there are too many friends to make in this world that I haven't met yet! I'd seen what happened to the kids at school who couldn't wait to leave as soon as it was legal. It seemed to me that most of them were happy to land tinpot jobs, if that – no challenge, no gateway to a wider world, no ambition.

Oh God, now I sound like my dad, judging people by what's important to me. I don't mean to – of course everybody has to do what's right for them. Good luck to them. It's just me over-reacting at the prospect of doing it myself. I'd had a taste of routine work in my Saturday jobs, and knew that full time and for ever would so not be for me. Though for all I know, those people commuting to work might have been going to fabulous, exciting jobs where every day was a thrill. Just hiding it very well…

Dad was talking again about me doing law, but that was never gonna happen. Now I started thinking, well, if I'm not perform-ing on stage, perhaps I should think about backstage work – I've always been interested in the technicalities. And while I'm at it, not just theatre, but TV and films too.

Media Studies, in short. A local college, Telford, was offering a one-year course that looked like a useful taster, so I signed up for it. Perhaps it'd show whether I really was cut out for this kind of thing, whether it was worth solid commitment. So, looking at the college as a kind of stepping stone, I got stuck in.

Much to my delight, Sasha, an old friend from school, was on the same course. Apart from the instant companionship and solidarity, she kindly gave me a lift to and from the college. I was still living at home and Telford was way out west in the outskirts of the city. I had learned to drive – Dad had given me lessons on private ground, and I took the test on my seventeenth birthday. I passed, but there was no way yet that I could afford my own wheels. Sasha's old Lada was a godsend. Actually, it was so beat-up and naff that we were embarrassed to be seen in it. We'd disguise ourselves with balaclavas – we must have looked a right couple of dodgy characters, out for a day's ram-raiding. Not that I'm a fan of flashy posh cars, far from it, but this old heap was pushing it a bit – and pushing it a bit is what we often had to do when it conked out. Sometimes we pushed it so far that we might just as well have walked, without the extra effort.

Still, we made it to the college most days. The course itself involved a bit of radio production, a bit of filming, plus some actual performing. The radio side does date me. If I talk about editing now, I mime the way we used to do it in the days before computers when we manually spliced tapes and put them back together – so I'm turning knobs, using scissors, holding strips up to the light. Gives younger people a laugh about the old days, though I reckon that kind of hands-on work gives you a more solid understanding of what's involved, rather than just pressing buttons on a keyboard.

One thing that tickled Sasha and me about the college was the great mix of vocational courses. There'd be blokes in boiler suits and toolbags wandering off to plumbers' workshops, and trainee beauticians clicking along in high heels, dressed in sparkling white uniforms with never a hair out of place and lashings of make-up. Sasha and I would slouch around in our grungy clothes, trying to look like hip media students.

Part of the image was, of course, drugs. College is the classic place to try out new stuff. You're with a bunch of new people, not your old mates. A diverse bunch, always with someone who's into one thing or another. Cannabis, of course, speed, ecstasy…E was just coming on to the scene, and everyone said it just makes you feel really happy, makes you want to dance, so that was enough for me. Bring it on! Apart from the fun, it kept those low moods at bay. I drew the line at ketamin, though. If it's a horse tranquilliser, God knows what it would do to people.

I'm not sure how much we really got from the course. It wasn't exactly demanding – in fact what stands out in that whole year wasn't what I was learning, but the fact that I left home.

It sounds like a big adventure, but in fact I had it easy. It was more of a halfway house, so to speak. Mum and Dad had acquired a couple of properties in the city, including a flat above the office where they ran their building firm, and that's the one I moved into. For me at the time, it was the best of both worlds. The flat was in a cool part of the city, the Grassmarket, right near the castle. It's packed with pubs and clubs and shops and has a real buzz. There's a nearby brewery too, and the smell of it hung over the whole place – no bad thing, except on Sunday mornings after the night before, when the heavy alcoholic fumes could get right up your nose.

Anyway, it was great to have more freedom. And if I was having a bad day, it was good to know Mum was working downstairs and I could pop in for a wee chat, saying, 'Mum, I'm feeling a bit low.' Then it would be maternal tea and sympathy. The only drawback was what you'd expect when your parents are your landlords. Sometimes Mum would just walk in without knocking – 'Mum!' I'd protest. 'I could have been doing anything!' Though truth to tell, chance would have been a fine thing.

I was more than happy to leave home. Apart from the positive side of growing up, having my own space and organising my own life, there was the negative side. Even in my last year at school, things had got more strained at home. I'm not prying into my parents' private lives even if I could, bearing in mind how reticent they both are when it comes to emotion, but it was obvious their relationship was getting rockier. Keith and I would have dinner with Mum, then Dad would come in much later. I noticed that they took to sitting in separate rooms in the evening, both watching telly – but the same programme. It was as if they worked together during the day, and that was all they could stand. Talk about unresolved issues! And there were more narks between them. Keith and I could always pick up on the vibe. Not that Keith was at home a lot. Unlike me, he went out when he liked and did his own thing, rebelling against Dad and all his pressures – 'Do this, do that.' I really felt for my brother. He didn't know any more than I did at his age what he wanted to do. How can you, when you've no experience of life?

Jumping ahead about five years, no one was really surprised when Mum and Dad eventually split up. They married for love, built up a good home and business and raised two kids – then grew apart. Not exactly an unusual story. After their separation, Mum stayed in the family home, where she's lived ever since, always an anchor for the rest of us.

As I meandered through the Telford course – as I say, it wasn't tremendously demanding – the year was ticking by and I had to think about the next step. I hadn't been put off Media Studies, but I definitely wanted something more challenging that I could get my teeth into. I scoured prospectuses from colleges around the country. Locally, Napier had a promising-looking course, but I didn't get a straight offer, just a place on the waiting list.

Meanwhile, my dad had got me an interview with a bloke he knew, some kind of accountant or lawyer, I can't remember which. I think Dad was still hoping that I'd do something solid and respectable, and this guy would be the one to persuade me. In fact Dad's plan backfired. After the guy and I had been chatting for a while, he said to me, 'Do you know, it'd probably be good for you to get out of Edinburgh, broaden your horizons.'

That chimed with me. Don't get me wrong – as I've said before, I love Edinburgh, it's a fantastic place. Apart from all the history and culture, there's a real buzz from the university, there's always something going on and I'd got to know quite a lot of people. But by now I was longing for a change of scene, to see what else was out there in the wider world.

'Why don't you go to London?' asked the lawyer/accountant guy.

Another capital city – natural choice, really. I had applied to a London college and been accepted, so when Napier put me on the waiting list I thought, Soddit. I'll go for London. And I did. London – rock'n'roll! It held a magic for me ever since that memorable trip to the theatre when I saw Joanna Lumley.

Though when I say London, I should be more specific. It was Watford. All I can say is that I'm from Edinburgh – how could I know? On the map it looked pretty close to the city. Just a step away, I thought. Like the rest of London, it was bound to be cool and trendy...mistake. At least I could enjoy the anticipation after I finished at Telford.

There was something else to enjoy that summer, too. For the first time I went abroad on holiday without my mum. Just me and my mates Lynne and Michelle and Michelle's sister Debbie. We all marched into a local travel agent's and said, 'We wanna get away from here, go somewhere fun.'

'Right you are,' said the travel agent. 'You want Faliraki – you'll love it.'

'Faliraki?'

'It's in Greece, on the island of Rhodes. Sun, sea, sand and all the nightlife you can shake a stick at.'

Yup, that sounded like fun, so we went for it. An all-girls holiday to Faliraki it was, then...

And lucky for us we went at just the right age. Any younger and we'd have been with parents, and wouldn't have appreciated the freedoms – much older, and we'd have run screaming from the place. As it was, we had the time of our lives for two whole weeks.

We had an apartment a bit outside the resort, nice and quiet and comfortable. It didn't prepare us for the town itself. The main square was heaving, girls and guys knocking back the drink from ten o'clock in the morning, couples snogging and practically having it away in public, while music blared non-stop out of pubs and clubs. The beach was packed too, a mass of baking bodies. At first we just stood there gawping at it – 'Oh my God, is this what people do on holiday?' Then it was 'Wa-hey!' It didn't take us long to get into the spirit. We were all single, away from home and away from parents for the first time, and we knew how to party all right. So it was drinking and eating and laughing and dancing and snogging random fit boys, staying out all night and having a blast. OK, there was the vomit and piss to negotiate in the streets, and unwelcome advances from grotty boys, but we were young, we could take it.

We all felt so liberated. I can't remember a time we weren't laughing – at ourselves, at other people, at the madness of it all.

Then the two weeks were up and it was time to go home. And I found myself crying and crying, unable to stop.

'What's the matter with you?' my friends asked, reasonably enough.

'I don't want to go home!' I wailed.

'What? You've got to – you can't stay here for ever.'

Of course I couldn't, but I wished I could. I passionately wanted to stay, having a good time. I didn't want to go back to work and responsibilities. And that set a pattern that's lasted to this day. I love holidays and cry my eyes out when I have to go home. I want the magic to last for ever.

I don't know how I square this with my work ethic, my insistence

on earning my own living. Maybe deep down under all that condi-
tioning I'm a lotus eater, never happier than when I'm carefree in the
sun. Pity I'm an industrious Scot, then. Oh well, that's another
contradiction to add to the mix, another indication that I was never
destined for a smooth emotional life.

There'd been another sign of this before the holiday, in fact.
After college ended, I was back living at home before I left for
Watford. One morning, just before we were due to leave for
Greece, my mum had noticed a bikini in the front garden. Odd,
she thought.

It turned out that I was back to my old sleepwalking ways. As
I had my own room, both at home and in the Fountainbridge flat,
normally nobody would know if I wandered about during the
night, if I stayed in the room. This time, the holiday must have
been on my mind, as I got up, sorted through my drawer, chose a
bikini, opened the window and threw it out into the garden. After
that, Mum took to locking all the windows at night and pocketing
the key.

At least the tears of leaving Faliraki didn't last long. When I got
home, I clicked back into normal mode. Though maybe not
normal, as there were still some weeks of holiday before term
started, and I made the most of them. In fact I got caught up in
what you might call a rough crowd.

It could be an object lesson for people like my dad: make
something prohibited and you make it more attractive. He had a
fixed idea of who would and who would not be suitable company

for his daughter. I especially remember one time when I was in my room, working as usual, and there was a ring at the door. I heard a murmur of voices, then the sound of an engine driving away. I glanced out of the window and saw it was a van belonging to a local firm that a friend of mine had joined when he left school. Apparently he'd called to see me – just to say hello – and Dad had actually said, 'Don't come to this house again. You didn't stay on at school, so you're not fit company for my daughter.'

What can I say? I was mortified. Good job Dad had never got wind of Andrew – he'd be out of the house when I was making all those long lovelorn phone calls. I couldn't see mad Andrew meeting with paternal approval. Another time I was with a friend of mine, a girl called Jocelyn, mucking about on our bikes in the street. We were around sixteen. Something upset Jocelyn and she swore – 'For fuck's sake!' – and Dad heard it. He must have been in the front garden. He went mad, ordered me into the house and forbade me to speak to her or invite her to the house. That took a while to settle…

I don't think he ever knew that for ages when I'd gone to the local beach with my friends I'd always found myself attracted by the 'rough' bit, the far end with the funfair and amusement arcades that we weren't supposed to go to. In the summer, especially in Trades Fortnight when factories closed down, it'd be taken over by the Weedgies – Glaswegians – taking their regular holiday. That livened the place up even more, all rolled-up trousers and fish and chips. I thought this glimpse of another world was thrilling…

Not the sort of place for me, of course. It's all about standards, I was told. Yeah, sure, I thought, someone else's.

After Faliraki, I started going out with a young guy called Hughie, younger than me (I was nineteen). He knew some colourful characters. Not that they were bad people, they weren't. They just had bad habits, mostly revolving round drugs of all kinds. By now I was up for almost anything – 'Wa-hey, this is brilliant!' Good Gail was well and truly finding her naughty side. We'd all go out to rave clubs and go mental. Sometimes we went off to Glasgow and hit the clubbing scene there. A whole gang of us cheesy quavers – our name for ravers – would gather in Portobello on a Saturday night, some of us off our heads already, and pile into the hired coach. I hadn't been on a coach since I was a kid and going to Spain – now I was the noisy boozy grown-up! Though at this time, booze wasn't a big deal for my crowd. We liked pubs, sure, but never got stuck into the heavy stuff. It would be quite a few years before I'd start to use alcohol to blot out the misery in my life.

When we went to Glasgow, we always stopped at the same service station on the motorway, and each time we drew into the car park I swear I could see the staff battening down the hatches – 'Not them again!' Nothing violent, though. Just a bunch of unnaturally happy people on a night out. But with grungy clothes and wild hair and eyes popping out of our heads, maybe nicking the odd flower from the displays – we weren't the kind of customers to inspire confidence. I'd usually stay on the coach, scared there might be an argument. I'd be bolder once we got to the club, the Hacienda. This is most definitely not to be confused with the Manchester club of that name. The Weedgie version was a grotty dive in a very run-down part of the city. If it wasn't actually the Gorbals, we liked to think it was – it sounded excitingly dangerous, edgy.

I'd have taken just half a tab of E. I might be finding what passed for my wild side, but I was still cautious. I'd see how I got on before taking the second half. Meanwhile I'd hurl myself into the sweaty darkness of the club, techno music thumping out and making the building shake, and jump up on to the podium. That was my stage – I'd dance and dance in the limelight all night, with supernatural energy, feeling I could go on for ever.

When it was time to leave we'd wake up the coach driver, and wind down on the trip back. I loved everything about these times, not just the high-octane energy kick. There was the quieter side – people opening up their hearts, a feeling of real loving friendship, cuddles and warmth. If E did this to people, it could only be a good thing.

In fact when stories started to appear in newspapers, with dire warnings about sudden death, I thought, Hang on, this can't be the same thing I'm taking, it just makes you giggle and dance and feel drunk without falling over and throwing up, it makes you love people. Revels for the older generation, in more ways than one.

Then one day this pretty balloon was well and truly burst. Of course, people had started cashing in and adulterating the stuff, and I took a bad tab. I was horribly sick and ill. Blackout. Spent most of the night in the club toilet. When I recovered, I thought, That's enough. Taking those pills is like Russian roulette. I'd rather live. Looking back, I realise how naive I was, dicing with death. But even that experience didn't put me off trying something different later on...

Meanwhile, Hughie was sweet, and I was happy to stay with him. Amid all the mad partying, I was never promiscuous. Choosy,

I like to think. Probably everyone I've ever slept with has been off his head one way or another, so at least I've kept to a pattern. Most of my friends would go for the good-looking boys, but I've never been one for just looks. I'm attracted to boys with a bit of an edge, like Andrew at school. And I've always had a nurturing side – I like to look after people. Not like a surrogate mum, I hasten to add. But there's something about a dark side, a troubled soul…

By now, my brother Keith had been doing his own share of raving – in fact he was much deeper into it all than I ever was. He'd gone to college, but erratically. All Dad's strictures had backfired and Keith had cut loose from what was expected of him. He's very bright, but the formal academic route was never going to be for him.

Not that Keith ever lost the plot. His head's screwed on all right – both of us had that grounding, even if it doesn't always show up in me. We both knew people who overdid it, got hooked on drugs and got wasted. Some turned to crime to fund their habit, and ended up in jail. Some died. Like many people I experimented and, frankly, had a lot of fun, but eventually drugs lost any appeal they might have had. It's possible to just grow out of them.

Our mum and dad didn't know much about drugs. I think Mum suspected that Keith and I dabbled, but she didn't say anything. She probably realised that at heart we were sensible kids. There was one time, though, that Dad confronted me, and went completely off his head.

'If you touch that filthy stuff I'll lock you in the cellar and you won't come out!' he yelled.

Good one, Dad. I know parents worry – I would myself – but as usual Dad was more likely to provoke the opposite reaction. Something bad enough to get you locked in a cellar? Wow, must try that.

And London was on the horizon now. The big city – who knew what I could get up to there...

# * 6 *

# Going South

Sunday, 16 September 1990. This time I really was leaving home, going hundreds of miles south to start at Watford College. As ever, I was torn by conflicting emotions. I knew it was the right thing to do, to strike out on my own. By now I was chafing at the life I'd been used to, finding it claustrophobic, and what's more I was having trouble with a boyfriend who was getting a bit heavy, a bit possessive. But wouldn't you know it, when the day came I could hardly do anything for crying.

Mum had woken me up early to get ready to leave. I finished my packing through a haze of tears, feeling I was wrenching myself away from everyone and everything I loved. Mum couldn't hold back the tears either, and Keith was in floods. Even Dad, that monument to Scottish hardness, was choked. Perhaps the reality was dawning on him – his little girl actually leaving home. It was a big thing, the first child moving out. For all our differences, there's no wiping out that family bond.

Then my friends arrived to see me off – Joanne, Kieron, Lynne, Lesley and Simon, and of course my troublesome boy-friend, who was really upset.

Simon, Lesley's brother, was a particular friend, one I haven't mentioned yet but have been close to for years. We used to call him Fat Boy Simon for the obvious reason – hardly sensitive, considering how much I hated being called fat. But Simon genuinely didn't mind, he took everything in good part. His heart was as big as his appetite. He lived round the corner from us, and would stroll into our house and head straight for the fridge.

'Hi, Sandra,' he'd greet my mum.

'Stay away from the fridge!' she'd say like a TV cop.

To no avail. He'd stick his head in the fridge and make himself something to eat.

My mum would try again. 'Simon, I'm not your mother and this is not your house. Get out.'

But it was impossible to be hard with Simon, he was so lovable. For some reason, his mum was convinced that we were going to get married. Don't know where she got that idea from. She was a nice, funny woman, who suffered from brittle bones, but she never complained. In fact the whole family used to joke about it. Simon used to say, 'Come round to our house – if you poke my mum I'm sure something'll break!'

Now I looked at his big, round, smiling face and realised I was going to miss him and everybody more than I could say.

Eventually I finished saying my goodbyes and kissing every-one, and got into the car with all my stuff. Mum and Dad were driving me to Watford, a journey that would take about eight hours. I was quite calm most of the time, but if I tried to speak to Mum I started to cry again.

At long last we drew up outside my new digs, which the college had arranged for me. When the landlady let us into the house, I felt like crying again – and I could see Mum did too.

Talk about culture shock. I suppose we all take our homes for granted. That's the norm for us. So I associated home with order and tidiness – not showpiece stiff, but comfortably clean and immaculate. My new home looked chaotic, with stuff piled all over the place. I was taking over the room occupied by the landlady's daughter, who'd moved out to live with her fiancé. But much to my dismay she hadn't yet shifted her belongings, or even cleaned up. She was on holiday, and would pick up her gear later. Meanwhile I was going to have to live out of a suitcase.

God, this makes me sound like a prissy little cow, an anal-retentive control freak. After all, the landlady was a lovely, welcoming woman, generous and kind. But if anyone was coming to stay in my house I'd have cleaned it from top to bottom. I may not be much into housewifery, but I'd make everything perfect for my visitor, make sure they were comfortable.

OK, I was meeting a different way of life – more casual, less uptight. Nothing wrong with that, but a shock to my system all the same. Probably a good one. Though I didn't take to the dog. I'd never lived with a dog before, and this was a yappy little crea-ture that left shit all over the back garden. We had a cat, and the thought of leaving crap in the garden would have sent my mother into a fainting fit.

Not a good start, then. My mum, casting anguished looks

around the messy place, kissed me goodbye, eyes streaming, then Dad did too and they were gone. I sat alone in that cluttered room wondering if I'd made the most enormous mistake.

But then Bridget, a fellow student, arrived. She was studying electrical engineering, having been sent on the course by her employers. Her work was a closed book to me, but she was really nice, and things were beginning to look up. A guy called Rob came round to take her out for a drink that first evening, and they invited me. I was more than happy to go out. Sitting in The Hare, just up the road, chatting away, it took my mind off Mum and Dad and everyone. I told myself to quit griping and give this new life a go.

Next day, Monday, was the first day of term. I got up and went to have a shower. Oops, another assumption. There was no separate shower, just a rubber hose contraption, so I had to get used to hosing myself down! After breakfast, time to go – and here Bridget came up trumps. She had a car, and kindly offered me a regular lift. Just as well, as we were some distance from the college.

Then it was a matter of finding my way around, getting used to another place, enrolling, sorting out timetables, meeting fellow students…nothing too taxing. In the afternoon I walked into town, and with sinking heart realised that Watford wasn't the most hip and happening place around. The next day, Tuesday, I wasn't due in until 11.30, long after Bridget had to be in, so I tried public transport. I waited at the bus stop for half an hour, then the driver dropped me off at the wrong stop and I had a forty-five-minute walk through grey, uninspiring streets.

Sorry, Watford. Your charms were lost on me.

The course I'd started was lost on me too. I'd cocked up here.

Graphics, printing technology…boring or what? I heard about a media production course, leading to an HND – higher national diploma – that sounded more my scene. Not being one to endure boredom more than was strictly necessary, I had a quick chat with the sympathetic head of department and I was transferred, thank goodness.

My very first lecture in this new subject – video production – showed I'd done the right thing. It was good fun, and my classmates seemed much happier and livelier than the last lot. To round off this promising day, Bridget and I went to a couple of pubs, then visited the tackiest nightclub I have ever been to – Paradise Lost. They were right about the name. Quite an experience.

By the end of that month, life had settled into a routine. Get up, hose myself down, eat breakfast, lift to college, lectures, work assignments, staying in and going out.

I left my old digs after a few months and moved into a sweet little granny flat attached to a big house owned by a lovely lady. It was in a leafy avenue, and much nearer the college – I went from dodgy public transport and a long walk to a five-minute stroll to lectures. I loved my new flat. Surroundings are important to me, and here I was now in a beautifully appointed, self-contained, ground-floor apartment, all to myself. There were other students in the house, though, and everyone was very friendly. I even loved the family dog, a big alsatian that would wander round the back garden under my window. That was when I changed my opinion of dogs.

I made some good friends – Sandy, Yemisi, Richard, Steve…a real mix of people; we all had a great time together. I especially liked a guy called Paul, who had big fluffy hair. We did such exciting things. I'd say to him, 'I'm making a collage out of newspaper – d'you wanna come and help me?'

'Yeah,' he'd say. 'Great.' Really.

So we'd hang out in my little flat, listening to Pink Floyd and cutting paper into odd shapes, joining the most peculiar items together for a laugh. Believe me, for Watford this was real entertainment.

Less innocuously, drugs were still around. As I've said, I did experiment with stuff, but nothing too heavy, at least intentionally. The bad experience with E didn't entirely put me off trying something new, especially if it came with assurances of a good time.

I was in my Watford flat with a couple of other girls, just chilling out, and the boyfriend of one of them came round.

'D'you wanna try this?' he asked, showing me something in a twist of paper.

'What is it?'

'Acid – fantastic stuff. You won't believe it, it'll blow your mind.'

It did that all right.

Before long I was tripping insanely, awful images flooding my head. I was sitting on the carpet and it was swallowing me up, taking me down into its depths. I staggered up and looked in a mirror – my face was melting, my eyes, nose and mouth all running into each other. I could hear screaming – that was me.

I remember one of the girls shouting in my ear, saying that orange juice is good, it numbs the effect. So off I staggered to the fridge, tearing open cartons of juice and dropping them. Then I couldn't keep still – jumping, dancing. Every time I sank to the floor, the carpet would swallow me up again.

Madness. Twenty-four hours of hell – by which time I was a twitching, weeping ball of paranoia, and utterly exhausted.

I suppose I was naive. Other people say acid is cool, it expands your consciousness and you have a really fun time. I hated it, and it put me off for life. Anyhow, maybe my brain is just the wrong sort to have this mind-altering stuff. It's away on a natural trip of its own much of the time…

And I'd seen what drugs could do to people, even before I went to college for the first time. People died. And while I was at Watford, I knew someone who drank liquid acid. It was in a small phial, and you're supposed to get just a tiny drop on your finger and lick it. This guy had no idea and he drank the whole lot. He's still tripping – in and out of institutions for the past fifteen years. Another guy I knew overdid it and tried to cut his own throat. I don't think he's ever been let out.

Then there was Calum. I went out with him for a while in Watford. He had his problems, which I found irresistible as usual, and for a while we had a kind of dalliance. He lived in another part of the country, but we'd meet up and go out dancing – a bit of a giggle. Then things petered out and I didn't hear from him for a long while. Eventually I phoned up a mutual friend and asked if she'd seen him.

'Oh,' she said, 'haven't you heard? Sorry – but he's dead. Hanged himself.'

Oh God. Everything must have got to him. What a way to go, what a waste, like all those other young lives cut short. Looking back now, I can see how easy it is to try and blot out problems, rather than sorting them out. Block your mind and maybe the bad things will go away. It shakes me to think that I could have done that too. If I'd been hooked when my life hit rock bottom, I could easily have overdone it and gone the same way. What a temptation. As it is, years later I nearly killed myself with legal drugs.

Back when I was a student, though, it was boredom rather than despair that could have led me to binge on the drugs – and the drink too. After my initial enthusiasm, the course had settled into a pretty dreary routine. Nothing actually wrong with it, it was me. The work seemed increasingly pointless. And my body was getting as sluggish as my mind. I couldn't find a martial arts club nearby, and for the first time in years didn't keep up my fitness regime. Stuffing my face with ice cream and chocolate didn't help, either. Sometimes I'd eat a whole big bag of Maltesers, all to myself. Talk about comfort eating. I was in the classic spiral – feeling low, eating to cheer myself up, putting on weight, then depressed at being fat. I did try an aerobics club, but felt too self-conscious as I was the youngest person there.

I was conscious of being a bit chubby when I first went to Watford, and joined a local WeightWatchers club with Bridget. I was now a bit over nine and a half stone. That must have been the heaviest I'd ever been, not good for someone who still hadn't grown taller than five foot two.

This struck me as gross. Sitting there looking at all the other fat women, I resolved to take myself in hand. Living on a student budget, I'd often buy just lardy, filling food, like bread, as well as chocolate. No wonder I was swelling up. I started to cut down immediately – but I wasn't stupid about it. I knew I had to have a certain amount of protein, carbs and veggies to keep going, so I switched to lighter, healthier stuff. I remember a lot of fruit and bowls of WeightWatchers soup. I cut down on my intake, and found it pretty easy, so I cut down some more, and some more.

People started saying to me, 'Wow, you've lost weight.' That gave me a great buzz. I might not be able to make things better in my life, but at least I could control my own weight, and the pounds fell off.

When I went home the next vacation, Mum took one look at me and was shocked. 'My God! There's nothing of you – you have to eat more!'

'No I don't,' I said. 'I'm fine.' And I meant it. I felt fantastic. I'd gone down to under seven stone, and was thrilled to see my cheekbones back. I could see my ribs, too, but that didn't seem to matter. I felt quite proud in fact.

I recently found an old photo of me taken by Mum around this time, and hardly recognised myself. I looked positively gaunt. What is it about ourselves that blinds us to reality? Blinded me, anyway. I thought I was doing fine, not realising the damage that was accumulating in my body as I effectively starved myself.

Anyhow, those trips home helped to alleviate the boredom of student life in Watford. I had to wait for the holidays as there was no just popping up for the weekend, with such a long distance involved. I had reminders of home, though, during term. Family and friends wrote to me, and I've always loved getting letters. Emails and texting just aren't the same – I like something tangible that I can treasure. Fat Boy Simon did a cheeky thing. On one of his regular visits to our house he nipped into my room and pinched some of my own stationery supply – and had the nerve to write to me on it!

'Hi,' he wrote. 'I've moved into your room and it's great, really comfy. I just love the easy access to the fridge...'

He's always been a great one for taking the piss. He used to make these crazy videos and send them to me. One time he filmed himself and my brother Keith mucking about behind a great big cake.

'We love you, we're so missing you!' they chorused, breaking into theatrical sobs. Then lifting up the cake and grinning – 'Yeah, now we got more cake to eat!'

Daft stuff, but it helped keep me sane. When the three of us – Keith, Simon and me – go out together, it's a case of taping up the ribs so you don't bust them laughing.

For a break from routine I'd also get the train into real London when I could afford it. A twenty-minute trip by train into Euston, then the underground to wonderland. Along with a girl-friend or two I'd hit the town. We'd splurge out in the Rock Garden in Covent Garden, and go shopping – or window-shopping, at least. Paul Smith, Whistles, fantastic gear. I'd always head to the Tintin shop too, one of my favourite places. I've always loved cartoons and comics. I've still got a membership card for Forbidden Planet.

As I say, money was usually tight, and I didn't always keep within my budget. When I was skint, and trying to lose weight, it was no hardship to go without food. I remember one time I didn't eat for about three days, but that was pushing it, even for me at the time. Then I found something like 47p down the back of a chair and went out and bought a choccie bar and a Diet Coke – the best food I'd ever eaten! Another time there was a big scare when I had to pay a big bill I wasn't expecting – bit of a blur now, which is what usually happens when anything to do with accounts pops up. Could it have been the poll tax? Did students have to pay part of it in those days? I can't remember, but I needed fifty quid pretty fast. I was never one to borrow money ad hoc from my parents – I knew some kids who just phoned up and said, 'Can you send me a couple of hundred?' We weren't like that.

I sent Dad a letter: 'Dear Dad, you've got to help me. Please send me fifty quid or I'll be in trouble. Enclosed photo shows what will happen to me if I don't pay up.'

I'd taken this photo of myself in a booth. I was lifting my arms as if I was holding bars in front of me. Then I carefully drew in the bars, and there I was – instant convict.

Well, it worked – and Mum thought it was so funny she kept the photo for years.

I mustn't make my time at Watford sound like a total miseryfest, though. For all the scrimping, the boredom, the unwise dieting, positive things did come out of it. Great friends, of course, and – something that was to define my professional life – a deepening conviction that this whole theoretical academic approach wasn't for me. I know we did practical stuff, working out storylines and producing videos, but it didn't seem real to me. I found myself feeling arsey towards the lecturers. I felt like saying, 'You're supposed to be showing me how to get into telly? If you're so great, how come you're not working in it yourself then?' I loved the whole film business, but wanted to do it for real – as a job.

In my second year, I didn't put in much of an appearance. I

started hanging out with a guy called Warren. He was mates with a gang of squatters, and I used to go with them to raves all over the place – there were some even in obscure parts of Watford. Usually, though, we'd get on buses and end up in Birmingham or Manchester, anywhere there was a good party and good vibes. More and more I was realising that this was the only way to stave off those times when nothing seemed worthwhile, and I'd start to feel paralysed with misery, depression, whatever it was called. So – keep busy! And if you're enjoying yourself to the hilt in the process, that's a bonus.

Then I got a letter from the college threatening to kick me out if I didn't do any work. That brought me up short. OK, I thought, I've gotta go back there. My basic common sense told me that I shouldn't leave college with nothing to show for it. So I got my head down, caught up with the course work, did OK and got my Higher National Diploma.

'Stay on a year and get a degree,' they told me.

You must be joking, I thought. Not another year of fannying around making home movies. I wanted to get stuck into the real world. Real work is the most important thing you can do. It is for me, anyway.

I had a plan. I'd been writing hundreds of letters to companies asking for a job – any job. I'd do anything, I said, be a runner, make the tea. I'd even work without pay. Anything to get my foot on the bottom rung of the ladder. It never occurred to me to expect to walk into a job with good money and status. The industry has always been hugely competitive, and you've got to have something solid to offer.

That was my thinking, anyway. I probably sound like an old fogey now, but even at the age of twenty-one I knew that to learn a job from scratch, watching people around you, is the best way to get a real grounding in anything. Watch and learn.

And I did the proper research – I didn't just fire off letters to all and sundry. I got a book called *The Knowledge* listing all the production companies in the country and their specialities. I focused on those who did the kind of thing I was interested in. Only they weren't interested in me. Rejection after rejection – that's if they bothered to answer at all. I kept what replies I did get, including a 'thanks but no thanks' from Chris Evans's company. But I kept going. And then – result!

I heard from an outfit called In Video, based in Edinburgh of all places, my very own home city. 'Come in and do some work experience for a couple of weeks,' they said. That meant no pay, but what the hell. I knew Mum and Dad wouldn't mind supporting me while I found my feet.

I bid a quiet farewell to Watford and packed to go home. I was determined to do my best. I wouldn't screw up and land on my arse. As it happened, I'd be too busy working it off...

# * 7 *

# Run-up to the Big Break

I started at the bottom, all right. But the way I saw it, the only way to go from there was up! As I've said, I'd never taken it for granted that you just walk into a good job. Nothing's just there for the taking – you have to work at it.

So I went and saw the people at In Video.

'Fine,' they said. 'We need a runner – give it a go for a couple of weeks.'

If you don't know what a runner is in the industry – well, it's got nothing to do with athletics. Though come to think of it, you do need to be pretty fit to do everything that's expected of you. You're a gofer, a dogsbody. Anything that needs doing, any errand that people want, that's what you do. And not just in the office. I was expecting the tea-making, the cleaning, the photocopying, the filing, the deliveries, all those small jobs that keep a workplace ticking over. I wasn't quite so prepared for picking up people's dry-cleaning, getting their shopping, babysitting their kids, waiting in for the gas man…

No strict division between work and home, then. But I threw myself into everything with enthusiasm. If I'd had to wear a badge (like the one at B&Q that had 'Hi. I'm Gail. I'm here to help') it would have read, 'Hi. I'm Gail. I go anywhere, do anything, no job too small'. I was like a perpetual motion machine. My ambition was to learn as much as I could, then go on and get a good job. I wasn't sure just what kind of good job it would be – even if it would be in front of the camera or behind it – but I was determined to make a splash one way or the other.

That unpaid trial fortnight turned into three years or so. And I did get paid, though not much for the amount of work I did. About a tenner a day, as I recall.

Whatever the job entailed, there was the great big plus of meeting new people – something I never tire of. And they were a great bunch of characters at In Video. This was the early nineties, and firms like this, making TV ads, were still pretty laid-back, long pub lunches and all. One of my duties was keeping the office bar well stocked.

They were mostly men, all Scots, from the boss to the graphic designers, the cameramen and the editors. If I had any favourites among them they'd be Jack, one of the graphic artists, and Tom, one of the cameramen. Jack was great, really laid back. He just used to laugh at me, shaking his head. Tom was like a big shaggy teddy bear, really tall, his long hair tied back in a pony tail, and famous for being grumpy. When I started work I irritated the hell out of him, all bouncing and keen as I was, and he deliberately tried to make me miserable.

'Pack up ma stuff,' he'd growl. 'Don't drop it. Drive the van. Do this, do that...' without so much as a please or thank you.

Even if he stomped off I'd run after him, saying, 'Can I get you anything? Can I do anything for you?'

And he'd rasp, 'Go away, child. Stop bothering me.' And he'd roll his eyes and ask the room at large, 'Where did this girl come from?'

But I'd insist to him, 'You're not gonna break me. I know you like me really. You do, don't you? Don't you?' Only to get another 'Och, away with yer.'

I must have worn him down, as eventually we got on well. I realised he wasn't really a Scots grouch, just rather aloof. I got to know his kids, and we're all still in touch – in fact I recently took those kids to a Snow Patrol concert. Only they're grown-up now, which always amazes me. 'Wow,' I said to them. 'I knew you guys when you were babies, now I'm taking you to concerts.' I know – what am I expecting? They'll be little for ever?

I did a lot of babysitting, including for Katie, the little daughter of Jamie, one of the bosses in the office. I still see her too, and she's another proper grown-up. She's even babysat for my daughter, which gave me a weird feeling of history repeating itself.

One of the few girls at work was Charlotte, the receptionist. Can you imagine a Scots lad as a receptionist? Charlotte was tall and pretty, very feminine. Compared to me she was quite fluffy and girly. She was engaged to be married, and loved being in love. She was always talking about weddings and stuff, which to me at the time was pretty boring – I just didn't get the whole settling-down thing. Still, she was a lovely, kind-hearted person, and we got on well.

It was she who organised a memorable birthday present for me. I turned up at work and was presented with a huge parcel – I couldn't imagine what it could be. The airholes in the wrapping paper should have given me a clue. It was a rabbit hutch. Complete with tiny little black bunny curled up inside.

'Er, thanks, guys,' I managed. I remembered that Charlotte and I had been talking about rabbits recently and I'd probably made the mistake of saying they were sweet, or something. Good job I was borrowing my mum's car to get to and from work – I wedged the hutch in the back seat to take it home.

When I got in, I called out to Mum, 'Hi, we're home.'

'Who's "we"?' she wanted to know.

'Oh, me and Flopsy,' I said.

'What? What on earth are you doing with that thing?'

'Birthday present. Charlotte's idea.'

I'd talked to Mum about people at work, and she knew about Charlotte's penchant for all things cute and fluffy.

'That explains it,' she said.

We put the hutch and its occupant in the back garden, and the bunny proved to have an unquenchable wanderlust. When it was older it kept chewing through the wood and escaping. We nailed on extra bits but it chewed through them too – and one day it disappeared for good. It was sweet while it lasted, but our relationship was not to be.

As I say, I'd gone back home for a while. It was good to have that support while I was working all hours and getting knackered.

To earn more money I'd tried bar work in the evenings, but being at everybody's beck and call inside office hours and outside too, it made extra commitments difficult, so I scraped by on my pay.

It wouldn't be long now before Mum and Dad split up; Dad was the one who moved out. The atmosphere was sometimes chilly, but with my long hours at work I wasn't at home that much. I kept my head down and didn't get in the way. It was great to see more of my brother Keith, though, when he chose to put in an appearance. After a year or so I was back in the Grassmarket flat, which cut down on journey time – given my work schedule, this was a blessing. As well as independence again, of course.

There was the same drawback to my parents' generosity – Mum especially was likely to walk in at any time just to say hello, even if I was in bed.

'Mum!' I'd remonstrate. 'I could be up to anything!' Though, as before but with a different reason (I was usually knackered), chance would be a fine thing.

'Well,' she'd reason. 'It is my flat, I should be able to walk in any time.'

'Yeah,' I'd protest. 'But I'm paying rent now. Doesn't that make me entitled to some privacy?'

Paying rent – that was when I was allowed to. Often Mum would put the money in an envelope and give it back to me. I'd say, 'I'm supposed to be looking after myself here, aren't I?' And Mum would say, 'Och, don't worry about it this month.'

I know she just wanted to look after me. She was still worried that I was so thin – by her standards, that is. I thought I looked pretty good. After all, I wasn't exactly a skeleton, and I had plenty of energy, even if it tended to run out quickly and suddenly. My periods had become very irregular – seemed to have stopped, in fact – and I knew that could be linked to low body weight, but it didn't bother me at the time. It was a hell of a lot better than bleeding half the time. And I could always tell myself that I just didn't have time to eat.

I did appreciate Mum's concern, and felt bad for being grumpy. But there was one unsettling time when I came back in the evening and found the bathroom entirely repainted. I phoned home – 'What happened here?'

'I had a couple of hours spare,' Mum said, 'so I thought I'd brighten the place up while you were at work...'

Right. When your mum's your landlady, there's no arguing.

By the time I'd been at the company for around a year, I was feeling pretty well established. There were a lot of ropes, but I was learning them, and getting more confident.

I remember one time when I felt sufficiently relaxed to have a bit of fun. I used to do a lot of parking cars for visitors – these big advertising execs would sweep up in their posh cars and I'd drive them to one of the allotted spaces. One day this guy drove up in a spanking brand-new Saab, and as I sat in the driving seat I thought, 'Soddit. It's a nice day – I'm off.' And I drove out of the parking lot – I could see people gesturing at me from the big upstairs conference room window, but I waved and mouthed, 'Just five minutes.' I drove round the block – what a lovely motor it was – and back to the car park, where one of my bosses was waiting for me.

'What d'you think you're doing?' he ranted. 'You can't take the client's car!'

'Well,' I said, 'the guy asked me to park it so I thought I'd take it for a wee runaround. Very nice it was, too.'

I thought, What are you gonna do? Sack me? No one else is going to do what I do for ten quid a day. Who else would wait all evening while the big guys were at a meeting in case they wanted something? In those old relaxed days they'd often be knocking back the scotch and smoking big cigars in full red-braces mode. One bloke might pop out and say, 'Gail, get me forty Marlboro Lights, will you?' And I'd always say, 'OK.'

One night a meeting went on even longer than usual, into the wee small hours, and I was asked to go and get pizzas – at three o'clock in the morning; at which time Edinburgh was shut. So I drove home, got a stack of frozen pizzas out the freezer, cooked them in Mum's oven and took them back to the office. There you go. If I was going to be a runner, I'd be the best bloody runner ever.

Sometimes I had company on those evening vigils – Vicky, one of the VT operators and, again, one of the few girls employed there. We'd do what was necessary, tidying up stuff in the office, waiting to see if the bigwigs needed anything. She had a more important job than me, but she didn't mind helping out. I suppose the guys could have said, 'Piss off home, we'll see to ourselves,' but I think they liked the idea of someone being on tap. If things were very quiet on our side of the door, Vicky and I would whisper to each other, 'Shall we get a bottle of wine?' One of us would slip out to the offie and we'd enjoy a drink or two. It was fun, we often had a good laugh. A few times, if nobody was needed in the office, we'd hit the town together and have a great time in pubs and clubs. Usually, though, I didn't have the time or the energy to go out raving.

Meanwhile, I was gradually taking on other bits and pieces of work, to help out people when they were extra busy. I used to work in Facilities, mostly in the VT room. I was a VT operator and offline editor – and unofficial library lady. In those days people stored tapes for reuse. We had thousands of them, and every shot had to be catalogued. So when somebody said, 'Can you find out if we ever did a shot of the Princes Street gardens in 1978? It must be early afternoon with not many people in sight,' off I'd trawl through the records. Everything was done manually back then. When, years later, I worked with an American production company, I was amazed at how much reshooting they were prepared to do. Quite a shock to my Scottish frugality.

The making of the ads themselves was pretty intense, all these advertising types running around and shouting when things went wrong. I was on hand as usual to help out or try to find things – 'Quick, Gail, we need a dark brown handbag and this one's too light – get a dark one now!' It was a lot of fun, if exhausting. On the technical side, I had a chance to learn how to operate a rostrum camera, and I tried my hand at writing scripts too.

I really got to learn how a production was put together, how one person's job linked to another's to get the whole picture. Ads are films in miniature, after all, and the principles are the same whatever the size of job – and my experience here was to help me enormously in the future. These days, when I meet kids who call themselves producers or directors, it usually doesn't take me long to work out how limited their experience actually is. (Old Fogey Alert!) Give me a solid all-round grounding any time.

I actually rose to the dizzy heights of assistant producer, which still sounds quite grand to me. I had my own assignments, my own budget – pretty small, but still a budget. It felt like a real achievement. Not that I put my old donkey work behind me. One bit of film I did wasn't an ad, but a short documentary shot on the west coast of Scotland. The local people were talking Gaelic, so we needed an interpreter who transcribed the speech. Then after filming all day, I had to sit at night with my little machine and catalogue each separate shot. I paused it after each scene, identifying it as 'Mrs McCready talking about her father' or 'Farmer describing storm' or whatever. God, I could never have got my head round the old Gaelic – all those consonants – but it sounded wonderful. And in these days of digital and computers, that way of working now seems like it's from another time too. But it was a very useful discipline, and I still use it to catalogue my own personal shots.

As I say, I got on well with my colleagues, once I'd proved I was useful and knew what I was doing. There was a bit of friction, though, when a new Facilities manager arrived. I suppose it's the same in any office – a tightly knit group of people don't always take to being swept up by a new broom. What's more, this new manager was a woman, Marnie, in an industry still dominated by men. I think it made her determined to be ultra efficient – anyhow, she gave me a hard time at first, and was very much the one in charge. Once she settled in, though, she realised she could trust me, and we became really good friends. It must be tough holding your own in a man's world.

We were both at a festival recently, and were having dinner with a bunch of friends. I was a bit tipsy, and decided to wind her up.

'I used to work with Marnie,' I informed the person next to me. 'And she was a real bitch.'

I turned to Marnie. 'You were a real bitch, Marnie.'

'Aye, I know.'

'You were a bitch,' I repeated. 'A real bitch.'

'Aye, I know I was a bitch, Gail.'

'You were a real BITCH,' I insisted. The drink must have been dredging up the resentment I'd initially felt with Marnie, when I thought she was being unfair.

'Bet you thought I'd never get a job on telly,' I spluttered.

'No, Gail, I did not.'

Her quiet forbearance got to me and I shut up. She wasn't always that tolerant!

I got along with most of the clients I met, too. The only time I had any aggro as an assistant producer was when we were doing an ad for a Saudi client. I know it's sensitive, all this cultural awareness stuff, but frankly I was insulted by the clients. They wouldn't acknowledge me when I tried to talk to them about the account, simply because I was a woman and they didn't take me seriously. I'd go, 'Excuse me, but I'm responsible for half this account, half the budget...' and I'd get waved away. The only time they did address me was to say, 'You go and buy my wife a present from Marks and Spencer.' I complained to my boss but he said, 'Gail, just go along with them, go to bloody M&S.' What's more, it was hinted that I should wear a short skirt when they came over – of course I knew why, as these guys never looked me in the eye, just at my tits or legs. Did I wear a short skirt? Did I bollocks. I dug out an old tracksuit. (Or would they have approved of such a modest covering too? Can't win.) You'll gather I was most indignant. When I'm abroad I make an effort to conform to local standards, respect the culture, and I think it should work both ways.

Well, that's my small contribution to Saudi–Scottish relations…

Thinking back on my days as a humble runner, lowest of the low, I marvel at how much I put myself through. Not that I regret an instant of it. It's just that when I'm working in TV now, I try to be considerate to people in that position, always polite – 'Could you possibly get me a coffee, please?' Apologetic, really, even if the runners are there to do just that sort of thing, that's their job. And I often get raised eyebrows, rolled eyes and heavy sighs. I've tried empathising: 'I used to be a runner – hard work, but it's worth it in the end.' Fat lot anyone cares, of course – just a shrug and a 'Whatever'. I daren't ask anyone to actually leave the building to get me something in case they faint from shock.

This, of course, is yet another Old Fogey moment. When I were a lad we lived in a puddle and ate coke from t'road and worked more hours in t'day than are theoretically possible…

Anyhow, after a few years I reckoned I'd learned as much from In Video as I could, and had the pleasure of working with a great bunch of people. I thought it was time to move on, and got a job with an outfit called Picardy Television, which produced short films, just up the road from my old workplace.

And what good job did I step into? Runner.

So had my grand plan been for nothing? Not at all. Though it might seem at first sight like a step backwards, the way I saw it was that it was a new environment, with new people, contacts who could lead anywhere in future. And in fact I had a similar job progression here, doing all the old routine work and finally becoming assistant producer again – just on a quicker timescale.

It was quite different in character from laid-back, sometimes flying-by-the-seat-of-the-pants In Video. I found Picardy a more serious, focused set-up, good in many ways but not perhaps so hot on the camaraderie. I missed the laughs. But it was while I was at Picardy that something crystallised in my mind. I realised what kind of job I'd really like to do in television. Much as I enjoyed the production side, my old acting ambitions had never really gone away. They'd just become dormant while I was first racketing around at college and then working my arse off. The performer in me, which got me singing, dancing and acting at the drop of a hat when I was younger, was coming more and more to the fore. I'd look at people presenting TV shows of all descriptions, and, with the confidence of not only youth but also experience, thought, I could do that. Looks like a load of fun.

So that was it. I'd be on the telly!

How to convince the telly people, though? Thousands of people have the same idea, of course, so how could I make myself stand out from the crowd, make myself noticed? I'd have to put my money where my mouth was, so to speak, and show the kind of thing I could do. A show reel, in fact.

I wanted to project the kind of image that I thought would have a wide appeal – nothing serious, but bouncy and energetic while being tongue in cheek. So: presenting…Gail Porter as Wonder Woman!

Remember those old shows? Lynda Carter as the all-American heroine with her star-spangled pants, high boots, satin tights, magic golden lasso – not forgetting the bracelets that made her bullet-proof (handy accessories, those). I was only a kid when she hit Scottish TV, in the late seventies, I think, but when I saw the shows I reckoned she was my kinda fantasy heroine. Like a female Clark Kent, one minute she's plain and bespectacled Diana Prince, then a quick twirl and she's Wonder Woman, ready to kick the ass of the enemies of democracy.

My incarnation was, let's face it, a bit bargain basement. My mum made the costume, a blue two-piece like an old-fashioned swimsuit, and I dug out from somewhere a weird-looking helmet affair. I already had a pair of high boots, so that completed the outfit. To start the performance, I stood in my mum's back garden, dressed in everyday jeans and sweater, then spun round and round till – ta-da! Wonder Woman went into her act, full karate mode, battling invisible foes. I leapt and crouched, and jumped and skipped and generally hammed it up, complete with a range of wide-eyed goggling. As a climax I leapt over the garden gate – or rather ran slap bang into it and fell back on my bum. I tried scrambling over it but got caught up in the trellis. Collapse of fantasy heroine.

It was a real home movie, not only shot at home but actually filmed by my mum, using the old camera that had captured the efforts of me and my friends years before. Well, it was a lot of fun to make, and it made me laugh. A VT editor at Picardy helped me cut the tape, and dub the jazzy theme tune – 'Wonder Woman, the world's waiting for you-hoo…' All I could do now was send out a dozen or so copies on spec to TV producers, asking to be considered for an audition, and wait with fingers crossed. In those days, before the explosion of satellite and cable, there weren't that many production companies, but again I tried to pick those I thought would be appropriate for this sort of larkiness.

Meanwhile, I'd been babysitting for a woman I knew, a make-up artist called Irene. Her husband Dougie was a TV director, and when I was chatting to them I mentioned that I'd done 'a wee show reel'.

'Yeah?' said Dougie. 'I've got a new kids' show coming up – why don't you send me a copy?'

Well, I wasn't expecting any special favours, but was very happy to do as he suggested. And much to my amazement it wasn't long before I had a letter asking me to an audition. An audition! I hadn't had one of those since my doomed attempt to get into drama at Napier. I could only hope that this one would go better.

The audition was for STV – Scottish Television – but the show would be broadcast nationally. I left home bright and early on the appointed day, catching the train to Glasgow. I got to the studio, all keyed up. Then I saw the competition and I immediately thought, My God, I'm never gonna get this job. There seemed to be hundreds of other young women, all impossibly tall, impeccably blonde and immaculately made up. There was me: short, a bit unkempt and undeniably brown-haired. These women were pacing around, studying sheets of paper. I asked one girl, 'What are you all reading?'

She looked me up and down. 'It's the script, of course,' she drawled. 'We were all sent one.'

'Script?' I said. 'What script? I never got one.'

'Did you not?' she replied, arching an elegant eyebrow. 'What a pity.'

And I swear I could see her inner self light up – Oh good, she's out of it, she's off the list. Oh no I wasn't. Soddit, I might not have a script, but here I was in Glasgow and I wasn't giving up now. I'll just tell them and take it from there.

When it was my turn to be called, I strolled in, looked at the group of people sitting down, flashed them a grin and said, 'Hi, how're you doing? By the way, I haven't got a script.'

They looked startled. To my own surprise, I didn't feel nervous.

There was some muttering while I stood there, then I added, 'Honestly, I haven't just forgotten to bring it. If you sent me one it probably arrived this morning, after I left to get the train. But no sweat – I can wing it. Just give me an idea of what's going on.'

They looked doubtful, then one guy said, 'Right, OK. Well, the premise is you're playing an interactive game with kids at home. You're on the phone, fielding the calls. You and Al are doing a double act.'

Al was the guy they'd already chosen. He was huge – dwarfed me.

So I set to it, making it up as I went along, joshing with Al, just kind of mucking around. We jumped all over the place, pulled faces, cracked jokes to imaginary callers – all in all, a bloody good laugh. And it felt entirely natural to me; I had a blast.

What's more, being so familiar with the studio set-up, having worked behind the scenes for so long, I wasn't fazed by any of the technical stuff. I knew who was doing what and why. I even put on my own microphone as a matter of course – that got me a couple of sideways looks and mutterings of 'She's a bit cocky.' I said, 'Nah – I've worked in TV, I know what to do,' while thinking, Well, it's not bloody rocket science, is it?

I left the audition feeling pretty cheerful. I'd enjoyed it. The old performance bug was biting again, all right. I knew not to get my hopes up – just went back to work at Picardy. And not just Picardy. I didn't work such insanely long hours here, just eight-thirty a.m. to six p.m., so I had time to earn more money in the evening. I was working in a pub near the Mound (that's the artificial hill connecting Edinburgh's Old Town to the New Town), as a waitress cum barmaid, and I loved it: the constantly changing company, the badinage – and the fact that I was kind of looking after people. I sometimes think I'd be in my element running a bed and breakfast place – making sure everyone's room is clean and comfortable, getting them their meals, setting the table with a lovely cloth and flowers and all the trimmings. Bit odd, really, considering that left to myself I'm not domesticated. It's not so much the cleaning and cooking stuff, though. It's more about making people happy, I think, showing them I care.

By this time I'd been seeing a guy called Tony Penfold for a while. He was a really nice bloke, from Kendal, and we had a love of martial arts in common – he was a great judo player (that's what they're called, players), with black belts and all. I always tried to fit in a bit of practice when I could, but it wasn't easy. Tony would often meet me in the pub, and listened patiently when I blethered on about my audition and not hearing anything for ages.

I did ring up the studio several times, asking straight out, 'Have I got the job? Have I got the job?'

Well, I didn't have an agent, so I had to look out for myself.

They just kept repeating, 'We'll let you know...'

So I just kept working as usual. Then one evening I was working in the pub, with Tony hanging around waiting for me, and my mobile rang.

'Hi, Gail. We'd just like to let you know that you do have the job. Congratulations.'

Rock'n'roll! I've got the job!

'I've got the job!' I yelled to Tony and any other customer who might have been interested. 'I'm gonna be on telly!'

Thank you, Dougie!

# * 8 *

# Up and Down – And Up Again

I gave in my notice at Picardy without much of a pang, and got ready for this new life. It mostly meant meetings, when the format and content of the show were hammered out. The title was now officially *The Totally Interactive Game Show* (*T.I.G.S.* for short). They came up with a name for me – I was the Jeepster (not quite sure why), and big Al was, well, Big Al. Basically we were a couple of sci-fi zanies running round the studio, playing interactive games with our young viewers. There'd be a knockout competition and the winners battled it out in a virtual Scalextric game, the grand winner getting a Super Nintendo game or something similar.

And, of course, all the action was live.

I remember the time we actually went on screen for the first time, in October 1995. I made sure I'd told everyone I knew, family, friends and distant relatives, to look out for it. I was all of twenty-four-and-a-half years old, and I felt like a hyperactive kid, standing there in my wacky silver space suit. We'd shot all the title sequences, and I was thinking, 'My God, in twenty seconds we'll be going live to the nation!'

Some guy was counting down: 'Ten, nine, eight, seven, six...' I need the toilet! '...five, four, three, two, one...lift-off!'

'Hi, kids!' and so we were launched. For all our planning, things kept going wrong, sequences got out of order. Many a time I'd hear a squeak in my earpiece from the producer – 'Just fill the time!' And I'd go something like, 'Right, OK, everyone, everything's going crazy here – but hey! We're gonna send out the prizes anyway...'

Just keep the show on the road. After that baptism of fire, I never found live TV daunting ever again. If you can keep your head while all those around you are losing theirs...well, you'll have one more head than they've got.

I must say I was absolutely bloody well stoked by the whole thing. I could hardly believe it – and it was great to see how chuffed my family and friends were too. 'That was you on the telly!' 'I know!'

But behind all the madness and mayhem, I'd had to be a bit more calculating than usual. My contract was for just six weeks – there was no guarantee that I'd be wanted after then, or even if the show itself would be continuing. So I had to look ahead.

While we were still in the planning stage, I'd sent my show reel to a guy called Alan Marke, who worked for Channel X – this outfit used to do all the Vic Reeves and Bob Mortimer stuff, which I loved. Alan got in touch to tell me that although he didn't have anything for me immediately he was impressed by the tape. He sorted me out with an agent, my very first, a lovely lady called Vivian Clore.

Vivian was a little hesitant. 'I usually look after comedians, not presenters,' she said. 'And I don't really know much about children's TV. But Alan has faith in you, so I'll keep an eye out in London, see what I can do.'

Cool! I've only landed one job and now I've got an agent, and in London at that. Everything seemed to be happening at once.

So now my career in TV was well and truly launched? Er, no.

*T.I.G.S.* did make quite a splash, I'll say that for it. People noticed it, kids liked me and wrote fan letters. But, as I suspected, when the six weeks were up, so was I. Still, riding high for a while, I had some other auditions – and got nowhere.

I wasn't giving up, of course. I had to think positive.

I'd go to London, that's what I'd do. After all, my agent ('my agent'! Get me!) was based in London, so I should be on the spot. I was lucky enough to have a good friend in London, a documentary producer called Derek Guthrie. I'd met him when he came to work in Edinburgh, when I was still at In Video. I often used to babysit for him and his wife Dorothy, and when they were back home in London and heard about my plans, they said, 'You must come and stay with us.'

That was so generous – but I'd have to find a way to repay them. 'Great,' I said. 'I'll babysit every night so you two can go out.' Deal.

They soon made me feel at home, and I loved looking after

Gabby and Nick, their children. Like all the kids I used to babysit, they're now about ten feet tall, and Nick works in the HMV store in London. 'We all know you,' he teases me. 'You're the DVD lady.' Well, I might go in and buy the odd dozen or so…

Anyhow, it was great to have a secure base while I was testing the waters in London. I was called to an audition for another kids' show, an ITV series called *Wizadora*. Apologies to any old fans out there, but this was mental. Wizadora – 'You adore her' – was a trainee wizardess, a preschool girl, with a lot of puppet friends, including a talking telephone and a coat hanger. Shades of Paladin the talking paraffin lamp here (he of *Glen Michael's Cavalcade* fame). I really am not that enamoured with animated household objects, and found it hard to take it all seriously. Still, I thought of the money and gave it a shot. Not exactly a whole-hearted one, though, and I was surprised to make it to the final recall – just me and another potential wizardess.

I just couldn't summon up the enthusiasm, the whole thing was so not me. Quite rightly, I didn't get the job – and was over the moon. Went out and got wankered to celebrate. Not the usual reaction to rejection, I know, but if I'd been stuck in something twee like that, I would have ended up resentful and bored. I know me.

I had to think again. I couldn't stay at Derek's for ever, kind though he and his wife were. Which way now?

Well, it wasn't exactly down…

First, I thought, I'd go home for a wee while – the break would do me good. I'd been dashing about like a mad thing, running on adrenaline. Much as I like the buzz, even I was beginning to feel the strain. And it would be good to see Mum again, find out how she was getting on now that Dad had well and truly left. He was living in another part of the city, with a girlfriend, I believed – not that I was interested enough to find out for sure. I felt very remote from him.

I found Mum her usual stoical self, 'Och, I'm fine, don't you worry.' She did seem OK, busy as ever, so that was a relief. She had a few things to say about me, though.

'You're still looking skinny, Gail – you need feeding up.' And: 'You look tired – you must have been overdoing it.'

I wasn't bothered about the skinny bit. I was still watching my weight, eating low-fat foods and other diet stuff. Mum wouldn't be getting me to stuff down haggis any time soon. TV puts at least ten pounds on you, and I had no intention of being a fat presenter – when I finally got another job. I was bothered about the tiredness, though. I shouldn't be feeling this bad. Yes, I did get tired, but after a rest I usually bounced right back up again. The human yo-yo. Now the 'down' side seemed to be taking a long time to lift.

I dragged myself round the house, forced myself to go for walks, to see old friends, but my heart wasn't in it. 'What's the matter with you?' people would ask. They obviously thought I should be on a high, what with my glittering TV career. I just wanted to hide somewhere and cry. Nothing seemed worth doing – why was I even bothering?

Ever since college days I'd got used to my cycle of up and down moods, and knew that working and playing hard was the best remedy for keeping blues at bay – at least, for a time. But my emotional states now seemed to be getting more intense, more pronounced. The highs higher, the lows lower. You could call the highs manic, and the lows depressed – no prizes to see where I'm heading! But I never thought for an instant that I had something that suggested actual mental disorder. I was just me. I'd snap out of it eventually.

Well, it was more like crawling than snapping, but one day I did wake up with a lighter heart and the old familiar feeling of get-up-and-go, rather than pulling my duvet over my head again.

'You're looking more cheerful,' my mother observed. Which I promptly proved by ringing round all the old friends I could think of and inviting them out. That evening in the pub I was more like my old self, the life and soul of the party, safely surrounded by a wall of people.

With a renewed zest, I started thinking more positively about what I should do. I fired off more letters to production companies, and individual producers. One of them was Peter Richardson, driving force of the Comic Strip in London. I'd been just a kid when the first film, *Five Go Mad in Dorset*, hit TV in the early eighties, but when I was older I loved them all, and made a point of searching out old episodes. That kind of mad, clever comedy is right up my street, and I wrote to Peter Richardson telling him so. I embellished my letter with little sketches, plot outlines, whatever my imagination threw up.

I was used to my letters being ignored, or barely acknowledged, so I was thrilled to get a proper reply – from Peter's assistant at the time, Robert Popper. He sounded encouraging and seemed to appreciate what I was getting at, though of course he didn't have anything for me. I wrote back straight away, with more far-out ideas and jokes and little drawings, and from then on we had quite a regular correspondence. I'd pour out my ideas, and took to sending weird photos I'd come across. It might not be leading anywhere, I thought, but it was fun, and made London seem not such a hopeless place to aim at.

In fact I decided on another visit. Derek and Dorothy were happy for me to come and stay again, and I always loved looking after the children. I was chatting one day to Derek about what was happening in London and he said, 'Come on, I'll take you to the Groucho. Get in the thick of it.'

On the way there I was thinking, Wow, the Groucho – everyone's heard of that. I hadn't known Derek was a member, and I was seriously impressed.

Sitting in the club, over a few glasses of wine, I looked surreptitiously round the room, trying to look cool, forcing myself not to exclaim, 'Blimey, look over there!' every time I recognised a famous face. This was proper media land all right.

Then one particular man walked in and my heart gave a leap. I recognised him straight away – it was Peter Richardson of Comic Strip fame. I'd seen his picture lots of times. Right, Gail, I thought, now or never.

I walked over to his table and said, 'Mr Richardson?'

He looked up and said, 'Yeah.'

Then I nerved myself and said all at once, 'Mr Richardson, please don't think I'm stalking you, I'm not, but I'm Gail Porter, the Scottish girl who's been writing all those letters to you – or rather to Robert.'

He just gazed at me and said, 'Oh my God.'

I babbled on. 'Honestly, I'm not dangerous or anything – I've just come down from Edinburgh for a while and the chances of bumping into you again in my lifetime are not huge so I thought I would just come over and introduce myself. And I'm not a stalker.'

Peter smiled. 'I got that the first time,' he said. Then he added, 'Well, now you're here, our office is just down the street, so why don't you join me when I go back, and I'll show you around.'

Fantastic! That's my motto – Strike while the iron's hot. Seize the day. She who hesitates is lost…when you see a chance, grab it with both hands!

So a while later I said bye, and thanks, to Derek and walked with Peter to the office, which was in Dean Street in those days.

He introduced me to Robert Popper.

'This is Gail Porter, the one who writes those letters from Scotland,' he said.

Robert's jaw dropped, and I swear I could see a look of panic on his face. She's come all the way down here to track us down! Is she insane?

'It's OK,' I assured him. 'I'm not stalking anyone. I just happened to bump into Peter and thought I'd say hello…'

Well, we all had a friendly chat and they obviously believed that I (a) wasn't off my head, (b) was harmless, and (c) could actually be useful to them. They offered me a job on the spot.

Three guesses for what kind of job. Well, no, you'd only need one. Runner.

*

Not that I was complaining – it was tremendous to get a foot in the door of such a cool company. And as I've said before, every new job brings a whole lot of new prospects, new people. Who knows where anything might lead?

And this time it was a new medium for me: radio. It was a Radio 4 series called *Fry's the Limit*, starring Stephen Fry. It was based on *Round the Horne*, if you remember those old shows – a mix of stand-up and sketches. Very clever and very funny, not unlike Mr Fry himself, who I found rather intimidating, to tell the truth. Not in himself, I mean his talent – awesome. Though years later I did have a touch of fellow feeling when he talked openly about his mental-health problems, at the same time as I was trying to deal with my own. Curiously comforting, in a way, to know that even the biggest brain isn't immune. And as the man himself says, it's what makes you who you are.

Anyhow, back in my radio days, the duties were mostly the same, running (literally) around making sure everything was where it should be and everybody had what they wanted. The show was recorded in front of a live audience and the cast wore old-fashioned formal dress – I remember many a trip to Moss Bros to pick up the penguin suits. There was only one downside. One particular person associated with the show, who shall be nameless. How can I put this delicately? He was very fond of alcohol and assorted illicit substances, so fond that he found it a tad difficult to get up in the morning. When he should have been at rehearsals he was sleeping the sleep of the totally wankered.

It was my job to get him to rehearsals, and I'd be outside his place for hours, hammering on the door, ringing the bell, yelling through the letterbox, 'Get up! You're late!' Eventually he would emerge, saunter into rehearsals when they were half over, and say, 'Sorry, everyone.' But it would be me who got the bollocking. 'What else could I do?' I'd protest. 'It's like raising the dead. The only thing I could do is break into his house and pour a bucket of cold water over his head.'

Still, all part of life's rich pattern. As ever, I absorbed everything I could from what I was experiencing. Except I'd draw the line at my living accommodation at the time. No way I'd like to absorb that.

I hadn't wanted to impose on Derek and Dorothy any more than I already had, although they were always amazingly generous. I was earning some money so found my own place. Only the money, frankly, was not a lot, so my choice was limited.

'What's it like?' asked my mum when I rang her up.

'Brilliant,' I said. 'It's a lovely little hotel tucked away in Victoria.'

Well, the 'Victoria' bit was true. But really I had a room in a squalid bed and breakfast that wouldn't have been out of place in a documentary about the seamy side of London. Dodgy clientele, too – the sort who book by the hour. My room was really disgusting, especially the mattress, which smelt peculiar and had unidentifiable stains all over it. I had to cover it up with thick blankets before I dared lie on it. The shower didn't work properly and there were little beasties running around in it. Total yuk. What's more, there was no lock on the door, so I had to wedge a chair under the handle at night. I could hear odd noises during the hours of darkness – shouts, crying, grunts, and heavy footsteps echoing up and down the stairs. The front door was slammed a lot too.

My poor mum would have gone out of her mind if she could have seen me, and I wasn't greatly charmed myself, but it was all I could afford. I'd get to work in the morning – snatching something to eat on the way as the breakfast part of the deal was as bad as the bed – and people would say, 'How's the new flat? Are you settling in?' I'd say, 'It's great, a nice little place, really cheap for London.'

A girl has her pride…

In any case, I only had to endure the place while the job and the money lasted, a matter of months. The work was fine, it was really interesting to see another side of broadcasting, and I'd met some lovely people. Especially Robert Popper himself – we became firm friends, as it turned out. In the future he and his flatmate would often put me up when I was in London for an audition or a meeting.

Going through the grind of audition and rejection, I must admit there was a time when I feared *The Totally Interactive Game Show* was a flash in the pan for me. A one-off. From my interactive beginnings I was worried I'd only be inactive where telly was concerned. Sometimes I'd be seriously in the running for a show, only to fall at the last hurdle. One time I even got down to the last two for *Blue Peter*! Though it's probably just as well I didn't get that job. Don't think I would've been a good fit, somehow.

Then I tried out for another kids' show, called *Fully Booked* – and got it. What's more, that title could have been predicting my fortune!

# * 9 *

# *Exposure!*

After half a dozen years working my arse off, keeping my ambition alive and dreaming of presenting on television, I finally cracked it. Or had it cracked for me. Whatever, I got this gig on kids' TV, in the late nineties, and then the doors opened – offers flooded in. For little Gail Porter, this was the big time. I could safely assume that my days of being a runner really were behind me (touch wood).

*Fully Booked* was another Scottish TV show, also broadcast nationally, which had been running for a couple of years. I was part of a trio of new faces joining in 1998 – the others were Chris Jarvis and Tim Vincent. We went out live on Sunday mornings, from our fictional hotel that saw a stream of celebrity guests passing through (hence the title). Cue for much mayhem and merriment. The hotel receptionist was a cow called Morag – well, she would be. No kids' show is complete without at least one talking animal or household implement. What would they do without puppets and cartoons to back up us humans? Anyhow, it was all great, crazy fun and I was in my element.

As if I didn't have enough manic energy to start with, there was always a big bowl of jelly babies for me in the studio – I'd eat them for breakfast before we went on air. All those E numbers would send me loopy. I felt my feet hardly hit the ground – and the show did set a fast pace. By now I was renting a flat in West Hampstead, so on Friday evenings I'd fly to Glasgow, rehearse all day Saturday, then broadcast Sunday morning. By eleven a.m. work was over, so it was another flight back to London, all wired up and ready to go out on the town. Those weekends were packed – and weekdays would soon be filling up with other jobs too.

Meanwhile I was getting my first taste of what felt like real fame. I'd had fan letters after *T.I.G.S.*, which were good for the ego, but now there were always crowds of people waiting outside the *Fully Booked* studio. An autograph and a chat? No prob, happy to oblige. Nothing stops me talking, and anyway the people – mums and dads as well as kids – were always so friendly. Mind you, I did get some rather odd letters from dads. 'I was watching you with my son and daughter the other day and I just wanted to say how well I think you're doing...' Hmm, I'd think. Sitting there with your kids, gazing at a young woman who's bouncing around, pigtails flying, and looks like a child...dirty old man! I still meet people who say they remember the show fondly – I always hope it's for the right reasons.

I think *Fully Booked* set the mould for me as a children's presenter. In fact I was to do loads more shows for adults and families generally than I ever did for kids, but the 'children' tag stuck for a long while. Maybe it was because I did look a lot younger than my age. At twenty-seven I could have passed for twelve, in the very unlikely event of ever needing to. Half-price at the movies?

Most of the kids' shows I was involved in followed the same kind of format – all whizzy and busy, music and mayhem, guest stars from TV and film and pop charts, cartoons and quizzes, the whole shebang. Got to keep those young viewers glued to the set! I presented the 'Electric Circus' showbiz bit for *Live and Kicking*, then went on to *Scratchy & Co*, *Up for It*, *Megamag*, *Sticky*...I was fitting in more and more shows, grabbing everything that was offered. And I loved it all.

Looking back, it all seems like a mad kaleidoscope, the shows blurring into one colourful blob. It's hard to disentangle one from the other. A few high points do stick out, though, like the time I was working on *Sticky* – and it was literally a high point. One segment of the show was suggested by viewers: 'Challenge Gail'. One week I had to go to Blackpool and ride the big rollercoaster eight times, one after the other, each time doing something different – eating a banana, say, or trying to put on lipstick. That rollercoaster was big, really big – readers with a nervous stomach look away now. I was on my own on the thing, all the other seats being occupied by sandbags. So we'd grind inexorably to the top and for a moment stay poised on the brink of a humungous sheer drop, a little camera in front of me filming my reactions. The first time I looked down, a loud 'Shi-i-i-i-t!' burst from me. Cut and retake. Made the same mistake next time: 'Motherfuck-e-e-e-e-r!'

I lost count how many times I went on the bloody contraption, till we had enough film of me not uttering profanities. I certainly tried the patience of the crew. Charlotte Wheeler, the assistant producer, had a few pithy comments for me. I'd first had a taste of her acerbic wit when I auditioned for the show – interesting, I thought. That's practically rude...Anyhow, we hit it off, and we've been close friends ever since. Or partners in crime, as we call ourselves.

Back on the set that day, my brother Keith had been watching the filming, and he thought it was all a big joke, hilarious. Maybe not so much on the train home, though (I was going up to stay with my mum). I kept dozing off, and dreaming of the big drop. Which meant that at random intervals I'd jerk awake, eyes staring wildly, and yell, 'Fuck!' It was like Tourette's on a train. Keith would explain to everybody staring at me, 'Sorry, it's my sister, don't take any notice.'

Oh, and I had a *Blue Peter* moment on this show, of the excreting animal variety. Only it wasn't an elephant shitting, it was a bunny rabbit pissing all over me as I was holding it and asking viewers to suggest a name for it. I could have thought of a few.

While I was hurling myself whole-heartedly into these shows, I never stopped to think if they might have been contributing to my swinging moods. If you're inclined to be manic, is it a good idea to be working in a manic environment? Was I feeding off them or were they feeding off me? If you'd asked me at the time, I would of course have replied, 'Who gives a toss?' Show time, play time – bring it on! With hindsight, maybe the best job for my mental health would have been in a quiet corner of Radio 4. Like they used to have in the old days – I once caught a clip from a *Woman's Hour* archive show and someone was talking about knitting your own stair carpet. Or a whatnot. There's a thought...

I did actually work on a couple of kids' shows that weren't all pumped-up mania. There was one called *It's a Mystery*, where I was one of a couple of detectives investigating spooky phenomena. 'Just why did the wind chimes chime the way they did?' we would intone, sepulchrally. Now I think of it as a junior version of *Dead Famous*, of which more later.

The other show was more of a national treasure: *How*. It had been running for years before I joined, and was now called *How 2*, though still with the legendary Fred Dinenage in charge. Adrian, the series producer, had brought me in – he'd seen something else I did and thought I'd be right for the show. Which was very perceptive of him, as this was explaining real science to kids. I think Adrian saw that I could work in a team and build up a rapport with them and the audience. And he knew that I'd had a lot of studio experience: I was familiar with the technical side as well as the presentation angle.

For *How 2* there was a hefty script to learn – not much scope for ad-libbing. We presenters demonstrated four or five experiments in the show, and I quickly realised that you had to understand the principles yourself to explain them properly. If you made a mistake in the middle of an experiment, the recording couldn't have the usual cutting and pasting job to cover it up. You'd have to start again, right from the beginning. If someone cocked up here, there'd be an explosion of colourful language unsuitable for children, to say the least. Many a 'Bollocks!' rang round the studio. So the pressure was on to make everything perfect.

Fred was wonderful to work with; I loved him. In our first

rehearsal, when we were sitting down and saying, 'How', I just burst out laughing. 'Sorry, sorry,' I said to all and sundry. It was the thought of me, little Gail from Jop, sitting here beside none other than Fred Dinenage, saying 'How' to the nation. At least I didn't disrupt an experiment, and I managed to stifle the giggling.

All these shows, light-hearted and serious or whatever, may have been aimed at kids, but I felt right at home. And if you could see what I've got at my home now, you'd think a kid is what I am. Ever since *Star Wars*, I've collected toys, games, posters, everything to do with my favourite movies and comic books. As I write this, I've got a life-size figure of Darth Vader looming to one side of me, miniature action figures of Princess Leia, Luke Skywalker, Han Solo, Chewbacca and Obi Wan Kenobi artistically arranged on one shelf, a mass of robots and stormtroopers on another, light sabres and spaceships hanging from the ceiling...and every wall covered with movie posters. Not just *Star Wars*, of course. I wouldn't be that fanatical. There's *Spiderman*, *X-Men* – you name it.

I don't know what this says about me, other than that I'm probably a textbook Peter Pan (or whatever the female equivalent is – Petra Pan?). That early sense of wonder and enchantment has never left me. I love being transported to another universe, especially when, at times, this one doesn't seem so hot.

Of course I don't live entirely in a fantasy world, even if I wanted to. Here I am, a mother, with responsibilities. A child to look after, a house to run, a mortgage to pay, bills, contracts... all the paraphernalia of the adult world. I'm a grown woman, all

right. A fact, now I mention it, not lost on the publishers of a
certain men's magazine…

There you go. I've got boobs, as I believe I've said already. And I
have an arse. And do you know what? Under my clothes – I'm
naked. There's a novelty. At least, you'd think it was, if the mad
reaction to nude photos of me in a men's magazine was anything
to go by.

I bet most of the fuss was linked to the fact that I was known
as a children's presenter. As such, I'd had a wholesome image, girl
next door, all laughs and nice teeth and nice hair and big eyes. I
was bubbly and sparkly. And now images of my private parts (or at
least boobs and arse) were being revealed to a mass audience of
slavering men. How disgusting. That's an attack on childhood
innocence and purity, dirtying children by association.

By sheer coincidence, another children's TV presenter had just
been in the news for unbecoming conduct. Richard Bacon was
sacked from *Blue Peter* after being outed for taking cocaine. There
was a very strong feeling, especially in the tabloids, that this was
unacceptable in anybody connected to children's entertainment,
especially such an iconic show. He was a role model to impres-
sionable children. He'd let himself down, the show down, the
BBC down, and the millions of loyal young viewers down.

I thought at the time that the Bacon fuss was overkill – he
hadn't mainlined on live TV, had he? It was in private, I understand,
in his own time. And taking cocaine, or any other illicit drug, is
not exactly unknown in the entertainment industry, even in the

hallowed corridors of Television Centre. Not that I'd recommend his example, of course, but there's more than a whiff of hypocrisy involved. It just goes to show what strong emotions are unleashed whenever children are involved, even indirectly. Hence the over-reaction to the photos of me. You'd think I was doing unspeakable acts with the Archbishop of Canterbury and the Andrex puppy.

As it happens, the image I projected on kids' TV wasn't a million miles from the real me – which is why the shows were a good fit for my personality. But of course I was playing a part to a great extent; I was simply acting. How can anybody think a presenter is just being herself? A show might look natural and spontaneous – which is part of its appeal – but it's not exactly slung together without any planning (though, granted, some do look like it!). There's a script, which might allow some ad-libbing but must basically be learned and followed. You're hardly likely to go on air and actually speak your mind – 'Frankly, I've had a shit day and I don't give a flying fuck about the penguins...' It's a performance. Viewers may think they know you but all they really know is your professional persona. If they like what they see, then that's great, you're doing your job right. But if they think they know you, they're mistaken.

There were reports that I was sacked from children's TV in retaliation for the nude photos, but that's just not true. By the time they were published, I was moving on from kids' shows to those with a wider appeal, like *The Movie Chart Show* and *Top of the Pops*. I'd really enjoyed the kids' stuff, but in my late twenties I was interested in branching out, and music and movies were natural choices for me.

The people who said I was sacked were probably the same ones who told me why I'd posed for the photos in the first place.

*a) You wanted a quick way to get famous.*

*b) You did it for money.*

*c) You wanted to sex up your image.*

*d) All of the above.*

Yet if you'd asked me during the photo shoot in question why I stripped off, the answer would have been quite simple. Why not? At least it certainly wasn't the money – I never got a penny for any of the nude shoots I did. I don't know if that's common practice, then or now, but money was never an issue.

It's not that I ever set out to be a lads' pin-up. What sort of ambition is that for a girl? But I'd always liked the look of show-biz glamour, ever since I used to pore over old film magazines with my grandma Mary. There was no *Hello!* or *OK* in those days, but you'd find celebrities in magazines like *Photoplay*. My young self gazed at pictures of such stars as Marilyn Monroe, heavily made up with hair sculpted into place, dressed to the nines (or sometimes undressed to the nines in sophisticated swimsuits) and thought they just oozed glamour. If ordinary mortals lived their lives in black and white, the stars were in Technicolor. Later I had my hair dyed blonde as a tribute. Also to see if it was true that blondes have more fun. Well, from my own experience I must say they definitely don't have any less.

When I began to make a name for myself in TV, I was often asked to pose for photos – nothing sensational, just fashion shoots or personality pieces, in family-type magazines or media supplements. Part of me wondered why anyone would want to see a photo of me, then I'd shake that thought off – why shouldn't they? Though I say it myself, I can be pleasing on the eye, and I was back working out in the gym, keeping up my martial arts again, so I was pretty fit. Go for it! I was only too happy to try on a lot of cool new clothes for the camera. When I was off duty, I'd slob around in any old thing – baggy jeans, old sweatshirt – but now and again it was fun to scrub up.

I'd appeared in a men's magazine already, when I was still working on *Fully Booked*. When *Arena* asked me, out of the blue, I did wonder why. I'm a children's presenter – why on earth should they be interested in me? Was it anything to do with those enthusiastic letters from dads? Whatever, I gave it my usual up-for-anything shot, and was photographed wearing a parka with a big fur-lined hood pulled up around my ears. Nothing revealing there. The caption was something like, 'We've got to keep an eye on this one...' and they christened me Cornflake Girl – there I was on telly at breakfast time on a Sunday. Apparently I was a bit crazy, a bit kooky. They spoke truer than they knew.

For the particular shoot that would hit the headlines, for the men's monthly *GQ*, I was going through the usual routines, dressed in borrowed finery, when the photographer said, 'What about getting your kit off, just showing your bum? You could lie there looking cheeky.'

Yeah, I thought, my bum cheeks will look cheeky anyway. Other than that, I never really thought about it. Just shrugged and said, 'OK.'

'Really?' said the photographer.

'Yup.'

That's all there was to it. I was asked, and thought Why not? It'd probably be good for a laugh.

So there I was, heavily made up and hair loose, striking a number of artful poses that didn't reveal very much at all. Though I was of course completely naked at the time. The poor little runner – a boy who couldn't have been more than seventeen – didn't know where to look. He passed me a cup of tea, hand shaking and eyes firmly fixed on a point above my head. 'Anything else you need?' he stuttered. Perhaps he'd seen me in one of the kids' shows and thought the world had gone mad.

I just asked for a glass of champagne – always helps to smooth things along, I find. Not that I had qualms, exactly. As I say, it didn't seem a big deal. And in the event, the photographer used a blue light, all very tasteful, discreet and sophisticated, and when I saw copies of the pictures I thought, Wow! That's me – I look really glamorous! Thank God for digital retouching!

But at first it didn't seem as if *GQ* was that bothered. They sat on the pictures for ages, so they couldn't have thought them anything out of the ordinary. Then one month they used one of the shots, printed quite small, with the caption 'Look at our little Gail'. Then came the insane overreaction, after which they hurriedly plastered the rest of the pictures over the next available edition.

Yes, of course men will be looking at it. So what? *GQ* isn't some horrible, squalid little rag catering to sad wankers. It's stylish, upmarket, and I think I look great in those photos. In fact when my daughter's older I'll show them to her. She'll probably never believe I was ever that young and fit!

Anyhow, of all the hang-ups I've got, being seen without any clothes on has never been one of them. I just don't see why people make such a fuss over something so trivial, especially when, as I say, the pictures weren't pornographic. Pornography is another area entirely, one I'd never get involved in. I did wonder what my family would think – it'd never been a Porter trait to go starkers in public, as far as I know. I thought I'd better warn my mum.

'I've done something a bit risqué,' I told her on the phone.

'You what?'

'I've posed for a magazine, with no clothes on.'

Now she yelled. 'You WHAT?'

'Just bum and boobs,' I said hurriedly.

After more splutterings, Mum calmed down. She's learned to expect the unexpected with me – in fact one of her favourite sayings to me is, 'What have you done *now*?' In the end she's always there for me.

I didn't bother thinking about my dad's reaction. We were hardly in touch anyway. No doubt he'd think I was besmirching the family name or something – though being a builder I daresay he was used to pin-ups. Not that he would ever have associated his daughter with them. My brother Keith was a bit flummoxed when his mates said, 'Wa-hey, that's your sister!' I remember him shaking his head, saying, 'Tha's no' reet, man. It's just no' reet, ma sister on a magazine!' But like Mum he accepts me for what I am, what I do. In fact he even got me to sign a few photos for his mates.

My own mates had reacted in a predictable way. They weren't shocked, of course they weren't. Like Mum, they thought along the lines of 'What have you done now? Don't you ever stop? You're always doing something to wind people up...' Some of my girl friends even said, 'God, I wish I had an arse like that.' And as I told them, 'You probably have!' I must admit there is something seductive about photo shoots, whether you're clothed or not. Whatever your shape and size, you could go into one of these studios looking and feeling like shit and you get what amounts to an extreme makeover: make-up, hair...the works. Good for the ego, I must say.

Once I'd made this splash in *GQ*, other men's magazines were knocking on my door. I bet it had never crossed their minds before then that I could be seen as a pin-up. After all, it had never crossed mine. I was happy to go along with more sessions, though always insisting the photos were tasteful. In all, I was finding this new venture quite amusing. It's no hardship to be told I was attractive, even sexy. And maybe there was something in me that got a kick out of not being the eternally good little girl. Snobby Porter well and truly laid to rest! I had no plans to make a career out of it, but as a sideline it was fun, and I knew I wouldn't do it for long.

What I didn't like was one time when a picture of me was taken out of context, without my permission or even my knowledge – and when I say context...well, there's not much resemblance between the pages of a men's magazine and the Houses of Parliament. I'd posed for *FHM* magazine, in a shoot to be published in the June 1999 edition. Then one evening in May, the cover shot, of me naked, back to the camera, looking over my right shoulder, was projected on to the Houses of Parliament as a stunt. It was blown up to the size of a house – bigger, even: the image must have been sixty-foot high. The first I knew was when it was on the TV news.

I was gobsmacked. It's one thing to agree to be photographed for a men's magazine. You know where you are, so to speak. But to take an image and blow it up to an enormous size on an iconic public building for all to see…Nobody asked me, and I thought it was well out of order. As for the point of it all – well, there was some stuff about encouraging young people to vote. Yeah, a huge nude picture of me will immediately inspire any young person to trot along to the polling station and put a cross on the ballot paper. My bum on the seat of Parliament. Vote Porter? Bollocks.

Or maybe it was an ironic comment on shallow celebrity culture. Dumb young folks would rather see me with no clothes on than get seriously involved in political debate. Yeah. Or maybe, just maybe, it was a publicity stunt to boost *FHM*. Certainly it had its fifteen minutes of fame.

I did my last nude shoot a couple of months later, for *Maxim*. I was getting bored now. As far as I know, the magazine didn't go around projecting my naked image on to any other national government buildings. People had their say about me one way or the other, and that was it. A storm in a teacup (or in my case at the time, a D cup).

The repercussions rippled on for a bit. I expected lairy comments from men who didn't know me – after all, they've seen my naked arse, so that gives them a chance to say, 'Wa-hey! I've seen your arse.' So then they say, 'Can I have my picture taken with you?' One guy asked me to sign his arm, then went and got the signature tattooed. Strange. Though at least it was only his arm…

Though I couldn't do anything about the headlines, I'd say what I thought in interviews. One journalist from a feminist magazine interviewed me in Groucho's, maintaining that pin-ups are degrading, encouraging men to rape. I wasn't having any of this. 'Look,' I said, 'if a man has it in his nature to rape, seeing my bare bum wouldn't push him over the edge.' Rape is violence, and whatever my photos were, they weren't violent; if anything they were pretty anodyne. Not a naked nipple or crotch in sight. By the end of our session, the journalist shook my hand and seemed persuaded, saying, 'Fair play to you.'

I said the same sort of thing when I was invited to the Oxford Union, to one of their debates. In fact I did the Oxford gig twice, and Cambridge once, and loved them all, though it was about as far from my usual haunts as possible. The first was about TV in general, not just presenters posing for nude photos, but of course I was grilled on that 'degrading to women' angle.

'Well,' I said, 'women without bums might take exception, might think it's degrading. I wouldn't want to upset anyone without an arse...'

The students loved it, they were brilliant and a group of them ended up taking me out to dinner and we had a lot of laughs. Another time I got some stick was more public and not so much fun. I was guesting on *Never Mind the Buzzcocks*, and you expect Mark Lamarr, the host, to wind up the guests. That's what he does. Even so, I was a bit taken aback when he said straight out, 'What's the point of you being here if you're not gonna show us your tits?' I thought, O-kay...Then it was the round where you guess the next line of a song, and up came a sexy little number.

Mark said, 'I like you a lot right now...' and I buzzed the buzzer. Turning my head away from him, I spoke the next line: 'Would you go to bed with me?'

'That's right,' said Mark. 'But why aren't you looking at me?'

I could only say, 'The thought of actually saying that to your face makes me feel quite ill. And I don't want to give you any false hopes.'

Not exactly Oscar Wilde, but a bit of a touché! Afterwards Mark said, 'Bloody hell, you got one back on me.' I said, 'You don't slag me off and don't expect something back – I may take my time but it's coming!'

No grudges, though – we became really good friends after that. He's a lovely bloke, really funny and quick. We kind of went out, in a friendly way, and once were photographed together, which gave us a good laugh. He came round to my flat in West Hampstead one afternoon, when I was going to Marks & Spencer for some food shopping.

'I'll come with you,' said Mark, and off we went.

A week later a magazine ran a photo of the two of us, with the most bizarre caption: 'Spotted – Gail Porter and Mark Lamarr buying a cucumber from M&S.' What are you supposed to read into that?

When you're in the public eye, you soon learn that photos sell newspapers, even on the flimsiest basis. You're fair game for paparazzi – if you worry too much about them, the intrusion into your private life, you'd go crazy. Much better just to laugh. And the way I was stretching my telly wings was certainly bringing me more and more into the public eye.

I was happy to try my hand at anything. As I've said, I was leaving kids' TV behind me in favour of programmes like *The Movie Chart Show* (self-explanatory), *Gail's Big Nineties* (a nudge and a wink at my boobs, of course, but a show that gave me a chance to write my own script to link clips of performers) and *Top of the Pops*. I especially loved *TOTP*, always a total buzz, off screen as well as on. It wasn't a regular gig – I'd be told a short time in advance when I'd be on. There wasn't a lot of preparation to get your head round, just a set of links written on cards that you had to memorise.

Then you were off...And what a guest list! Where else could you see everyone from Madonna and Prince to the Wombles and the Tweenies? And everything going at a fast pace, lively and fun. In my time this was due mainly to the producer, Chris Cowey, a fantastic guy with really innovative ideas. He kept the thing afloat.

When I joined, the show was recorded at Elstree, quite a trek to get to but worth it for the atmosphere. It was like a social club, very friendly. We'd hang out with the guests – I'd make a beeline for any from Scotland – and go to the pub afterwards. A lot of top-liners, though, especially the Americans, would just come in, do their thing and go out again. Having a pint in a not terribly trendy pub wouldn't have been their idea of style. We also rubbed shoulders with a lot of actors – *EastEnders* is filmed at Elstree, and the actors would often come and look at *TOTP* on their breaks, while we'd pop next door to see what was going on in Albert Square. In the BBC canteen you'd see Barbara Windsor at one table and Cliff Richard at another.

A behind-the-scenes highlight for me was when one show coincided with my birthday. NYC rappers Cypress Hill were on the bill, one of my all-time favourites. Before we started recording, the band stood up and sang 'Happy Birthday' to me, and I was thrilled. Life doesn't get much better than this, I thought.

Well, it could certainly get a lot worse…

# * 10 *

# Losing It

It's quite a shock to the system, I can tell you. One minute you're pretty much a nobody as far as the media world is concerned, then you're right out there, on a high-profile show. Now it's your turn to have runners looking after you: 'Can we get anything for you? Can we get you a car?' Not, as I've said before, that I've ever been comfortable with that. I've never been one to say, 'I want my dressing room painted white!' or 'I must have tulips!' or 'I must have puppies about the place!' All of which requests, by the way, are not unknown. When I started being successful, even though it was what I'd been aiming at, I've always had a sneaking feeling that it wasn't right, that I didn't belong here. Any minute now and I'd be rumbled – but no, it was all 'She's amazing, brilliant, the new big thing...' Flattering though this was, my hard-nosed Scottish sense was not deceived. After all, I did love my job, but what did it amount to really? Talking to the camera, talking to other people on camera.

But the fuss went on all around me and I began to feel I was losing my bearings, getting out of my depth. For God's sake, I was just a girl from Joppa – the other day I'd probably have been back in Edinburgh having a laugh with my mates. So what's with the big time? Was I mad or was it other people?

I'd never thought of myself as actually mad, even when I was at one of my really low points. If I could sum up myself at any time after adolescence, it'd be in one word: confused. I can't pretend I ever understood what was going on in my mind – except that given a choice I'd rather be up than down. I'd get a massive buzz from my pick'n'mix of presenting jobs, high as a kite just on adrenaline, and after work kept up the momentum, rounding up my friends and going out on the town. If ever I found myself at home alone, I'd have to phone someone, get them to come over.

I've always known that I don't like being alone. Without distractions, I tend to sink into a low state of fear and worry that can paralyse me. Better not risk it, I reasoned at some level. If a spinning top slows down, it starts to wobble. So don't stop spinning. Keep going, so when your head hits the pillow you're spark out till the next day. That had been my mantra ever since I'd come to London. I could stave off depression, panic, misery – whatever it was – by being active. This included a demanding regime at the gym: a two-hour workout from six o'clock in the morning, seven days a week, running on the machine or any kind of cardio exercise. All that toning would keep me fit, just as rigorously controlling my food intake kept me slim. I thought of myself as disciplined, not compulsive, and aimed to keep myself between six and a half and seven stone.

That was what I had to do. I might not be able to figure out the world, but I could at least control my own body. That's what I told myself, anyway – that it wasn't being skinny for its own sake, to look good on TV, but to be in control.

When I came to London I'd stepped up the dieting I'd been doing at college and at home. No one'd ever call me Big Bum again! I didn't trouble with WeightWatchers meals now, but was going more and more for watery food that had few calories, like cucumber and tomatoes and grapes. So after the gym I'd have a breakfast of grapes. At work, it was no more sandwiches from the canteen, but some chunks of cucumber. In the evening, a bowl of tomato soup for dinner or occasionally some prawns. Eventually I had to have exactly the same things every day. I never ate out – if I had to go to some function, I'd order the least disgusting option and just push the food around on my plate, pretending I was eating it. At least I couldn't drink much – with an empty stomach I'd fall over after two glasses of wine.

When people around me started saying, 'You're looking really thin – are you all right?' I just accepted it as a compliment. Yup, that's me in control of my own body – I was as chuffed as when I'd first lost those extra pounds in college. But then people would say, 'You're too skinny,' and up would go my defences.

'Good,' I'd say. 'That's what I want.'

Then someone would say, 'You must eat more.'

And I'd say, 'Nope. I'm not gonna eat anything.'

Perverse or what? In fact, the more you starve yourself the harder it becomes to eat. Your stomach gets used to it. I was heading for a fall, literally.

My energy started to fail. I'd drag myself through the odd presenting job – and always managed to get through, I must say – but that was about it. Just as well my main work at this particular time was now on Virgin Radio, where the audience couldn't see me! I found myself unwilling, and unable, to keep up the after-work stuff. I couldn't go to meetings or parties, which are usually part of the job. I didn't want to see anyone, do anything. I think for about three weeks I ate hardly anything. Just the odd nibble on grapes or cucumber, while dragging myself to the gym every morning. My stomach seemed to be shrinking and shrinking, and it was an effort to force anything down.

I was really tired, tired beyond any tiredness I'd ever experienced. My mind must have been affected, because when I looked in the mirror I saw someone who was fat. I'd always told myself that I controlled my eating for my own ends, not to fit the ideal of the perfect body. But now I realise I had a completely distorted image of myself.

My God, I thought. I'm huge. Every morning I'd try on clothes and fling them over the floor, screaming and bursting into tears. Most of them made me look even more huge. I'd pick out the baggiest tops and trousers I had to cover up my horrible bloated body. At home I'd just wear my outsize pyjamas.

Then one night I woke up feeling sick and dizzy. I put the light on but couldn't see properly. I managed to reach the bathroom, but then collapsed and hit my head on the sink. I lay on the floor stunned. What the hell was happening? When the pain died down I crawled to the living room and phoned my friend Angie, my personal trainer at the gym.

'I'll come round first thing,' she said.

She hadn't realised what I'd been doing to myself – nobody at the gym did, any more than people at work, or so I thought. The baggy clothes covered up my arms and legs, while I didn't lose much weight from my face. I've always had a clear skin, so what with my shiny hair as well, I didn't look ill at all.

When Angie saw me next morning, she was very concerned, but I insisted on going to the gym as usual, despite her objections. Mind over matter. Once there, I collapsed again, sick and dizzy, and Angie overruled me. 'You're going to hospital,' she said.

At the hospital, in Paddington, I was put in a small room and weighed. Just six stone, the lightest I'd ever been. I wasn't as happy as I thought I should have been. Then I waited for a doctor who, when he arrived, seemed to be more angry than anything. 'You're seriously underweight,' he said. 'You must eat more – what's the matter with you?'

What indeed. Then a nurse came in and handed me a sandwich. A huge, thick doorstep, Mother's Pride white, dripping with butter and strawberry jam. 'Eat that,' she said brusquely.

What? I'd barely eaten anything for weeks and now I was supposed to force down that heap of stodge? 'No thanks,' I said. 'I'm not eating that.'

Doctor and nurse looked at each other.

'Well,' said the doctor, 'if you won't eat there's nothing we can do for you. You may as well go home.'

At the time I thought they were really rude and unsympathetic, but I can see now they must have felt frustrated and saw my condition as entirely my own fault. This was nearly ten years ago, when anorexia wasn't as widely discussed as it is now, size zero models and all. They probably had enough to do with people who were ill or injured through no fault of their own, and thought that I was just being selfish.

Shortly after I got home, I had a call from my agent, Craig. (Vivian had helped me for a few months, then advised me to go with people who knew more about my side of showbiz.) He wanted to come round. He didn't say whether he'd been told anything, but as soon as he came in I could see he was serious.

'I'm worried about you,' he said. 'People are starting to talk.'

Apparently my baggy clothes hadn't altogether disguised my thinness. Also, my non-appearance at parties and other dos had caused some comment.

'What's the matter with you?' asked Craig.

I was tearful by now, and choked out, 'I'm too fat.'

We both sat and stared at my arms, sticking like bony twigs out of my short-sleeved top.

Craig sighed. 'OK,' he said, 'we've got a problem here. But Gail, we're all concerned about you, we all want you to be well. You really can't go on like this.'

Any moment he was going to mention seeing someone, I was sure. Instead he said, 'Think about it. You've got to take yourself in hand.'

'OK,' I said. Easy as that. But even I realised that I couldn't go on like this, not if I wanted any semblance of life back. I'd have to do something.

So, who could help? Doctors? I went to my GP, and set a pattern that would recur for years.

*

Sitting on my mum's lap, 1971. Mum has a very groovy hairdo
going on and I have more hair than I do now.

In my first competitive dancing kilt,
practising the Highland fling in
the front garden.

Me and my brother Keith with our
brand new kitten Leia. She lived
to the grand old age of 22.

One morning I woke up in my
Supergirl nightie and decided
I would adorn myself with a princess
hat and head out to my street
looking for evil I could rectify.

In my early twenties
with boyfriend Tony.

A girl has to have a mental
18–30 type holiday: Faliraki
was mine. Sitting next to
me is Debbie, Lynne is
lounging in the back (with
Debbie's sister Michelle,
who you can't see).

My dad doing what he loves best.

At my mum's house with my Uncle David and my grandpa, the redoubtable Horatio Walter Stanley Twiddy.

My first ever calendar shoot, in a luxury house overlooking Cannes. My mum came as moral support.

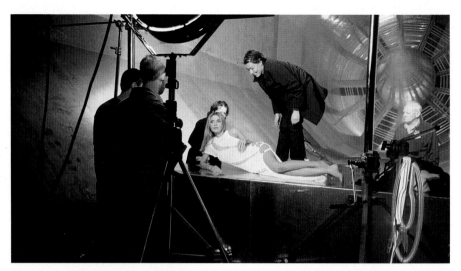

In a wind tunnel at an abandoned air field – I was bloody freezing so the photographer dressed me in as little as possible.

Just larking about on a shoot, as you do in Gina heels and a bikini.

More photo shoots. Blimey I miss my hair!

The *FHM* shoot that ended up on the Houses of Parliament. The first I learned of this was the morning after, on the news.

**CELEBRITY BLIND MAN'S BUFF**

Three days of simulated blindness – a totally moving and educating experience.

Another kids' show, another pair of shiny trousers – *Scratchy & Co*, Saturday mornings, ITV.

Ali G serenading me with 'Every Breath She Takes'. A highlight of my life.

It's still number one. It's *Top of the Pops*. I'm a rather overexcited Gail Porter.

The start of the cover photos. Never quite understood how I managed that one.

**Gail force**
MASTERS

*Esquire*

THE SHARPER READ FOR MEN

AUGUST 1999 £3.10

**GAIL PORTER**
THE LAST EVER NAKED PICTURES

SHOOTING PUMAS IN DEVON

EVEL KNIEVEL
'I'VE LIVED BETTER THAN ANY PRESIDENT'

THIRTYSOMETHING WOMEN WHO WANT YOU FOR SEX

The last ever naked pictures, until the next one!

CHRIS MOYLES
RADIO 1 BAD BOY MOUTHS OFF

9 770960 515081

In Spain with my mum.
I wasn't a great fan of
food at this time.

Hiding in my baggy
Frank Skinner t-shirt.

Claire Holdsworth, me,
Charlotte Wheeler,
Nicola Davies, Carlos
Ferraz and Geoff Lloyd.
Great friends and
champers – perfect.

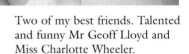

Charlotte checking my boobs
before we hit the town.

Two of my best friends. Talented
and funny Mr Geoff Lloyd and
Miss Charlotte Wheeler.

Cat Deeley and me at a Chelsea
celebrity football match.

Me, Melinda Messenger and
Jordan at Silverstone.

I was at Virgin Radio at
the same time as Chris
Evans – he is a very
clever and fun man.

My first ever Oxford Union
talk. A nerve-wracking but
fantastic experience.

Dan and me doing a shoot shortly after we announced our engagement.

Dan acting out what he probably would have loved to have done to me many a time.

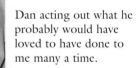

Our angel – four minutes old.

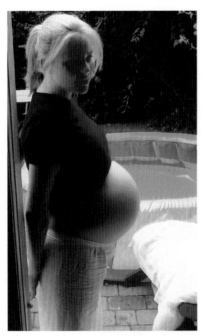

The biggest bump
ever and I still had
two months to go.

Doing what we love best – snuggling!

Honey at four
weeks old.

At the Scottish Baftas, with a hat created by my friend Woody.

Accepting the baldness and being happy with my lot.

Michelle Chapman and myself, having just been caught by the paparazzi.

Dressing down for my divorce party. Dress and jacket by Laura Lee – hair by Hamleys!

James and me in New Delhi.

© CORBIS

A ragpickers' project in New Delhi which I visited for Action Aid.

© FAIRTRADE

My brother Keith and me in Uganda for Fairtrade.

© FAIRTRADE

The children in Uganda thought my hair was hilarious.

Sitting in the waiting room staring glumly at the old dog-eared magazines, waiting for the sign to light up: MISS PORTER TO ROOM 2.

Off I go, and as soon as I walk into the doctor's room I burst into tears.

'So what appears to be the problem, Miss Porter?'

'Nothing.'

'So why the tears?'

'Oh well, you see, the thing is, well, it is, I feel, how can I explain it, I feel kind of, you know...actually I'm fine.'

Then he gives me the 'You can tell me, I'm a doctor' look and I want to punch him on the nose and leave right then.

Instead I say, 'I'm just tired and I don't want to leave my house sometimes and I feel rather worthless and I get ridiculously happy, then I burst into tears and then I freak out when bills come through my letterbox. But I want to help everyone and I need constant reassurance that my friends love me and then I want to sleep again. I know I'm not eating enough but I find it very difficult. Other than that, I'm fine.'

'Well, that does sound rather tiring.'

No shit, Sherlock.

'Perhaps you need a holiday.'

Fine. Are you going to pay for it? Look after my life and pay my bills while I piss off and chill out? Life just isn't like that, Doctor man. I stand up and start edging towards the door.

'Sit down, Miss Porter, and we can discuss options. Would you like to talk to someone?'

I'm talking to you and it's freaking me out.

'We can put you on an NHS waiting list and a psychiatrist will contact you and give you a date to go in. It may take up to six months, though.'

'Yeah, do that.'

I just desperately wanted to get out of that room and get away...

As it happened, I was sent a letter after only four months saying I had an appointment the following Friday. Unfortunately I was away working and got home three days after that Friday. And what else did the letter say?

'If you do not keep this appointment, you will go to the end of the waiting list.'

I thought, I can't believe this. I've waited all this time and then I'm not able to make this time and now I have to start all over again? There must be a better way of organising appointments. Is it really such a rigid, bureaucratic system?

Well, yes. There are probably variations round the country, and maybe things have improved since then, but it was that kind of bureaucracy that drove my brother out of the caring profession.

After his 'wild' days, Keith had had a variety of jobs and then worked for some years with autistic people, doing really good work. He has a massive heart, and he always wanted a career where he would help other people. And this was a tough, demanding job. He told me how he felt the system failed the most vulnerable.

'This kid needs help,' he'd say. 'And he needs it now.' Only to be told, 'Well, fill this form out and then we'll take it to here and to there...' He reckons health care got mixed up with politics, and he can't stand it, any more than I can. When help's needed, that's when you should get it. As a matter of fact, Keith still visits the people he used to care for out of concern for them, but as a private individual not an official health worker.

So the only professional advice for me was (a) sleep more, (b) eat more, and (c) er, that's it.

I knew I could control the eating. If lack of it was doing me in, then I could do something. I'd been running on empty for too long, I could understand that. No miraculous conversion – I wasn't about to start stuffing myself. I gradually stepped up my intake of food, eating more carbs and protein, while not pushing myself quite so hard in the gym. My weight slowly increased. I was weighing myself twice every day – that had become my habit – and the needle on the dial eventually reached seven stone. That was my weight when I had my first nude photo shoot, and I looked pretty good then. By the time of my next nude shoot, I was back on form, looking like a woman with boobs and an arse, not a scrawny sparrow.

God, that was a narrow escape – I could have done myself a severe damage. As it was, I didn't do my metabolism any favours. My periods seemed to have disappeared for good. And although I resolved never to get so thin again, it was as if losing weight was a default action whenever I was stressed. I might at last admit I had anorexia, but that didn't mean I could always control it.

Meanwhile, fitting the old adage that you never know what's coming in life – with all my hang-ups and inadequacies behind me, for the first time in years there was the chance of a real romance, true love…

# * 11 *

# Love at Last

Whenever I was interviewed by a newspaper or magazine, sooner or later the subject of my love life would come up. To which the only honest answer was: 'What love life?'

My relationship with judo player Tony, who'd shared my anxious waiting for the *T.I.G.S.* job, had run its course, and for some years – years, mind you – I hadn't had a proper boyfriend. Or even an improper one. Sure, I went out on dates, had dinner, went to clubs, danced, had fun, but I never met a man I knew would be The One. Not even remotely. I'd put on a bit of a front – 'Who needs a man? I'm happy as I am' – and while I didn't exactly sit at home moping, at heart I did get to feel a touch wistful.

Not that I didn't love my friends – I did, and do. They're massively important to me. Some of my best times have been going out on the town with a bunch of friends, girls and guys; we'd have a blast. And it wasn't always party, party, party. We had good times just chilling out, talking, building a real rapport and confidence in each other. I'd do anything for them, and I know they'd do anything for me.

There were even times I could combine friends with work. I was still working for *Esquire*, only keeping my clothes firmly on. I'd write monthly articles called 'Gail's Night Out'. The mag would give me enough money to take half a dozen girl friends out to dinner, and we'd discuss a specified theme. I'd record us all and then put the article together. So off I'd go with a bunch of mates, we'd order dinner, and I'd open the envelope with the theme of the day. Sometimes the hot topic was ridiculous – 'Boys' pants: discuss' – other times it was more serious, and we could really get stuck in. Everybody would be chipping in, going off at tangents, and at least once someone would ask, 'What was the topic again?' What with the copious amounts of wine we were getting through, the discussion could get heated all right! A lot of fun, though – and quite a challenge for me afterwards to decipher the tape.

There was another spin-off from my nude modelling. I got asked to places I wouldn't normally go. One memorable time I was invited to a bash for Hugh Hefner, of Playboy Bunny fame. I went with my friend Charlotte – I certainly wasn't going to go into a lions' den on my own. Apparently Hugh spotted me and said, 'I'd like to speak to the little blonde girl.'

I dithered a bit and Charlotte pushed me – 'You are so going over there!' she hissed.

Quite an experience to shake hands with the Hef, while being dwarfed by three of his super-blonde Barbie Playmates, Sandy, Brandy and Mandy. And being entertained by the floor show, a bunch of lesbian dancers cavorting around. At such times I think of myself digging sandcastles as a kid on Portobello beach – the contrast between my early life and what I do now is so bizarre, and to tell the truth I like it. I like wondering, 'Why am I here?'

There was another funny follow-up to this. I made the front page of the *Daily Sport*, with the best caption ever: 'TV's Gail Porter in lesbo sex shock'. I loved it so much I got lots of copies and gave them to my friends. I even gave one to my mum, who wasn't exactly thrilled, though possibly relieved to read the inside story. There I was at the Hefner party, and after I saw girls cavorting with each other I was 'in shock'. Yeah, right.

Of course I'd known for ages not to take seriously anything about me in the tabloids. It was just a laugh. They'd put labels on me – I was the new Zoë Ball or the new Sara Cox or the new somebody else. No reflection on those girls, but I didn't want to be the new anybody, just the one and only Gail Porter. Tabloid shorthand, I guess. All of us were young, had blonde hair and presented TV and radio shows, so we must be clones of each other. In fact I hardly knew Zoë – we've only met a couple of times. I've seen more of Sara (and I have a particular reason to be grateful to her), but it's not like any of us were joined at the hip.

We were all called 'ladettes', though, a label that's been done to death – except that it keeps popping up even now. Ever since the Spice Girls and Girl Power in the mid-nineties, there's been all this stuff about 'sisters doin' it for themselves', challenging men at their own game and so on. Fine, if that means earning your own money, being independent, going out and having a great time. That was me all right, and still is. But ladettes were supposed to be into beer, football and fags, acting like lairy blokes, getting drunk, throwing up and throwing punches. Well, beer makes me sick, I hate football, I don't smoke and I'm not into violence. My idea of a good time was being out with my mates, sure, but if I drank too much of anything (and I must say I did now and then) it was champagne at the Ivy. I had other regular haunts – the Alphabet Bar and Balan's in Soho, and Little Italy, presided over by the wonderful Veronica. And by now I belonged to the Groucho, which I'd loved ever since Derek took me there. He nominated me, someone seconded (all very formal), and I became a member. I'm also a member at Soho House, which somebody else nominated me for. It's great going to these private clubs – you know you can relax and there won't be photographers poking their lenses in your face.

Maybe my love of martial arts and sci-fi suggested a blokey side to some people, but frankly, so what? It all seems a bit arbitrary to me. I must say I've never had the slightest inclination to pretend to be a man, or rather, a lad. And my idea of fun probably wouldn't have fitted the stereotype either. One of the best fun things I've ever done, that I enjoyed more than I can say, was so silly, so innocent. It was when I was working at Virgin Radio, co-presenting a show with my best friend there, Geoff Lloyd, who's just about the nicest, funniest man on the airwaves. We used to bust our guts laughing on the show. We'd say daft things like, 'Right, today we're going cliff jumping. We have to find Cliff Richard and Cliff Michelmore and jump over them!' I know, I know – groan. But a real laugh when you're mucking about with someone on your own wavelength.

One day after work we got a fit in our heads – whizzed to

Hamley's toy store in Regent Street and bought ourselves some pretend tap shoes. They're great, these. You just strap on the tap bit to the toe of your own shoes, and off you go. Very realistic. Geoff and I hit the pavements and did a Fred and Ginger all the way to Villiers Street near Charing Cross, a performance probably not appreciated by people trying to walk and shop. We danced all the way to Gordon's Wine Bar and did our final twirls at the counter. 'Can we' – tap tappity tap – 'have a' – tap tappity tap – 'bottle of wine' – tap tappity tap – 'please!' We thought we were hilarious, and giggled our way downstairs into the dark caverns of the wine bar, tapping as we went.

Mind you, to show that variety is the spice of life, the next day I got my nipple pierced. I was out with a girl friend, and when I asked her, 'What can top tap-dancing in the street?' she said, 'Get your nipples pierced.' Not sure what the connection is there, but anyhow, I thought, Why not? It hurt a bit at the time, but then I had a dinky little silver ring adorning the nipple, and for some reason I felt really feminine. So much so that I had the other nipple pierced, and kept both rings for a couple of years, till I got bored with them.

My holidays weren't exactly typical ladette style either. No more Faliraki with the girls for me. These days I usually went with my mum. In fact the first time was to celebrate her fiftieth birthday – at last I was earning enough money to say a big thank you for all her support over the years. We went to Monte Carlo and stayed in a really posh hotel, where we had a beautiful room. The first evening we got all dressed up for dinner, then went to chance our luck in the casino. Where they wouldn't let me in.

'You have to be over eighteen,' they told me.

'I am!' I insisted, to no avail.

My mum was hooting with laughter. 'You'd better go and get your passport, love,' she said, and then only went and sailed in by herself.

Once I'd shown my passport, I went to find Mum. She was sitting at a machine surrounded by buckets of money, and laughing.

'What are you doing?' I asked.

'Dunno,' she said happily. 'It just keeps paying me.'

She walked away from there with about three hundred quid, and we never did work out how she did it.

We certainly had our moments. I remember one time in Barcelona when we did fit the ladette bill a bit more and got tipsy. (Would that make my mum a blokette?) We had a few glasses of wine at dinner and made our unsteady way back to our hotel, taking the lift to our floor. When we got out, Mum said, 'Look at the carpet! It's different!'

'So it is,' I said, focusing my eyes on an unfamiliar pattern. 'That's a lot of carpet to lay in an afternoon.'

We staggered up the corridor, giggling, and I tried to fit the key in our door. I couldn't make it work.

'Bloody bastard key,' I muttered, only to find the door opening and a lady asking, 'Can I help you?'

'Um, is this room 216?' I asked.

'No, it's 416.'

That explained the carpet, then. In retrospect, perhaps it's not a lot to get hysterical about, but it's a good memory. Mum and I were getting on really well.

There was a little friction another time, though, when we went to Puerto Banus in Malaga. On our girls' week away, Mum pulled! She met an English doctor, a very distinguished-looking man, who was working for an Arabian prince. They spent a lot of time together, going on proper dates. I heard a noise outside our hotel door late one night, and when I opened it, there they were, snogging!

'Do you know what time it is?' I demanded, tapping my watch and turning instantly into my own mother, or Saffy from *AbFab*. 'You know what? I'll give you just five more minutes!'

Then she came in all giddy and laughing, saying, 'Whee, more wine!'

My attitude may have hardened as I didn't have any similar success, and moped about a bit by myself. When I bumped into Declan Donnelly (the Dec bit of Ant and Dec) I was really chuffed – we go back years, he's a great bloke, very funny. He was having a romantic break with his lovely girlfriend Claire, and invited me to join them for dinner one evening. I jumped at the chance, though I imagine Claire wouldn't have been too keen on a Scottish gooseberry. Anyway, I was past being considerate – I was dying for company. When I saw Mum and her bloke swimming in the hotel pool, with all the other mature guests, a malicious part of me thought of that old film where all the wrinklies get rejuvenated in a pool by an alien pod.

'Look at 'em frolicking about down there,' I said to Dec, nodding at the pool. '*Cocoon* or what!'

Not very nice, I know, but I thought it was funny. So did Dec. Anyway, Mum enjoyed herself, and that was what really mattered.

The doctor fizzled out after a while, but he was nice while he lasted. One up to Mum – it did her good after her split from Dad.


Whatever image of me was projected in the press, I guess the old-fashioned romantic side of me didn't figure much – I certainly didn't play it up. Yet at heart that's what I am. Ever since my puppy-love days with Andrew at school, I've loved everything about being in love. I might have been a bit scathing about the whole hearts and flowers thing, never seeing myself as a fluffy bunny, girly sort of girl. But to be honest, I love that thrill, that connection with a man, the knowledge we're both special to each other. And the sex, of course. Sex without commitment was not on the cards for me, but I don't think I've ever been one of nature's celibates...

So I would have loved to give my heart to a man, but where was he?

Funnily enough, while I'd been looking for someone and keeping my eyes open, I actually found him on a blind date. Though as I knew who he was in advance, I suppose it wasn't strictly a blind date.

We were set up by Sara Cox. She invited me to a birthday party she was throwing for her boyfriend, and I must have been moaning more than usual about my single state as she said, 'Look, Gail, I know someone you'll like.' This someone was Keith Flint, front man of hard-core techno band The Prodigy. Sara's boyfriend was Leroy, another member of the band, hence the connection.

Hmm, I thought, Keith Flint? Interesting...certainly a force to be reckoned with. Ever since The Prodigy had burst out of the Essex house scene, they'd made a name for themselves as in-yer-face techno ravers, and of all those wild men, Keith was the wildest. Mad clothes, mad hair, ripping up the stage like a windmilling dervish. And he'd actually go on a date with me? Apparently so.

It made me smile when I imagined how my aged relatives would have reacted if they'd seen Keith on *Top of the Pops* when they visited my family for Christmas. (Not that *Top of the Pops* would have been the venue of choice for The Prodigy.) I could just hear them: 'Is that a man? Look at his hair – it's purple! It's sticking up all over the place! And his clothes – they belong on a scarecrow! Is that an earring? Look at those tattoos – he should be in a circus. Why is he shouting all the time? And why doesn't he ever stand still?'

Yup, definitely not the clean-cut, boy-next-door type. Good.

When I mentioned my upcoming date to my Virgin Radio colleagues, there was great excitement.

'Wow,' said my producer Sara-Jane. 'Keith Flint of The Prodigy. Oh my God.'

'What do you think he's really like?' said Daisy, another producer.

'I've heard he's really quite a private person,' said our colleague Pam.

I simply didn't know what to expect. We'd arranged that Keith would come to the production office after work and pick me up, and I sat there quaking with nerves. I was convincing myself that the whole idea was insane, he'd never like me, it was going to be a nightmare.

Then he walked in, not so outlandishly dressed that he turned heads. We shook hands and I went into my usual routine when I'm nervous. That is, non-stop talking.

'Hi, I'm very pleased to meet you, thanks for coming, how are you, where d'you wanna go, d'you wanna drink, what about the Groucho, I'm a member…'

As I burbled on, Keith just stood there gazing at me, and at the back of my mind I thought, He hates me, he hates me, he'll never go through with this, he'll go away, he'll leave me here…but at the same time another part of my mind was thinking, Hey, he's really good-looking, behind his glasses his eyes are beautiful…

At least he agreed to the Groucho and we sat in the bar. He must have been as nervous as me, as he drank a lot very quickly, again just like me. We were going on to Leroy's birthday party, and on the way there, I'm not sure how it happened, we had a wee snog. Good sign?

At the party my heart sank again as Keith wandered round the room talking to people, and I was just sitting there on my own, thinking, Oh great, he doesn't really like me, he's not interested. I felt like a spare part, but then things picked up and everyone was really nice, and we all got dancing. Keith and I clicked and got on like a house on fire, and for my part I fell totally in love with him. Quite a shock to the system, but I reckoned I could take it.

We saw each other whenever we could, and spoke every day on the phone. I thought this love affair would go on for ever. I'm like all the old pop songs rolled together – 'I give my heart completely…' How wrong could I be?

I was still renting the flat in West Hampstead, which was

owned by a lovely uncle of my friend Robert Popper's. It was great to have my own space at last. Especially with no chance of Mum popping in! Though Mum did get an unexpected sight of Keith one morning when she was staying over with me in my flat. There she was waking up in the front room when Keith wandered in from the bedroom, wearing just boxers and looking like the Illustrated Man – he's got tattoos up and down his arms and legs, all over his body.

'Morning,' he said to my mum. 'Wanna cuppa tea?'

Mum nearly had a heart attack but recovered enough to say, 'Och, hello.'

Keith was living out in Essex, so our time together would be in the city. Then there was a chance for us to go on holiday together – courtesy of my job. I'd been working on *Wish You Were Here*, the holiday programme, and my next assignment was in the Maldives, no less. Tough, but someone's gotta do it. The presenters could usually take a companion with them, for when they were off duty, and this seemed a perfect opportunity for Keith and I to go away together for the first time.

Yup, work. I mustn't get so caught up with my new love life to forget about that.

*Wish You Were Here* was my dream job – travelling, staying in new places, meeting new people, trying out new activities…OK, you have a camera shoved in your face most of the time, but that's the point: you're showing viewers at home what's around, what there is to do. We had great crews, too, which was just as well as we were all away from home and couldn't piss off if we got on each others' nerves. I always tried to pull my weight whatever was going on, sometimes to the bemusement of crew members.

We'd be at an airport and I'd pick up a piece of the equipment.

'What are you doing with that tripod?' someone would say.

'Carrying it,' I'd explain. 'Five pieces of equipment, five people, one piece each.'

'But you're the presenter…'

I always found it bizarre to be treated differently. If you're part of a team, you work as a team. That's what I think, anyway.

I have a lot of good memories from *Wish You Were Here*, even apart from the trip with Keith.

There was one time I went on a cruise – and that was a time and a half. Not my usual kind of stamping ground, but very popular with viewers. The ship was full of old people – in my experience great company when you're travelling around. The oldies have the best stories. I hooked up with one old guy who was sick and needed a heart bypass operation – which didn't stop him bopping around on the dance floor with me. It was like dancing with your grandad, a hoot, a good laugh. He called me his 'wee poppet', which was sweet. There was a lot of drinking, too, and I had quite a bout with one old lady, called Eileen, before toddling off to my cabin.

Next morning, I woke to find the cabin looked as if a bomb had hit it. Furniture all over the place, everything fallen on the floor, telly smashed. What the hell had happened? Surely it wasn't me stumbling about the night before! I went on deck to find someone to ask, and everywhere I looked there was puke. A few people sitting around were dead white, or slightly green. 'What the hell's been going on?' I asked a passing sailor. Apparently there'd been the worst ever storm at sea, and the ship had been tossed about like a cork most of the night.

While everybody else was staggering about and sicking their guts up, I'd slept like a log – and so did Eileen. 'What were we drinking?' I asked her. 'Meths?'

Oh well, all in the line of duty, I suppose. There was another time, when I took my brother Keith with me. It was like an 18–30 holiday, touring nightclubs in Ibiza. God, it made me feel old. I'd gone to Ibiza myself when I was much younger, with a girl friend. It was my second venture abroad after Faliraki and its madness, and I must have been about twenty or so. We hit the scene all right – drink, drugs, dancing, just chilling out…and, just like the Greek island, I loved it. In fact I didn't want to leave – I spun out my time there for ages, putting off going back to college.

Now I was in Ibiza with my brother, nearly ten years later, and I felt like a respectable matron amid a load of mad kids. Anyway, even if I hadn't got all the naughty goings-on out of my system, I was working, I had to be responsible. I couldn't act like a reckless teenager. What a strange time that was – my brother still laughs at it. Keith and I were staying in a package-holiday family-type hotel. Every morning we'd be sitting there waiting for breakfast and the tannoy would blare out a fanfare: '*Buenos días*, good morning, everybody.' Then, after an impressive drum roll, we'd hear what today's activity was. One morning it was – teabag tossing!

The things I do for my art. I was filmed with a teabag hanging out of my mouth by its string. You had to clench the string between your teeth, swing your head, and let the teabag go off towards the target. The winner was given a big glass of wine, which at nine o'clock in the morning certainly sets you up for the day. My brother was rolling around on the floor, crying with laughter at me.

One morning he tried to ask the waiter for breakfast. Not speaking Spanish, he mimed a piece of bread being put under a grill, and making a cup of tea. Tea and toast for breakfast, *gracias*. The waiter had seemed to know what Keith meant, so it was rather a surprise when he came back with a plate of hamburgers, beans and chips and a bottle of beer. Well, we thought it was funny.

My trip with the other Keith in my life was an altogether more classy business. No chips with everything here, or daft stunts. Just a tropical paradise. No wonder people call the Maldives a string of pearls scattered over the Indian Ocean. More than a thousand islands, with coral gardens in lagoons of the deepest turquoise, the clearest water, the most dazzling beaches…I seem to be doing my bit for the Maldivian tourist board here, but I love the place so much. I could live there for ever. And the first time I visit, it's with the man I thought I was going to love for ever.

We had a fabulous time. I had to do all my pieces to camera, obviously, but when I was off duty Keith and I soaked up the natural beauties, the tranquillity – at least when he wasn't being followed by fans. Quite a few people recognised him, with his sticking-up hair and tattoos, even though his everyday look was rather toned down compared to his stage appearance. At times he was a bit of a Pied Piper, with kids trailing after him. Keith was uncomfortable with this attention, genuinely being a private person, so we always headed for the quieter places. The islands are fantastic for diving, so both of us tried it for the first time.

Then it was time to go home. I had my usual crying bout, desperately sad to be leaving a place where I'd been so happy. I've always felt most alive in the sun, it calms as well as energises me. I'm sure I was born in the wrong country. Yet up pops the old work ethic: playtime over. Anyway, this time Keith was with me, which eased the transition. I had so much to look forward to at home – though not in the way I imagined.

When I arrived home, to my rented flat, I had a huge shock. It had been broken into and totally trashed. Everything valuable had been nicked, everything breakable lay in pieces on the floor. Even worse – my underwear was strewn all over my bed, and it was obvious that the burglar, or burglars, had wanked all over it. As I looked round at the scene of devastation, my legs gave way. I felt violated. I pulled myself together though, forcing myself to think, well, it's only stuff, nobody's hurt. But I couldn't stay here – no way could I spend the night here.

I phoned the police, and while I was waiting for them I phoned Keith, who'd gone home to Essex. Trying to keep my voice steady, I told him what had happened. His response was immediate. 'Right,' he said. 'That's it. You're coming here – you're living with me.'

My knight in shining armour! He told me he'd send one of his security guys to collect me – he'd help me pack up anything that could be salvaged. Meanwhile, I had to phone my landlord, Robert's uncle. I explained what had happened and said, 'I'm very sorry, but I just can't stay here.'

He was really kind, so sympathetic. 'I'm glad you've got somewhere else to stay,' he said. 'Don't worry about the flat – we'll clear the place up. You just look after yourself.' And he even waived the rent!

When I arrived at Keith's house, he was waiting for me.

'Are you all right?' he asked, a look of concern on his face as he handed me a large Bloody Mary.

'I am now,' I said.

But I wasn't.

# * 12 *

# The Pain of Loss

At first, everything was fine. I loved living with Keith; he's a wonderful man. His house is old and beautiful, tucked away in an Essex village. Quite an English country-house way of life, with dogs, wellies, log fires…idyllic. It was me who was going to press the destruct button.

The root of it all was that we wanted different things out of life. Keith and his band were taking a break, readjusting, working new things out. Keith himself was very happy to stay cloistered in his country life, he loved the peace and quiet and didn't like going out very much. But I was still working, mostly alternating between *Big Breakfast* that I'd joined recently and good old *Top of the Pops*. So that was a mix of very early starts, about two-thirty a.m., and late finishes. I was spending a lot of time on the motorway, either tired from getting up so early, or tired after a long day.

Working on those shows isn't just a matter of being on screen.

There's all the preparation, of course, for hours beforehand, then afterwards there's the winding down, where you talk things over. I always liked to relax after a show, but it's more than having a drink and a laugh – it's a way of keeping in touch with your network of friends and colleagues. That's always been important to me, and I began to miss it. I began to think, If only I lived in London, I could have an extra hour's sleep in the morning, and I wouldn't have to go home right after the show at night...

Then I'd think, What am I thinking? I love Keith, I love being with him. What if he moved to London? But it became clear that was never going to be an option, so I kept on commuting.

I was also fitting in the odd chat show – I rarely turned down work, and would dredge up the energy from somewhere. Apart from the buzz of doing different things, I was always conscious of my bank account. I was saving for a place of my own, more for a secure home than just getting a foot on the property ladder, and everything helped.

Talking of odd chat shows, the oddest was Ali G's. When I was invited on, I was a bit wary, the guy being so out there. Then I thought, Hey, Ali G is an anagram of Gail – we're made for each other! The show was hysterical, our host being his usual outrageous self. I do believe he even said to me at one point, 'Have you ever had a dwarf munch on your bits?' What! God, that man pushes every boundary – and somehow manages to deflect the shock waves while you collapse with laughter.

He invited me for lunch, fortunately as his real self, Sasha. 'Meet me outside the Ritz,' he said, and I thought, Wow, that's pushing the boat out. Only that's what he meant: outside. He brought a picnic and we went and sat in the park. Obviously a man for surprises. Very nice it was too.

One show I was very glad to get on was Chris Evans's *TFI Friday*. His company, Ginger Productions, was one of the very many that had rejected me years before. So I dug out the letter, and took it with me to the show.

Chris was saying something like, 'Well, Gail, you've done really well, we always knew you would, we love you...' when I interrupted him.

'Let me stop you there,' I said. 'Years ago I sent you my CV and a letter asking for a job – runner, tea girl, anything. You wrote back a really patronising letter: "Dear Gail, Thank you for your letter regarding being a tea girl. We're not interested, hope you find success in some area of your life, blah blah..." So you didn't always know, did you?'

Chris was mortified, his face going as red as his hair. 'You're joking, aren't you?' he said.

I showed him the letter, and he said, 'Bloody hell. Well, you're here now...'

Call me petty, but I found that very satisfying.

I was still doing the odd jaunt for *Wish You Were Here*, including a memorable trip to Wales. I was sent to an SAS camp in the wilds for a weekend, to sample the simple life for the viewers at home. All the blokes running it were old SAS types, and if most of them weren't pissed out of their minds half the time, they were giving a very good impression of it. We all went up the mountain and pitched our tents for the night. In the morning I said to one of the guys, 'Excuse me, but where's the bathroom?'

He pointed at a tree. 'There,' he said.

Right, piss behind a tree. Wash in the freezing lake, gather wood, make fires – great! And I mean that. I absolutely loved it, I was in my element. It was just like Ninja camp when I was a kid, only this time I was getting paid. The only downside was the food, mostly rabbits that the guys caught and killed. All very living off the land, but I don't eat meat so that was never gonna happen. I ate hardly anything that whole weekend, though at this time I was still struggling with anorexia so it wasn't too much of a change.

At the end of the weekend, I had a surprise. Keith actually drove all the way over from Essex to collect me. 'I missed you,' he said simply, and I was so touched. The only thing was, he was driving a bright red Ferrari, about the highest-end car around. You couldn't get more of a contrast – I'd been living the simple outdoor life on a Welsh mountain, all very basic, and here's this immaculate swish car, incongruous among the muddy 4x4s. I felt a bit embarrassed, and slunk down in the passenger seat with a baseball hat pulled over my ears. The last time I'd been embarrassed by a means of transport was my college friend Sasha's Lada, for completely the opposite reason – it was a rusty, unreliable old heap. Myself, I like a car between those two extremes. But it was a typical kind thought of Keith's to come and pick me up.

Back in the swing of things, I knew I'd have to live in London if I was going to keep up with work and social life. Living in Essex felt increasingly claustrophobic. Then one day I heard about a flat going in the heart of Soho, just about my favourite part of

London, and couldn't resist popping round to have a look. It was lovely, and not too expensive. While I was saving for my own place, I could live here very happily.

I asked the agent, 'When will it be available?'

'Tomorrow,' he said.

And it was bound to be snapped up by the next person to see it.

'I'll take it,' I said.

Now what I should have done was to tell Keith what I'd decided, that I was leaving. Not because I didn't love him, didn't value what we had between us. Just that I couldn't keep up this existence, splitting my time between his place in Essex and my work life in London. And I was so grateful to him, so thankful for his help and generosity when I'd been made homeless.

That would have been the proper thing to do. Keith is an intelligent, understanding man. He mightn't like this sudden break, he might feel hurt, but he would see where I was coming from, he'd respect my decision.

Except that I didn't do the proper thing. To my shame – and I don't often admit to shame – I did a bunk. I sneaked out the next day with my stuff and didn't tell him to his face that I wasn't coming back. Like a coward, I phoned him later in the day.

I can't work out why I did it that way. Of course I didn't want to hurt Keith, far from it, I flinched from it. But then made it worse by sneaking out. What's more, just to show how madly inconsistent I was, I hadn't been in my new flat for two minutes before I thought, I've made the biggest mistake of my life. I've walked out on the one guy I really love. What the hell am I doing?

Even though I'd brought about our split, I felt my heart was breaking. I missed him so much it felt like a physical hurt. 'Tough,' you might say, and I know I don't deserve any sympathy. Logic and emotions don't sit together well in my book, but I'd unmade my bed and I couldn't lie in it. I tried to undo what I'd done – not by confronting Keith and having a calm discussion about whether I could come back, but phoning him at all hours, declaring my love and generally irritating the hell out of him. I'd sit in my flat and get through a bottle of wine in an evening and phone him and burble on for hours. He was mad at me anyway for my sneaky behaviour, and now I was annoying the poor guy more than ever with incessant phone calls, crying like a lovesick schoolgirl.

He eventually agreed to see me again – in fact we did try getting back together a couple of times. But it didn't work out. The things each of us wanted most in life were ultimately not compatible.

Just as I'd hit the heights of happiness when I was with Keith, I fell into the deepest despair when I was without him. I know this doesn't make sense, any more than what I did to myself to make the pain go away.

It's got a name: self-harm. As if I wasn't hurting my physical self enough already by not eating properly again and drinking a lot, I took to more direct action, cutting myself with a blade.

One evening, I was sitting in my new flat, which hadn't yet started to feel like home. It was a bit bare, and seemed cold and uninviting. I hated myself for what I'd done, leaving Keith in the first place, and then hounding him. I must be a complete nightmare to him, I thought. Doing that to such a lovely man; failing him. Sometimes you come out of a relationship and think, You bastard. Not with Keith. I so wished that things could have worked out between us, and I missed him from the bottom of my heart. What a mess I was, what a worthless person.

I was drinking my way through a very nice bottle of Chablis. I finished it. I was vaguely aware of feeling hungry, much the same as usual. Then, without clearly thinking of anything, I just got up from the sofa and walked to the bathroom. I picked up the razor I use on my legs, and calmly walked back to the sofa and sat down again. I stared at the skin on my left arm. Smooth, still with a touch of sun. And holding the razor in my right hand, I slowly drew the blade across the skin, a very fine line that quickly welled up with drops of blood.

Euphoria. The pain was sharp, but felt clean and pure. Not like the chaotic pain in my mind. It was as if the new pain displaced the old one, at least for a while. A new pain that was actually a kind of pleasure, giving me relief.

I cut deeper. The pain was more intense, not so much a pleasure. This was more like punishment – which I deserved for being such a bad person. I brought it on myself.


That first cut wasn't the hardest. And it set a pattern for years to come. When I felt overwhelmed, confused, more messed up than usual, in my lowest moods I'd reach for the blade again. And again I'd have that strange reaction of relief and pain, always with a kind of self-loathing that seems to feed on itself. I cut myself because I don't like myself, and when I cut myself I don't like myself even more…

I know it's mad. We get pain for a reason, to show something is wrong. So if you deliberately inflict pain on yourself, and you're not a masochist, why do it? Is it that displacing idea, to play down the bigger pain? Or is it simply a punishment, to try and atone for the bad things you've done?

The sensible thing would have been to acknowledge I was messed up, and ask for help. At first, I was too stubborn, too proud (or stupid) to reveal what I thought of as a weakness, and I wasn't going to spill my guts to some psychiatrist who probably wouldn't know what I was talking about. My experiences with doctors had never been very fruitful – even if the problem was purely physical. I remember one time I did go to a doctor when my chest was very sore and I had difficulty breathing. He said after hardly a glance, 'Oh, it's a chest infection, you'll be fine, don't worry about it.' The next week I was in hospital with pneumonia. I'd been working on a feature for kids' TV about surfing in the north of Scotland, splashing about in freezing water in a wetsuit that was too big for me. I felt really unwell, but the doctor just fobbed me off.

So, whatever's wrong with you, doctors aren't to be trusted. Anyhow, what could they do about my mad habit? No, I'd rather lock myself in the bathroom and slash away.

Later, when I read about self-harming and realised I wasn't unique, that quite a lot of people were driven to do it, I tried going to another doctor. I probably didn't give him a chance, but as soon as he said, 'You have to stop this,' I was off. Of course

I had to stop it, I knew that, but it was like telling a drug addict, 'Well, you've just got to go cold turkey.'

On top of the self-loathing, there's the guilt. It's a completely selfish act, and it worries people who care about you. I remember once I went back to Keith's house to get some more of my stuff, and he saw the marks on my arm. I suspect that part of me wanted him to see them, wanted him to know how deeply I really felt. Anyway, I didn't take the trouble to wear a long-sleeved top.

'What the hell's going on?' he asked. I tried to explain, only as I was so confused myself, the explanation probably didn't make much sense. But he knew I was hurting myself, and he was really upset; he only ever wished me well.

I don't know how much other people were aware of what I was doing – bright, bubbly personality that I appeared to be. I haven't really spoken about it publicly, though I gather there have been rumours.

If I didn't know already that my mind was messed up, I started sleepwalking again. I hadn't been aware of doing it for quite a while. Keith had certainly never mentioned it. The reason I know about it is that I was found in the lobby of my block of flats in the middle of the night. There I was in my pyjamas, having left my flat on the eighth floor, got in the lift and pressed the ground-floor button. All on automatic. Trying to escape? I don't know. A kind neighbour led me back to my flat and I pushed the event to the back of my mind, where it joined all the other crazy bits.

And I was getting more than my usual quota of nightmares. Insane dreams where I was being chased. Not by Santa Claus this time, but by faceless people, tracking me through elaborate mazes.

I had to frantically find my way through endless corridors, in an eerie kind of half light, while my pursuers steadily gained on me. I'd wake up with my heart pounding, streaming with sweat, scared to open my eyes till I was sure I wasn't still in some kind of trap.

Bleeding, crying, bad dreams…good job I was all alone. Who could put up with that? All the while I was pushing myself at work – I had to keep the money coming in. I think I put on a convincing show. If friends asked how I was, I'd always head them off. 'I'm fine!' I didn't want anyone knowing what I was doing to myself.

Yup, there was always work to give my existence a focus, a function. And it was work that would bring me together with the next man in my life, and make a normal life seem possible – for a while.

# * 13 *

# Wedding Daze

'I'll never get married.'

Yup, that's me speaking – Mystic Gail, infallible guide to the future. Well, I meant it at the time, or thought I did.

After my split with Keith, I thought love would be off the agenda for ever. I just couldn't hack it, and the misery I was feeling was proof of that. But after a while the daily routine began to smooth away the raw edges. My feelings for Keith didn't go away – I'll always love him – but they kind of got absorbed into everything else I was doing. I found myself gradually climbing out of the pit of despair. I didn't feel the urge to cut myself so often.

One particular piece of work I did that year (we're up to 2001 now) played a big part in shaking me out of my self-centredness, making me think about priorities in life. An eye-opener, in fact – ironic, as the programme involved simulating blindness and making my way around the country. It was called *Celebrity Blind Man's Buff*, not the most sensitive title ever dreamed up, but the programme made quite an impact. Despite the rather gimmicky premise, it was a serious attempt to convey to sighted people what it's like to be blind, and also to show how blind people are treated in a society where seeing is the norm.

I was one of three people (along with comedian Sean Hughes and actress Linda Robson) making their way from Blackpool to London, wearing special glasses that simulated impaired vision. Carrying white sticks, we had to negotiate public transport, pavements, shops – all the usual ingredients of society – plus, of course, other people.

It was certainly a challenge. You don't realise how much you take your senses for granted until you lose them.

The only negative part of the experience for me was when I asked some girls to help me and they deliberately led me into a bollard. It might have been a giggle for them but not for me. It makes you realise how mean-spirited people can make life a misery for people with disabilities. I've always hated meanness.

The climax of the journey was a stunner. I'd been accompanied from Euston Station to the London Eye (the final destination) by a pleasant man who was a great help. Only when I took off my special glasses did I realise he himself was genuinely blind. I was overcome with admiration for him, and all visually impaired people who develop the skills and the confidence to take on the sighted world. What on earth did I have to complain about, really?

The whole experience was a world away from my usual presenting jobs, where I'd be relentlessly bright and breezy. I enjoyed the change, getting involved in something more thought-provoking, more meaty. I thought perhaps that might be the way my career would develop. Not the *Big Brother* kind of reality show – God, if you ever see me locked up in that house, it's a sign I'm totally skint or completely off my head – but something worthwhile. I never dreamed that one day I'd work on a documentary that was about me and the difficulties I was facing.

By this time, I'd met the man who would become my husband. In fact when the 'blind' programme was broadcast, we were planning our wedding – although for a long time nothing could have seemed less likely. And with the benefit of hindsight, maybe it should have stayed that way.

Our eyes didn't exactly meet across a crowded room. More like a crowded pub, though the meeting of eyes was not a meeting of hearts.

I was still at Virgin Radio. Chris Evans was working at the station too, and after the Friday show a crowd of us would pile down to Hammersmith where Chris's *TFI Friday* was filmed. We'd all hang out for an afternoon of madness, meeting the guests, drinking and generally having a laugh. I'd always go with Geoff (tap-dancing Fred to my Ginger).

This particular day on the *TFI Friday* set, Toploader were guesting. I watched them play, and – apologies to fans everywhere – their indie rock/Brit pop-style music wasn't my kinda thing. After the show we all dived over to the pub across the road. I was sitting with Geoff, and we both had a fair amount to drink. Then Dan Hipgrave was in front of me blocking out the light – he's a big guy, well built and over six foot – and speaking to me.

'D'you wanna come and see us tomorrow at Wembley?' he asked. 'We're backing Bon Jovi.'

What? I thought. Does he think I'm insane? Does he think I look like the kind of person who likes Bon Jovi?

Out loud I made some polite, vague reply. He asked for my phone number and I was happy to give it to him. He seemed nice, even cute, but I can't say there was an immediate spark. I thought no more about him.

Geoff came round to my flat next day (I was still living in Soho), to hang out as usual. Dan kept phoning, asking me if I was going to the gig that evening. I just said thanks, but no thanks, each time.

Geoff said, 'Are you gonna change your mind?'

'Not in a million years,' I said. 'I can't bear Bon Jovi and I don't reckon Toploader either. Why on earth would I go all the way to Wembley?'

'You don't fancy him then?' asked Geoff.

'Not specially,' I said honestly. 'He's fine, an OK bloke, but I'm not interested.'

And that was that, more or less, for about the next six months, though Dan did leave the odd message. Then I was presenting *Top of the Pops* and Toploader were on. Presenters always mingle with the guests, so I thought, Oh God, he'll think I'm really rude…

'Hi, nice to see you,' I greeted him. And to be honest, it wasn't actually nasty to see him.

After the show we went out together for a drink, had a chat. He was good company and had a great sense of humour. We had a bit of a goodnight kiss, and he said, 'We should go out again.'

'Yeah,' I said, noncommittally. I'd enjoyed his company and the laughs, but didn't feel anything like ready to even consider another relationship. I still had the remnants of my little achy breaky heart...

But by the time I went to Paris on a photo shoot shortly after, I thought of Dan again. I phoned him and said, 'Let's meet up when I come back.'

He didn't need persuading, and we went on one date, then another...We were going out constantly, having a great time. I don't think I'd ever laughed so much. We really got along fine. After the Keith Flint lows came the Dan Hipgrave highs...We were on a roll. I was working like mad, and Dan's band had had a big hit with 'Dancing in the Moonlight'. The future looked bright.

Anyhow, six months later we were getting married.


Talk about 'Marry in haste, repent at leisure'. I couldn't have predicted that being married would eventually play its part in my disastrous downward spiral. Then again, if Dan and I hadn't got together, we wouldn't have our daughter, who's the light of both our lives. Life without her is unimaginable. But, to be honest, I should never have actually got married. I think Dan did love me at one point, and I certainly meant it when I said I loved him. It took a while to realise that I was probably more in love with the idea of love, and confused the kind of love you have for your mates with the kind of love a marriage needs to survive. We were having the greatest time, sure, but that's not necessarily the best basis for last-ing commitment. Ultimately I wasn't fair to him. But I was at that place where security mattered to me. I may have left Keith, but I didn't want anyone to leave me; I didn't want to be on my own again. I thought that marriage would be the answer to everything.

I'd always said, when asked, that I'd never get married. Couldn't see the point. And to this day I'm hazy about how we decided to take the plunge. We must have got caught up in the madness of it all.

Dan had moved into my Soho flat. Living together didn't take the shine off our relationship, and we still got on well. We were out nearly every night in bars and clubs, and everything seemed a big laugh. Especially one night when we were coming back from the Alphabet Bar, having had quite a few drinks and intending to roll a joint or two at home. When we got to my block, Dufors Court off Broadwick Street (next to where the binmen hang out when they've emptied the bins), we saw a man reaching into my bin.

'He's going through my bin!' I said.

We went over to him and Dan said, 'What the hell do you think you're doing?' Then he looked again and said, 'You're wearing my old jumper!'

Sure enough, the man had fished out Dan's old woolly he'd chucked out.

The man didn't turn a hair. 'It's my job,' he announced.

'Bloody cheek!' I said. 'I'm gonna call the police!'

We staggered up to the flat and I made an indignant call to the local police station.

'Oh, we know about him,' the officer said. 'Calls himself a garbologist. Goes through celebrities' bins looking for stuff he can use or sell – he's famous for it. Don't worry, though, we'll move him on.'

That settled, Dan and I sat down and rolled a joint. We'd barely finished it when the door buzzer went.

'Hello?'

'It's the police – can we come up?'

What were we thinking? We staggered over to the windows and opened them all, waving our arms about to clear the smoke. Which struck us as very funny, so we were pissing ourselves laughing. Then I dug out a can of Airwick and sprayed it everywhere, which was even more amusing. So when we opened the door, a couple of policemen came into a room with curtains blowing about in the breeze and a strong smell of pine needles. And two people grinning inanely.

I guess the police are used to it. These guys were quite friendly, and one of them said, 'We've got rid of the garbologist. If you have any more trouble, let us know.'

'We will!' I said brightly. 'Thanks a lot!'

Then Dan added, 'D'you wanna mug that says Toploader on it?'

'Pardon?'

I was thinking, God, we must be really drunk if we're trying to fob off those mugs to the policemen.

While Dan wobbled off to the kitchen, one of the officers said to me, 'Gail' – we were on first-name terms – 'your carpet's on fire.'

We must have dropped a little bit of hot rock from the joint, and the carpet was smouldering.

'Dan!' I yelled. 'The carpet's on fire!'

'Shouldn't you put it out?' suggested the other officer.

'Yeah, right. Dan – fill the mugs with water!'

In he came with water sloshing out of a couple of mugs, and poured it randomly over the carpet. Then he beamed at the officers.

'Here's your mugs!'

'Oh, really, we can't…'

'Yes you can!'

Dan managed to make one of the officers accept a mug, and they backed out of the room, saying, 'Don't forget – any time you want us to help you with anything, give us a bell.'

Dan and I chorused, 'Brilliant!'

As we sobered up we thought, How come we didn't get arrested? There must have been more important matters in Soho that night, but it was typical of us to see the funny side of anything.

We approached the question of marriage with the same lack of seriousness. One night we were drunk again – there was always a lot of drink around – and possibly I proposed to Dan on the spur of the moment. Or he proposed to me, I can't remember. But we woke up next morning and we each had a ring on our finger. 'Shit!' we exclaimed, romantically. 'Where did they come from?'

Then we looked at each other and said, 'Oh well, why not?'

So, not the most whole-hearted decision, then…

I quickly realised that once you've announced a wedding, the whole thing becomes like a juggernaut, taking on a life of its own. What's more, it's not just the two of you who matter – other people evidently have a right to dictate terms, or at least put their oar in.

If I sound a touch bitter here, it's because I did begin to resent the fact that for this important day I couldn't have things all my own way. And I gather that's not unusual. Other people, especially your family, have a vested interest in this traditional rite of passage. At least I could set the ball rolling. Dan was happy to leave the actual organisation to me (though I'm not so much of a control freak that I didn't consult him!), and I thought, I'll push the boat out. If we were getting married then we'd go the whole hog. The sensible part of my mind was urging, 'Put the money towards the deposit on a house' – but what the hell! I'd have a bloody great party, the best ever, invite everybody – family, relations, friends, all the close people as well as those I hadn't seen for years. Friends and Relatives Reunited! I'd be paying for everything: ceremony, reception, party in the evening, accommodation for folk who needed to stay over – money well spent for a once-in-a-lifetime event (yeah, right). This wedding was going to be unforgettable.

I was dead set on having the ceremony in Edinburgh, my home city. Nowhere else would do. Dan comes from Eastbourne, and with all due respect to that venerable resort, his folks were gonna have to come up north.

Having fixed on the place, the venue was next. We're not religious, so a church was out of the question. That would be as inappropriate as me wearing white to signify virginity. We booked the Registrar's Office in Victoria Street, which is a beautiful little old-fashioned winding street, really atmospheric. We fixed the date for 10 August, just a few days after Dan's twenty-sixth birthday. (I am all of four years and five months older than him.)

It was when we planned the ceremony that rifts started to appear.

I'd asked my brother Keith to stand beside me during the ceremony, and that started my dad up. Despite our uneasy relationship, I didn't contemplate cutting him out altogether, but still, I wanted Keith to be the one by my side.

'I'm your father,' he said, 'I should be the one there. I should be able to choose what I do.'

'But I want Keith to stand by me,' I protested. 'He's not only my brother, he's my best friend.'

Arguments, bad feeling. My mum was getting upset too – not that she was exactly throwing herself into the role of bride's mother. She had nothing against Dan, but she had doubts about the marriage itself.

'It'll never last,' she told me bluntly.

As if to prove a point, she bought the first outfit she could find that wasn't black, her usual colour. It did absolutely nothing for her. She could have worn a sign on her back saying 'Am I bovvered?' and that would have summed up her attitude. And she was the mum who'd always stood by me, looked after me. Maybe I should have taken more notice.

I started to wish that Dan and I had kept things simple. After all, at the end of the day it was just about me and Dan. 'We could still jet off to the Bahamas by ourselves and just get married with no frills,' I said. His mum got wind of that, and it was her turn to get upset.

The last thing I wanted to do was upset my future in-laws. They're a lovely couple, Dan's mum and dad, absolutely devoted to each other. I don't think they've spent a night apart in forty-odd years – the kind of relationship I couldn't imagine having in a million years. In fact I never set out to upset anyone – it's supposed to be a happy day, for God's sake. When it came to it, I couldn't bring myself to go against other people's wishes, but in hindsight it really pisses me off. I wonder how many other brides have been caught in the same dilemma.

Well, all the preparations were eventually made, and Dan and I finally tied the knot. I'd compromised with Dad and Keith, and they both stood beside me, while Dan had fellow Toploader and best friend Joe Washbourne as his best man. About sixty guests watched as we made our vows. I was more nervous than I anticipated, and everything passed in a bit of a blur. I do remember the closing words – 'I now pronounce you husband and wife' – at which point there was a whooping and a hollering from the back of the room. It was my old friend Vernon Kay, whirling his arm about like a demented cowboy with a lasso. The other guests were taken aback, uncertain whether to join in or not. There was some hesitant lifting of arms, almost a little Mexican wave, scattered applause and the odd 'Hooray!'

I loved this unconventional finale. Typical Vernon, not one to hold back. I've known him for years, ever since we met at an awards ceremony, and he's been like a brother, always a good laugh. A funny thing – he'd brought his girlfriend, and next day there were photos of him with a 'mystery blonde' on his arm. Tess Daly isn't so mysterious these days!

Then it was time for the reception. We held it in the Witchery, the most beautiful, magical hotel in Edinburgh, right near the castle, and suitably historic. It's a place dripping with atmosphere, complete with suits of armour lurking in corners. Dan and I would be spending our wedding night in one of the bedrooms, which looks like Queen Elizabeth's spare room. Elizabeth the First, that is.

It had been another headache to sort out the 'top' table, with numbers limited to twelve. Both Mum and Dad had to be included, of course. Dad had brought his girlfriend Mary, and Mum was with the new man in her life, a lovely laid-back bloke called Derek, but partners had to sit at one of the smaller tables.

We laid on a grand spread for the traditional meal, all very Scottish, including lobsters, oysters, haggis and all the trimmings. I wanted people to have a choice, though, and arranged three separate menus: veggie, seafood and meat. It doesn't add to the fun of a party if people feel obliged to eat what they don't like, does it?

My grandpa Horatio was of course one of the guests, one of the special guests. At the start he put up his hand and waved it around.

'What is it, Grandpa?' I called out.

'Thank you very much for the lovely menu,' he said in his strong Edinburgh accent. 'But can I have ice cream for starters, ice cream for main, and ice cream for pudding?'

Er, of course. You dinnae get what you want if you dinnae ask for it. And he thoroughly enjoyed the three bowls of his favourite food. At least he didn't insist that the entertainment was non-stop playing of his favourite TV shows on DVD. *Only Fools and Horses* wouldn't have added to the occasion.

My family must have a thing about puddings. When it was Keith's turn for a speech, he departed from more traditional efforts.

'Hello. I'm only doing this cos my sister made me. Anyway, I'm up, I'm doin' a speech, congratulations. Can I have my puddin' now, for fuck's sake?'

Shocking! And in front of all the old people too. But he was so funny with it, people were falling off chairs, dentures were falling on to plates...As the bride, I wasn't supposed to make a speech, but nothing stops me talking, and I said my piece. Everything was great, we had fun – until someone happened to look out the window and saw a flash going off in the window of a flat across the road. It turned out that paparazzi had actually hired that flat so they could snatch photos of us.

That put a bit of a dampener on proceedings. It was gross intrusion into a private celebration, so we called the police to go round and sort them out.

What made me even more pissed off was the fact that we'd specifically refused offers from *Hello!*-type magazines to photograph our wedding. In fact we were offered £30,000, which would have nearly covered the cost. But it's not my scene. I once went to a wedding because the bride was a friend of mine, only to find my picture taken and printed without permission: 'celebrity' value. The bride and groom might agree to a photoshoot if they like, but why include all the friends and relations? I'd never inflict that on mine. Anyway, I can just imagine someone trying to get my grandpa Horatio to pose nicely.

Jumping ahead, it turned out that the magazine we'd turned down printed twelve pages of pictures taken by the paps. This was so out of order. I phoned up the magazine and said, 'You offered us £30,000 for our wedding and I said no, and you still managed to go behind our back and get twelve pages out of it.' I had an offer myself. 'You've saved money and I don't have any redress. Why don't you at least give £5,000 to a charity of my choice?'

Naive Gail. 'No. We got the pictures, end of story.'

Back to the reception – afterwards we had a big old do in the evening. I'd arranged for a marquee, to hold about four hundred people. I hired a ceilidh band – and we rocked! It went on for hours, and restored the good humour lost through the sneaky paps.

So, not a bad wedding on the whole, as weddings go. Now for the honeymoon – or lack of one, as it turned out.

A few weeks before the wedding, I'd had a phone call from BBC2, a bit of a bombshell.

'We really want you to present this programme for us – it's a martial arts show and you'd be ideal.'

'When does it start?' I asked, naturally enough.

'It starts on the eleventh of August,' they said.

So soon? 'But I'm getting married on the tenth,' I said.

'Yeah? Well...'

I had to think quickly. It was martial arts, my favourite thing, and what's more, it was for the BBC – good and solid, and there might be a chance of a long run. Regular pay packet. I was going to have to make up the cash I'd lavished on the wedding somehow!

'I'll do it,' I said.

The honeymoon had to be cancelled, which pissed Dan off. Then again, he wasn't exactly bringing in much money, so if I was going to be the breadwinner – which was fine by me – then I'd have to get out there and win the bread. It's a funny thing, which with my hazy grasp of finances I don't pretend to understand, but even high-profile bands don't necessarily have the money rolling in. I had to go for this job – no telling if such an opportunity would come round again.

Whatever, it was probably the first nail in our marital coffin.

So the wedding night was cut short as I had to get a plane to London at six o'clock in the morning. A few hours later I was in the Roundhouse in Camden, kicking into this martial arts show. I kept getting odd looks, and finally realised why. All the newspapers had photos of me and my wedding, even the front page of the *Times*. I found it hard to believe that was only the day before, and so did other people.

They looked at me in my little Chinese outfit, in full presenter mode, and said, 'My God, you were only married yesterday.'

'I know,' I said.

All in all, not exactly a conventional start to married life…


We did eventually get a honeymoon, though. When I had a good lot of filming under my belt, we went to Crete. For the first time after our wedding it was just us, nobody else, no work for me. It should have been bliss…but to my surprise Dan started showing signs of the green-eyed monster, quizzing me about my past affairs, real and imaginary.

Hang on, I thought, what's all this about? Whatever else I do to screw things up, I don't two-time anyone. I may be an imperfect wife, but I'm not unfaithful – Dan was talking about stuff that happened before I even met him. I've never been jealous in my life, and I certainly wasn't giving Dan the third degree about old flames. Still, the atmosphere soured and Dan didn't speak to me for a whole day of our honeymoon.

Just a few weeks into our marriage, had Dan changed from being a great laugh into a jealous husband?

But I suppose lots of marriages get off to a shaky start. Let's face it, there's a lot of adjusting to do after the Big Day, when real life kicks in. And in fact our next holiday was a lot more fun, maybe because it wasn't the official honeymoon where everything is supposed to be sweet and you're under pressure to make it so.

We went to St Lucia, which is heart-stoppingly beautiful – and, as I read in a brochure, a premier wedding and honeymoon destination. Bit late for that...But we got on much better, for a while, until we went sailing.

'Let's hire a catamaran,' I suggested.

'Yeah,' said Dan. 'I used to be a sailing instructor, I'll handle it.'

Really? I thought. New one on me!

So we hired the catamaran and the next thing we know we're floating out into the Indian Ocean heading for some rocks.

'You're the sailing instructor,' I said. 'Get us out of here!'

I was calling his bluff. He had never been a sailing instructor – in fact he was panicking as we drew nearer to the rocks, waving madly to the shore and yelling, 'Help! Come and get us!'

I was laughing hysterically, not from fear but from the incongruity of what he'd said and what he was doing.

'Why are you laughing?' he shouted at me. 'We might die!'

'Nah,' I said, when I was able to speak. 'They won't let us die – someone will see us and come to the rescue.' We weren't that far off land.

Sure enough, some guys in another boat noticed our predicament and helped us back to the beach. I was still laughing, much to Dan's outrage.

'How dare you laugh at me?' he ranted, and point-blank refused to speak to me for the rest of the day.

It's probably unfair to highlight his bit of play-acting – I'm sure we've all embroidered the truth a bit in our time. But the point was that he had no need to pretend to me. I wasn't going to think any more or any less of him whether he'd been a bloody sailing instructor or not. What made him think it mattered?

By now I was thinking, Uh-oh, we're in trouble...

We managed to weather that particular storm, and tried to settle back into married life, just like other couples. I'd even said I'd change my surname to Hipgrave, just like an old-fashioned wife. Didn't sound too bad. And there was the question of the marital home...

I'd been looking for the ideal house for ages, on my own account, even before Dan and I planned to get married. I thought of all the places I'd lived in my life – first the family home in Joppa, of course, then the flat above Mum and Dad's office, then a succession of student digs, then assorted rentals in London and that brief time in Essex with Keith Flint. I dearly wanted a place I could call home, where I could put down roots. As I've said before, it wasn't just a question of getting on the property ladder, though I knew I ought to do it as soon as I could as prices in London were going through the roof. I've never thought of home as just bricks and mortar, a commodity to be traded to make a profit. I wanted a proper home, one that I could love. Mind you, when I realised just how much property prices were rising, I thought, Hmm, how much did I spend on the wedding?

But I had been saving for years – about ten years altogether – and I'd put away a tidy sum for a deposit. I scoured the property columns, registered with estate agents and looked for places whenever I had the time.

I fell out with so many agents. I figure they must live in a world of their own. When I said I was looking specifically for two bedrooms, high ceilings (I'd got used to those in our old house in Scotland) and a garden, I'd be taken to view a dingy little box with one bedroom, low ceilings and not even a yard. 'What is wrong with you people?' I'd rage. 'You're wasting my time!' I know they're not supposed to actually lie on property specifications these days, but boy, can they still make a pig's ear sound like a silk purse!

One time an agent drove me to view a particular property, and as soon as I saw the outside I blew up. Another overpriced hovel.

'I'm not even going inside that one,' I said. 'You know what I want – how could you bring me here?'

He tried soft soap. 'Well, we're just keeping our options open...' he started.

I didn't let him finish.

'That's it,' I said. 'I'm getting out of the car, and you can piss off.'

I slammed the door with a satisfyingly loud bang, and he drove off. That'll show him. I'm hard and I'm Scottish and I don't take poncy southern crap.

Then I realised I was stuck in the middle of nowhere, all by myself, as it started to rain – heavily. That's what comes of making a point without thinking it through. Damn. And squelch.

But after all the false starts I came across the house of my dreams. I had to kiss a lot of property frogs but finally hit on the property prince. It was just five days after the wedding, when I was working on the martial arts show at the Roundhouse. I'd been sent particulars and photos of this house and immediately liked the look of it. It was in a long road in Belsize Park, and I nipped round there in my lunch hour. I rang the bell, the owner opened the door, I stepped into the hall, walked just a few paces, and said, 'I'll take it.'

'What?' said the owner, startled – but, needless to say, pleased.

The rest of the house confirmed my first impressions. Two spacious reception rooms on the ground floor, with the requisite high ceilings and, what's more, lovely Edwardian period fittings. A kitchen big enough to entertain in, leading into bathroom, shower and toilet. And a couple of further rooms downstairs in the half-basement. Oh yes, I call it a house, but strictly speaking it's only part of one – my neighbour goes up a flight of stairs to the rooms above. But it feels like a whole house, especially as there's a lovely little garden leading out through french doors.

I don't know what this arrangement is called in England, but funnily enough it's a similar layout to my old family house in Joppa: ground floor and basement, with stairs at the side leading to the neighbour's upper floor. Perhaps that's why I instinctively took to it.

Dan wasn't so smitten. He thought the bathroom arrangement was weird, and OK, it's all a bit higgledy-piggledy, but who cares? I'm buying it: money well spent (or anyway mostly mortgaged).

Great – done deal. Before long, with no chain our end, we moved in. All we had in the way of furniture was a mattress on the floor, though I soon brought in my familiar old toys and kids' stuff to liven the place up.

Marriage, house…what next? Oh yeah, a baby.

# * 14 *

# A New Arrival

When I announced to anyone who cared to listen, 'I'll never get married,' I probably followed it up with 'I'll never have a baby'. Except there was a difference in meaning. Where a baby was concerned, I believed I had no choice in the matter. I would never be able to have one. Bit of reverse psychology – I can't have a baby, so I say I don't want one. There's no point in wishing for something you can never have...After all, the anorexia, which wasn't so pronounced now but was still hovering in the wings, so to speak, had screwed up my hormonal system. My periods had practically stopped, and more than one doctor had told me it would be virtually impossible for me ever to conceive naturally.

So when I woke up one morning in the early spring of 2002 and felt nauseous, I put it down to just one of those things. Then that evening after work I met some friends in a bar and felt even sicker. The smell of the drink and the cigarette smoke made my head swim and my stomach lurch.

'What do you wanna drink?' people asked.

I just shook my head, hand over my mouth. I felt like I'd throw up any minute.

'What's the matter with you?' laughed my friends. 'You light-weight!'

Yeah, what is the matter with me? I was getting embarrassed. I mumbled an excuse and got home as soon as I could. And spent the next hour or two throwing up in the loo.

Dan was out, it seemed for ages, and I felt really scared. I rang him and begged him to come home. 'God!' he said when he came in, and called the emergency doctor. But the doctor just felt my belly and had no idea what was wrong. 'Just keep hydrated,' he said, 'and see how you are tomorrow.'

Hah, I could have said that.

I was feeling worse and worse, and I was supposed to be present-ing *The Clothes Show* in Birmingham the next day. I'd never make it, not if I felt like this. I couldn't sit for hours on a train when I could barely make it to the bathroom without throwing up, let alone stand up in front of an audience and perform. I had to ring my agent and say I couldn't make it. This would seriously piss off people, and I felt bad about it, but not as bad as I felt myself.

After a lousy night, I was still throwing up next morning. Dan went out, and I thought, I can't go on like this. I dragged myself to the local Boots, fortunately just a short walk away, and asked the nice lady behind the pharmacy counter if she had anything that would stop me being sick.

She gazed at me for a moment, frowning slightly. Then she said, 'Do you think you could be pregnant?'

'Oh no,' I said. 'No chance.' But then I thought – a couple of months ago I did have one of my very rare periods, quite light but definitely a period. Was that significant?

Of course I had to be sure. 'I'll take a testing kit after all, please,' I said.

When I got home, I duly peed on the little tube and waited. Positive.

I was stunned. Is it possible? I asked myself. Just the one period in months and months – talk about a small window of opportunity!

I had to be really sure, so I went back to Boots and bought another six testing kits. I thought I saw an understanding smile on the face of the same assistant...

Back home, six more peeings, all with the same result. I lined all seven little tubes up on the kitchen worktop, propped against the wall. Then I sat on one of our wooden chairs, staring at them, and waited for Dan to come home.

'Hi,' he said. Then he looked at the line of little tubes. 'What the hell?'

'All positive,' I said.

Talk about gobsmacked! But when he recovered from the shock he couldn't stop grinning. He'd accepted that I couldn't have children, and now I was pregnant! He was over the moon.

Myself, I couldn't work out how I felt. After the initial shock, shit scared. Me, Petra Pan, having a baby! I'd have some growing up to do. God, the responsibility...but then the thrill, the anticipation. I went round in circles.

We told family and friends, who were full of congratulations. Dan's parents, of course, could have wept with joy. My own mum was rather more circumspect.

'Oh,' she said when I phoned her.

It took her some time to adjust to the news. Of course she was happy if I was happy, but I reckon she was a bit knocked sideways with the thought of being a granny. Sign of getting old? Anyhow, she spent the first few months wondering out loud what the child should call her. 'I won't be Grandma,' she said firmly. Sandy P? Sandy Nanny? In the event she's called Grandma and nothing else and she doesn't seem to mind.

Of course, I wanted to know that everything was developing as it should, and I had all the tests and the scans. When I was asked if I wanted to know the sex, I said yes straight away. A girl, they said, and she's coming along perfectly.

Fantastic. I immediately knew what I'd call her: Pebbles. I once had a make-up artist called Pebbles and she was the cutest, loveliest girl. Pebbles Porter – or rather Hipgrave. If the baby had been a boy, I'd have called him Hopper, and not just because I'm a huge fan of Dennis Hopper. Like Pebbles, it's bouncy, cute, out of the ordinary. And it's not like his surname would have been Long.

Dan wasn't keen on Pebbles, and when his parents heard about it, they were simply horrified. No name for a baby!

Right, now I'm being told what I can and cannot call my baby. I couldn't disappear to the Bahamas to get married, and now I can't call my daughter what I like. When my daughter grows up, I just hope I don't try to dictate to her. But in the event, she would have an even sweeter name...

As I say, I went through all the scans and tests, but – and here I'll seriously piss off the ante-natal lobby – I was damned if I'd go to any classes. I'd heard about all those expectant mums and dads going to breathing and exercise classes, planning every detail of the birth down to the inspiring music and the wallpaper, usually with an embargo on drugs of any kind – 'We want a *natural* birth' – then it gets to the crunch and she's yelling, 'Fuck natural! Gimme all the painkillers you've got!'

My reasoning was what is the point of me sitting in a room with a bunch of other hormonal women discussing how we feel, how we're going to feel, all the rest of it, complete with models and diagrams, when first-timers just don't know how childbirth will affect them? I was reasonably fit already, thanks to my own exercise regime, so I didn't do any of the ante-natal exercises, breathing or otherwise. I figured that when it got to the point, the midwife would tell me what to do. I did know that what was in me was gonna come out, and it would probably hurt like hell. End of story.

Of course, this is just me. Stubborn and prickly when it comes to medicine. If other women do it differently, good for them. But cavewomen gave birth – did they have detailed birthing plans?

In any case, my pregnancy was awful. Not because I hadn't signed up for classes – it was a matter of scale. I'm slightly built, but my already sizeable breasts ballooned, till they resembled – well, balloons. They went up to 28J – not easy to get a bra that size, I can tell you. I could have killed a man with them. In fact I used to say that if I rolled over in bed I could have smothered Dan. How women can actually pay for plastic surgery to inflate their breasts is beyond me. Madness. Apart from the sheer cumbersome bulk of them, there's the drag on the back muscles. Sexy? Don't make me laugh.

Jumping ahead, after the birth they didn't go down very much. In fact I thought about getting a reduction operation. My chiropractor agreed that they're simply too big for my build.

What made it worse at the time was that I was pregnant during high summer, not only huge but swelteringly hot. I was still working, but nothing too energetic. Towards the end I stuck mainly to voiceovers and the like – in fact I phoned in my last job a week before the birth. Whether I was working or not, I liked to go out every day, walking the dog.

Ah, the dog. I've loved dogs ever since I met the Alsatian in my landlady's house in Watford, and I'd been looking out for one of my own now I had a garden. You can't keep a dog in a flat, not when you have to be out working during much of the day. I was about four months pregnant, hormones going all over the place, when I said to Dan, 'I want a dog.'

We were looking through *Loot*, and to my surprise I saw an ad – 'Shar Pei dogs for sale'. I'd always liked the breed, they're very individual dogs, and I hadn't even known the paper advertised animals.

I phoned the number, and took down the address.

'It's in London,' I told Dan. 'Not far.'

Dan was dubious. 'Have you thought this through?' he asked.

Probably not.

We got to the house and found uproar. Actually it was probably just an ordinary family home but it seemed to be bursting at the seams with kids, animals and parrots. We sat in the yard and the man brought out the boy Shar Pei we'd come to see – and he was manic, running around like mad. Oh no, I thought, I couldn't cope with that. Then another puppy wandered by, a girl, and put her paw on my lap. I looked into those liquid eyes that seemed to be saying, 'Please get me out of here,' and was hooked.

'We'll take her,' I announced.

'Are you sure you know what you're doing?' hissed Dan.

Actually, I thought it was sensible to have the dog before the baby, rather than the other way round. Then the dog would be part of the family first and wouldn't put the baby's nose out of joint. Dogs themselves can get jealous, I know, so I was going to make sure that the dog was involved from the start.

Shar Peis originated in China as a fighting dog. I read somewhere that the name comes from the Chinese for 'sand skin' – not from its colour but its rough texture. Missy, as I christened her, is a deep blue-black with characteristic loose skin round her head and neck, looking like deep wrinkles. Apparently this loose skin came in handy when the dogs were used for fighting – they'd be on the front line and attack each other, but because of the loose skin they weren't always hurt. Well, there's not much front-line fighting round Belsize Park, but Missy would certainly go for anyone who threatened me. In a funny way, she reminds me of a Scottish Chinese dog: I love you, she seems to say, but don't make a fuss, don't touch me too much. I love her to bits in return.

Well into my pregnancy I was taking Missy on her regular walks. Paparazzi were always hanging round the place now, pregnant TV presenters being irresistibly newsworthy, obviously.

I found this kind of attention very tiresome at this stage, and thought up a cunning plan.

If the paps were relying on selling different pictures of me every day, well then, every day I'd look the same. I had one voluminous outfit that was perfect for both my size and the weather, so I'd go out in the morning wearing it, with Missy on the lead, then come back, wash and dry it, and wear it out again the next day. Spot the difference, picture editors.

One of the paps noticed. 'You wear the same thing every day,' he said. 'Running short of clothes, are ya?'

'Nope,' I said, 'you don't see the logic. If I wear the same thing every day, same dog, same route, the papers will say they've seen the pic before. You might say you took it on Tuesday, but it's exactly the same as Saturday.'

'Get you!' was all he said.

I replied, 'That way, you won't make money out of my pregnancy.'

There was one time, though, when I could have done with some sympathy. I'd gone to Primrose Hill with Missy and was sitting on a bench when my back seized up. I had back seizures quite a lot, but this was severe. I struggled to get up, a swarm of photographers snapping away, nobody offering to help. It was no good, I had to phone Dan. As usual he didn't answer and I had to leave a message. Some time later he did arrive and literally pulled me up from the bench before driving me home. I had trapped nerves and had to keep lying down for ages.

While I was immobile, the baby kicked all the time, day and night. Wa-hey! I thought. It's like she's at a rave in my belly!

*

What with being huge, having painful back seizures and a mini breakdancer inside me, I was looking forward to the birth. It couldn't come too soon for me.

Contractions started on 1 September. By midnight I was in agony, and I told Dan, 'We've got to get to the hospital.'

Off we went – it was only a two-minute drive to the Royal Free. 'Yes, you're in labour,' they said, 'but you've got a long way to go. You can stay here, or you can wait at home.'

'I'll go home,' I said. 'Once I know things are getting serious, I'll come back.'

Fine. Dan went to bed – 'I need the rest,' he said. 'It might be a long day tomorrow.' Yeah, I thought, *he's* worried about it being a long day. I couldn't get comfortable. I ended up on all fours in the living room, watching reruns of *Trisha* on ITV2.

It got to about six o'clock in the morning and that was it. Things were hotting up all right. I crawled on all fours into the next-door room where Dan was sleeping. It was like waking the dead.

At last he regained consciousness – 'Get up!' I shouted. 'I must get to the hospital right now! It's happening!'

'Right,' he mumbled. 'I'll just nip to the bathroom.'

I stayed on all fours, hearing the shower run. I closed my eyes. I'm all for hygiene, but just this once...

Then there was silence. Where was he?

I crawled into the kitchen, and realised the grill was on and a frying pan was on the hob. 'Dan, what are you doing?' I called.

'It's OK,' he said, reappearing from the bathroom. 'I just thought I'd make myself a quick fried breakfast.'

I tried not to scream. 'Dan, I'm giving birth right now. I must get to the hospital right now!'

'Right,' he said. 'But can't I just have a quick fried breakfast before we go? It might be a long day.'

'No!'

He turned off the hob and said, 'What about a bacon sandwich?'

'NO! FUCKIN' GET IN THE FUCKIN' CAR!'

I just couldn't believe it. What about a nice cup of tea and a read of the paper while you're at it? It can't be all men who'd react like this, can it?

At least we got to the hospital quickly, then it was straight into a wheelchair for me as the contractions were so strong, I felt so ill. When I arrived at the maternity floor, a nurse took one look and said, 'My God! You must be in agony.'

You're right there.

Then people explained things to me. 'Well, we don't believe in giving women an epidural while they're giving birth, but we'll give you an epidural for a couple of hours to ease the pain.'

I don't know how far advanced I was, how dilated or whatever. I just thought, as I'd thought all along, she's coming out of there one way or another. And thank God for painkillers.

After a while the epidural wore off, and it was on with the gas and air. Good stuff. I was offering it around – 'Gas and air, anyone? It's brilliant!' It was all systems go, for hours. And hours. Close on twenty in all. The worst thing was towards the end when nurses kept pressing the emergency button. Other staff would rush in, there'd be a lot of activity and then they'd run out again. Nobody told me anything, and Dan, who managed to be with me most of the time, was as much in the dark.

We learned later that that she stopped breathing once or twice and then she swallowed some meconium, a baby's first poo that's floating around in the amniotic fluid. But evidently everything was put right, and after pushing and shoving and God knows what, she eventually came out. And she was perfect. I held her for just a moment, stunned, looking into her big blue eyes, then she was whisked away for the weighing and other medical checks.

Eight pounds twelve ounces. It wasn't that she was huge. She was very long, with wide shoulders. Naturally I had third-degree tears, so it was legs in stirrups and out with the darning needle. Dan was sitting beside me, and at one point I grabbed his hair. Being stitched up is not pleasant, even with a local anaesthetic.

'Ouch!' he cried.

And I said, 'If you say ouch to anything I will kill you. The minute I'm off these stirrups you're dead.'

I'd given birth to a huge baby who felt nearly as big as me. That's getting a quart out of a pint pot, all right. I could have told Dan I wished I'd married a midget and not a man well over six feet tall.

When our daughter was washed and ready, she was given to Dan to hold while I was still being worked on. I could see him take her gingerly, as if he was scared she'd break, and I could understand. Oh my God, this is mine! So precious!

He held her in his arms, wrapped in a shawl, and stood by the window. I could hear him murmuring to her – 'Um, hello. I'm your dad.'

He turned to face the window (we were quite high up), and with a sweep of one arm added, 'Er, this is London. This is where you live.'

Well, what *do* you say to your new baby?

When I was stitched up, I was helped into a wheelchair and taken to my little private room. I'd given birth on the NHS, the best care in the world, but I knew I'd crave peace and quiet afterwards. Not much chance of that on a general ward. Fortunately you can book one of the private rooms, and they don't cost much at all.

I was holding the baby in my arms. She'd hardly cried. She was lying still and calm, her enormous eyes looking deeply into mine, then moving away to scrutinise the rest of the world she'd been born into. There was none of that vague look babies can have. I gazed and gazed at her, drinking her in while my heart was full to bursting. All that sweat and tears and pain had been worth it. I fell in love with her on the spot.

As I was being wheeled along, I said to Dan, 'Oh, she's so beautiful. Just like Missy.'

'Who's Missy?' asked the nurse pushing me. 'Your niece?'

'My dog,' I explained.

She must have thought it was the after-effect of the gas and air.

That first night, I was in the room alone with Honey – we'd decided on that name. This enchanting baby wasn't a Pebbles, she was a little honey. So she was Honey.

I didn't sleep all night. I was convinced she'd choke on her own sick or stop breathing. I've got to watch over her, I thought. I've got to watch over her and I shall never sleep again for the rest of my life. My baby needs my care round the clock. In the dim light I fixed my eyes on her little face, smoothed her fine fair hair, listened for the regular noise of her gentle breathing.

At seven o'clock the lights came on in the hall, the sign that everyone was waking up. Ah, just five minutes' rest, I thought, and my head nodded forward.

'Gail!' a voice said sharply. 'The baby's been sick – didn't you notice?'

I jolted awake and saw to my horror that there was puke around Honey's mouth.

'You should have been watching out for her,' the nurse went on.

But I'd been awake all night doing just that! The moment I close my eyes she's sick. What a start. I felt like the worst mum in the world – a feeling that was only going to intensify.

For now I was shown how to bath her and dress her, and feed her of course. Fortunately she took to feeding straight away – the minute she got a nipple in her mouth, that was it. (Needless to say, I'd long since ditched the nipple rings.) Painful for me at first, which is often the case, but I got used to it. I was just thankful it was working out; I knew it doesn't always. Honey never seemed to stop feeding, the longest break I swear was an hour.

After a couple of days I was due to go home, but there was something important to arrange first. Not for Honey, we'd got all her stuff ready.

'What you have to do,' I said to Dan, 'is go to Primrose Pets and get a huge bone for Missy and keep it ready at home.'

'What?' he said. 'You're insane.'

'No I'm not,' I said. 'It's dog psychology.'

'Dog what?'

'I'm serious. I've been away for a couple of days, Missy must have been wondering where I was, and she's my baby too. I can't go home with my new baby and expect Missy to take to her right away. She might be jealous, and we can't take any risks.'

So when we took Honey home, Dan held her in one room while I made a huge fuss of Missy, gave her the bone and other treats. When she calmed down, I asked Dan to put Honey in her little reclining seat on the kitchen table, and brought Missy to her, talking quietly all the time.

Sniff, sniff, went Missy at this strange new object in the house. Then Honey woke, opened her eyes and gurgled. Missy was watching her intently, and I swear she was smitten in an instant. They were, and are, inseparable.

So that was the homecoming. The easy bit, as it turned out.

I went to work four days later, doing a voiceover. Just as well it didn't take long or require much effort. My legs were still a bit wobbly, and my stitches were killing me now the anaesthetic had worn off. I couldn't even pee in the loo – I had to run cold water into the bath, lower myself in and then pee, rinsing it out and then having a shower. I did that for four months.

After the end of our first week home with Honey, Dan went on a three-month tour with Toploader, and that's when the cracks in our relationship began to get wider. The tour was within the country, so if he was in Birmingham and the gig finished at eleven he could come home even though it could have taken a few hours. But he didn't. Maybe it would have wiped him out for the next day or maybe there were parties he was obliged to attend. Memories of after-show partying in my old single days flooded back to me.

I'd been there, done that, got the T-shirt – and not only had I been there, done that, got the T-shirt, I'd been there, done that, got the T-shirt and taken it back to the shop when it shrank in the wash.

Part of me understood that it was Dan's job, he was on the tour bus with the rest of the band, and he couldn't exactly come back and leave them there – and he did make the odd weekday home. But frankly I wasn't in the right frame of mind to think rationally – 'Just come home and stay here and help me!'

Having a baby changed everything. At least for me.

# * 15 *

# Baby Blues

'What have you been eating?'

The health visitor stared at me accusingly. She was sitting on one of the kitchen chairs, hands on knees that were so far apart that her navy skirt rode up and I couldn't help noticing her old-fashioned bloomers. I sat opposite her cradling Honey, who was fast asleep.

'Well…' I started to say.

'Any tomatoes? Grapes?' she said.

'Er, yeah, I've had some.'

'You shouldn't,' she snapped. 'Makes breast milk acid.'

Oh God, I'm poisoning my baby. I'm the worst mum in the world. I looked at the health visitor aghast, and scarcely took in the rest of what she was saying. Something about weight and the clinic. After she left, I held Honey tightly to me and cried and cried, but softly so as not to wake her up.

That early anxiety about Honey – she'd been sick when I wasn't looking! – stayed with me. I guess most new mothers are pretty uptight about their baby's health, until things settle down and both mum and baby get into a routine. It takes confidence. I was determined to do absolutely my best for Honey, to attend to her every need. I was feeding her on demand, which meant almost round the clock. I was straining so hard to be a perfect mum but I was convinced I'd never be good enough.

Every time the health visitor came, I felt sure she was criticising me for something or other, and what little confidence I had was draining away. It got so I wouldn't let her in – when she rang the bell I used to pretend I was out, just like all those years ago when Mum, Keith and I used to hide from the church elders.

I was too scared to take Honey to the baby clinic too, until one day I got a letter insisting that I took her in for a check-up. In the event, Honey was perfectly healthy, gaining weight, gurgling and smiling and kicking and generally developing as she should. Absolutely beautiful. So I must have been doing something right. It was me who wasn't thriving.

You'd think that once you've had your baby, gone through all that labour – with the added delight of stitches – your body can take it easy, get back to normal. And not just your body. Your mind, your emotions, your hormones, have gone through the mill too. So when the Big Event is over, it's back home and back to normal in due course. Whatever normal means.

I guess that happens to some women. Women whose physical and mental processes are pretty stable to start with – or maybe not even then. It seems to me that just as you don't know how childbirth will affect you, you can't predict how you'll feel and behave afterwards. I hadn't looked that far ahead myself, just assuming that I'd get on with whatever was necessary, much the same as usual. As I've said, it took months for the stitches to heal – not much fun, but I could understand that it was a straightforward process, just a matter of time. Another physical symptom alarmed me at first, though. As I said to the doctor, 'I think my arse is falling out.' Either that or a baby alien was choosing this exit rather than John Hurt's chest. Well, I'd never had piles before. And I never want them again, frankly. No, taxing though these physical symptoms were, what did get me down was something I couldn't put a name to.

It was more than anxiety about Honey. I just couldn't seem to get my energy back. I felt sluggish, as if I was moving through treacle. Everything was such an effort. And I felt bloated all the time, even less inclined to eat, though as I was breastfeeding Honey I had to be careful to eat the right things to make sure she had all the right nourishment. I'd put on a lot of weight during the pregnancy – I'd ballooned up to eleven and a half stone – but I forced myself to keep to a sensible diet, and very gradually I was heading towards my target weight of seven and a half stone. But even with the excess fat going, I still felt weighed down, emotionally as well as physically. If I hadn't been looking after Honey, I would have just lain on my bed and cried all day. I felt so hopeless, as if I was looking into a deep dark well.

I'd constantly try to give myself a metaphorical kick up the arse: 'What's the matter with you? You have a wonderful daughter, friends and family, all the people you love and who love you, you have a lovely house, you've still got work – what have you got to complain about? Look around you at the rest of the world! Wars and famines and babies starving...'

But all the mental talkings-to just left me feeling as guilty as I did when the health visitor used to get at me. But no, I must be fair – she was just doing her job. It was me who was prickly, defensive.

It didn't help when Dan went on tour only a week after Honey's birth. As I've said, it was his job, and he did manage the odd day home in between gigs. And yet...his absence just seemed to emphasise the enormous responsibility that had fallen on my shoulders. And not only caring for the baby – the mortgage still had to be paid. What Dan earned hardly made a dent in our monthly outgoings. I wasn't up for on-screen appearances for quite a while, so voiceover work was very useful. There was no question of having a nanny, so I had to take Honey with me. My good friend Charlotte helped a lot here. She wasn't working at the time, so while I was doing my thing in the studio, she'd be taking care of Honey in a nearby room. Then I could nip out between takes to feed her.

Some new mums might have a helping hand from their own mums, though of course mine was hundreds of miles away and could hardly just pop in. Mum wasn't the first grandparent to visit – Dan's parents were there in the hospital, over the moon. My mum came to the house shortly after I'd got back. She kissed the baby, made all the right noises, and for some reason known only to herself presented me with a big piece of cheese. Calcium? Then she was off.

Dad visited too, rather a stilted occasion. He said all the right things, though I couldn't wait for him to leave. It would have been nice if Honey had had another blood relative on the scene all the time, but it couldn't be helped.

As I dragged myself through day after day, I wondered if this was the same state I'd been in before, the highs and lows – only the highs didn't seem keen to put in an appearance. But you do get used to things, old habits assert themselves, and when I was offered a new job, one that meant a long-term commitment, I jumped at the chance. If there's one thing freelancers like, as well as the kind of work that looks interesting, of course, it's the chance of a regular income. I knew I'd manage somehow.

And the fact that Charlotte was involved made the project even more attractive – she'd just been appointed producer on the show. The only problem was that this job would take me away from home to the States. Well, it would have to, as it involved a tour round the haunts of American celebrities – 'haunts' being the operative word. The celebrities were all deceased, and the idea was to follow in their footsteps to see if There Was Anybody There... Appropriately enough, the show was called *Dead Famous*. Joke, see? I'd be one of two presenters, the resident sceptic (which was true to life), while a guy called Chris Fleming was the 'sensitive' who would try to tune into vibes from the Other Side. A kind of Scully and Mulder, without the aliens.

Sounded bonkers of course, but I love the States, and the prospect of touring round some fabulous places was irresistible. Perhaps that would shake out a few cobwebs, get the old fire going again. Then there was the attraction of the celebrities them-selves, posthumous of course. A lot were from the glam old days, including my childhood pin-up Marilyn Monroe, while others were more recent stars, dead prematurely, like Janis Joplin, John Lennon and Jim Morrison.

As Honey was so young, just a few months when filming for the first series began, there was no way I could, or would, leave her behind. So Dan came with us, to look after Honey while I was filming. There wasn't much else happening for him. After the tour, the band had broken up, and Dan went off to the States for a while, ostensibly to check out possibilities there. In reality, as I suspected while juggling childcare and work commitments, anxious and nervous and feeling low, he was hanging out with mates on a beach, strumming a guitar. Nice work if you can get it.

The *Dead Famous* schedule was three weeks in the States, then three weeks home again, seven or eight times per series, over a period of six months. I don't know how I held myself together for that first series. When I was filming I threw myself into work, determined as ever to give value for money. When the working day was over I looked after Honey – Dan always handed her over a bit sharpish, I thought, and went out on the town with the crew, including Charlotte. Was I getting refreshed with new places, new people? No – it was an endurance test. I did my work as well as I could, otherwise hardly speaking to people on the set. I found myself being snappy, quick to complain if someone wasn't on time or messed something up. Far from building up the kind of rapport I'd always tried to go for, I was pushing people away. I hardly knew myself. I was especially narked at Charlotte. Quite illogically, I thought she was neglecting me – never mind that as producer she had to look after everyone and keep the whole show on the road.

I was digging a hole for myself. I felt alienated from the rest of the people on set because they were so at ease with each other, like old friends, and I was the new girl. I resented Dan going out in the evening, and was jealous when I heard about everybody's adventures next morning. I was tired, bone-tired, and had to force myself on. Every night when Honey was asleep I'd lie in bed by myself and cry and cry.

Things eased a little on those six-month breaks from *Dead Famous* – though I still worked as much as I could. The mortgage wouldn't pay itself. Not that I ever wanted to be parted from Honey – I was besotted, as well as desperately anxious that something might go wrong with her. In fact she was a very happy baby, rarely crying. There was just one terrible time when she had colic, and cried for hours. Dan was away, so I was by myself. I held Honey in my arms trying to soothe her. I'd called the doctor and he'd given me some medicine, but it was hard to get it down her. I was so sorry for her, the pain her poor little body was enduring, yet I couldn't ease it. I felt like shooting myself. You feel so helpless.

In due course the symptoms did go away and she seemed no worse for the experience. But I was a wreck!

I always made a point of talking to Honey, in fact I've hardly stopped. I'd chat to her about anything, from the trees in the garden to what Missy was doing to what we were going to buy in the shops. Every night I'd read her a story or two, and persuade myself she was taking it all in.

Thinking to broaden her horizons, I once took her to a local music group for babies. All the mums (or rather nannies in that part of London) sat in a semi-circle with babies on their laps, helping them to shake rattles and tambourines or hit little drums. The lady in charge kept time, clapping her hands and chanting in a sing-song voice. Within two minutes I knew I had to get out of there. Just as I was thinking, This is ridiculous, the teacher lady went clap-clap, clap-clap-clap, clap-clap and keeping time she sang out, 'O-ver to Hon-ey's mum-my.' What? I'm supposed to be doing what? I tried la-la-ing a bit, when I really wanted to sing out 'I need to go home ve-ry bad-ly.' So at the end of the session when the lady asked, 'Would you like to sign up for the next eight weeks?' I just smiled and waved and clutching Honey dashed out the door.

OK, I'm sure some mums and babies like this sort of thing. The tweeness would finish me off. I'd see to Honey's musical experiences at home with proper music. In fact Honey hardly stops talking and singing and dancing about now, so she didn't lose out.

Honey was nearly eighteen months old when another spin-off from childbirth showed up. I'd been trying to control my low moods, and thought that getting back into shape would help. One morning I went for a bout of kick-boxing at the gym, and took the usual shower afterwards. It was when I was drying my hair that I caught a glimpse of myself in the mirror. There were two distinct bald patches at the front of my scalp, each about the size of a £2 coin. Bit of a shock, but I wasn't too worried. One thing I had heard was that new mothers did have a tendency to lose hair, and this was usually temporary. All that strain on the system. Still, I thought I'd better check it out, and actually made an appointment with my doctor.

This time I didn't burst into tears the minute I set foot in the surgery, as I usually did. I was there for something simple, I thought, hair loss. Nothing complicated. Sure enough, the doctor said that the condition was common, nothing to worry about, give it time. If it didn't improve, come back and see him again. Meanwhile…'Is there anything else I can do for you?' he asked.

That's when the tears did come and everything burst out in a rush.

'I just feel so awful. I'm worried about Honey all the time even though I know she's fine, everything is getting so much, and I have no energy…'

He let me rattle on, until I quietened down and wiped my eyes.

'I think we should run a few blood tests,' he said.

'What for?'

'From what you say, you could have an underlying thyroid problem, quite common in pregnancy.'

He turned out to be right. I had an underactive thyroid, accounting for the sluggishness and bloated feeling. It's often trig-gered by pregnancy, and my years of anorexia hadn't helped my metabolism either. Bit of a double whammy there. Fortunately it can be controlled by drugs, so I had to overcome my aversion to pill-popping. I've always hated taking tablets, it's galling for some-one who thinks she should be able to cope on her own. Every time I take a tablet I gag, and have to force it down.

The doctor also brought up post-natal depression. Of course I'd heard of the condition, but never thought it'd apply to me. I tend to think I'm the exception to any rule. The very word 'depression' rang alarm bells. I hadn't forgotten my earlier attempts to get professional help, for my mood swings and then the self-harm, which had come to nothing. But this time I was lucky to have a sympathetic doctor, who took the trouble to explain the causes and symptoms, the rollercoaster hormonal ride that can screw you up. I finally realised that my tiredness, snappiness and all-round dragginess could well be caused by this imbalance.

'Can it be treated?' I asked.

'Certainly. A course of mild antidepressants should help you.'

More pills. But if it meant my life would look up again, I'd be able to function as normal – bring 'em on! In fact I kicked myself for being so stubborn. I should have asked for help sooner, instead of wasting time thinking everything was my fault and I ought to be able to handle it by myself. In fact I've heard recently that a difficult birth can make women more prone to post-natal depression, and Honey's birth was not what you'd call easy.

With the new medication, I should have been sorted. And sure enough I did feel physically better, with my thyroid functioning more like it should. To a certain extent, I was feeling better emotionally too – it may have been the antidepressants, or simply knowing that I'd been suffering from a definable condition that wasn't uncommon. It wasn't anything I should blame myself for.

As for the hair loss, I kept a close eye on the bald spots, which didn't get any bigger – but neither did any new hair start growing. At the time *Dead Famous* was launching the first series, and there were a lot of publicity photoshoots. I wouldn't have looked too fetching with bald patches, so my great friend and make-up artist Carlos Ferraz actually coloured them in with eye shadow. Very effective too! When we were filming in the States, I had to be very open with the director. 'If my bald spots are showing,' I said to him, 'don't be too embarrassed to tell me.'

Luckily I still had a lot of thick hair, so I used to joke with my hairdresser – 'Gimme a comb-over!' Well, it's such a good look for balding men, isn't it? The subterfuge worked until at last the first signs of baby hair started growing into those lonely patches.

Thank God for that, I thought. I don't want to seem vain, but I'd really hate to lose my hair...

# * 16 *

# No Way Out

I was glad my hair grew back, but compared to what else was happening in my life it was hardly a big deal. The fault lines in my marriage were growing wider and wider. It didn't help that my work took me away from home so much that inevitably I'd miss milestones in Honey's development. One day I was at work when Dan phoned me.

'Honey's walking!' he said excitedly. 'She's just taken her first steps!'

Another day it was, 'Honey's talking! She's just said her first word – Dadda!'

I was gutted. A mean part of me thought, I did all the work and Dan gets to see her first walk and hear her first word – and it's bloody Dadda. Damn. At least I had the repeat performance to look forward to, and it didn't take her long to pick up 'Mamma'. And her walking – like a wee drunk tottering along. Hilarious and adorable. I so wished that I could spend more time with Honey.

I only took her with me to the States for that first series of *Dead Famous*. As she was getting older the jet lag might have got to her, and besides, now she was more aware of her surroundings I thought she'd be better with a regular routine. I'd miss her like mad, of course, but she'd have her daddy, who did everything for her, while my mum would always take the train down from Edinburgh and help out when he got involved with work stuff. I'd tell myself that it was only three weeks.

When I wasn't working on *Dead Famous*, I took on as much work as I could at home for the other six months of the year. I was game for anything. Chat shows, quizzes...you name it. One unusual direction for me was a spoof drama called *Sex, Lies and Michael Aspel*, which was just what it said on the tin. He had hordes of love children by different women – 'I've been a philanderer,' he confesses – and I was one of them. Daft, but brilliant fun to do. It's hard to believe that anyone took it seriously, but more than one person said to my mum at home, 'So you had an affair with Michael Aspel!' I even did one last ever pin-up photoshoot, for *Maxim* magazine – 'Goodbye, boys!' – which involved a few of the predictable poses but boobs and bum covered up.

Even if the work ethic wasn't knitted into my DNA, I knew I couldn't depend on anyone else to pay the mortgage, or anything else come to that.

It wasn't that I minded being the breadwinner, not at all. With a child to look after, either Dan or I had to bring the money in, and it happened to be me as I had the regular well-paid jobs. What I wanted, needed, from Dan was support – practical and emotional. Although he was great with Honey, it just didn't seem a marriage of equals. I was doing the lion's share, while he seemed to increasingly resent doing his part. I've often noticed this in couples – one person working their arse off while the other just seems to coast along. That's fine if both people are happy with the arrangement. Otherwise, the outlook is stormy. It's like a fault line running through the relationship, just waiting for enough pressure to trigger the earthquake.

Well, the pressure was building up all right. Over time there was a lot of anger, a lot of resentment, a lot of hard words. Dan started complaining, 'I gave up my career to look after Honey.' Yeah, right. I wouldn't put it quite that way. By then, the mutual bitterness was setting a pattern. Each of us would fly off the handle at each other at the slightest pretext.

The jealousy didn't help – Dan's, not mine. One evening when I was home and having a break, I went out with a friend of mine for a drink. We got talking to a bloke in the bar and the conversation drifted to sports and working out. He said, 'I play softball every Sunday with my mates in the park – how about you two come?' Sounded good, so I gave him my number. He later texted me, saying simply, 'Hi. Great to meet you and your friend. Hope to see you in the park.'

Does that sound incriminating? Dan thought so. He went through my messages when I wasn't looking, and went ballistic. He even phoned my friend's husband – 'Do you know what your wife's getting up to?' Blah blah. I was stunned. I'd known Dan was prone to jealousy, ever since he quizzed me about old flames on our honeymoon, but this incident was utterly innocuous. Exactly as straight as it seemed. While Dan was raging around, I thought,

This is mad. One minute I'm having a fairly banal chat with a bloke, nothing in it, just a casual invite to play softball with a group of people, the next minute we're having a wild affair. I tried to reason with Dan: 'If I was gonna have an affair, d'you think I'd be back home at ten o'clock at night, for God's sake?'

I really didn't have anything to hide. In fact he never had cause to doubt my fidelity, while for my part I had no interest in being jealous about him. I realised that my early illusions about my marriage had shattered.

'I don't love you,' I told him one day, not in a temper but quite calmly.

It was true. I really didn't love Dan in the way a wife should love her husband. I really should never have married him. That was my mistake, much as I pushed any reservation to the back of my mind at the time. It was unfair to Dan. He had a strong marriage ethic, raised as he was by a devoted, indissoluble couple. He might have been justified in expecting the same deal for himself. All I can say is that I never set out to hurt anyone.

'You don't mean it,' he said. He didn't believe me then, or later when I said it again. And again. When I tried to talk about us, to bring things out in the open, he'd brush me aside.

This was no way to live. Neither of us was happy and, much as we both loved Honey, she was coming up to two, old enough to pick up on the vibes. I had to bring things to a head.

Dan had gone back to the States, saying he had some gigs. I'd even sorted out his flight. Then I heard on the grapevine that actually he was just bumming around again, hanging out with his mates. That was it. I phoned him.

'I told you I don't love you, and I genuinely don't,' I said. 'I don't miss you, and I can't be with you any more.'

Immediate explosion.

'You bitch! How dare you do this to me when I'm this far away?'

I said, 'But I've been telling you for months that I don't love you, and what do you do? You get on a plane and hang out with your mates in LA. That's not a relationship. If you really wanted to save it you would never have gone away.'

Mind you, even if he had stayed, things probably wouldn't have worked out. The fault lines in our relationship ran too deeply. Nearly three years to the day it started, our marriage was effectively over.

Yet I can't ever regret being married. If it wasn't for Dan, I wouldn't have Honey. And the same goes for Dan. Whatever he went through with me – and I know I'm not the easiest person to live with, with my mood swings and self-harming – he has a daughter he loves with all his heart, and she loves him. Whatever our feelings towards each other, we've always tried to shield Honey from the rift in our relationship, do what was best for her.

And in fact at first, home life wouldn't have seemed very different to Honey, unless she noticed that Daddy was sleeping in the spare room. When he got a new girlfriend, that complicated things a bit. He wasn't around as much as he had been. In fact when I went to the States for my stints on *Dead Famous*, it was often my mum who looked after Honey full time. I'd take her – and Missy the dog, as there'd be no one to look after her either – with all the luggage on the train to Edinburgh, go to my mum's house, then get the train back to London and fly to the States next day. When I came home it was the same operation in reverse. Took some doing, believe me.

When I was working in the States, there was one reason to be cheerful at any rate. Dan might have got himself a new girlfriend, but it never occurred to me to look for anyone else. As it happened, he was there all the time – I didn't need to look far.

James was the cameraman on *Dead Famous*, part of the team travelling round the USA in the footsteps of departed celebrities. After that first series, when I was really tense and unhappy, I'd built up more of a rapport with the team as a whole, and James and I always got on fine, had a laugh – I'd take the mickey out of him because he was always dropping things. No way did I fancy him, and while I was committed to Dan it wouldn't have crossed my mind anyway. In fact I thought of James as a boy, though he's only two years younger than me. (I must have a thing about younger men...)

This particular schedule took us to a town in Texas, on the trail of John Wayne. One evening James and I went out for a post-work drink, drank a lot and sang karaoke. Now that's a romantic setting if ever I knew one. I found myself looking at him, at his handsome, smiling, friendly face. I knew he'd recently split up from his girlfriend, just as I was separating from Dan. Fellow feeling...a kind of recklessness overtook me.

'Come on,' I said, 'let's have a snog.'

'Gosh,' he said. 'That's dreadfully unprofessional.'

What?

'Oh God, I'm not thinking about being professional. I'm a bit lonely, you're a bit lonely, we're both single...'

We did kiss. After that I looked at him in a different way – one day a friend, plain and simple, the next – what? I was drawn to him, at the same time as I knew there'd be problems. For a start he also had a daughter, some years older than Honey, with the ex-girlfriend. And he was very much the type to do his own thing, not get tied down…Wouldn't it be easier if we could just choose who we fell in love with?

Meanwhile, a relationship with James may have been developing, but my life as a whole was the same crazy mix. Commuting across the Atlantic, working long hours, having some light moments but missing my daughter, coming home to the house where my estranged husband still lived some of the time. Arguments, bills, hassle, more work, the prospect of a messy divorce made it feel like I was on a relentless treadmill. Every day I seemed to feel a bit more tired, unable to sleep, glassy-eyed with fatigue but still plodding on.

'Oh for God's sake.'

One of my friends at the gym, Clarissa, was looking me straight in the eye.

'You look awful,' she said.

'I feel awful,' I replied.

Clarissa had a medical history quite similar to mine: mood swings, a touch of thyroid trouble, depression…

'You've got to see someone,' she said. 'I know you keep banging on about the NHS, but do yourself a favour. Go private. I did, and it was the best thing I ever did. Sorted me out.'

Yeah, well, you're richer than me, I thought. Then again, could I not afford to get myself sorted? If I went on like this, where would it end?

So I made an appointment with Clarissa's doctor – waiting days rather than months. I took a taxi to Harley Street, climbed the front steps of a dauntingly grand house and rang every bell on the big black door till I hit on the right one. The huge waiting room looked like the interior of an old-fashioned country house, with leather sofas, thick carpets and oak tables. Bit different to my doctor's waiting room. The magazines were different too: *National Geographic* and *Country Life* instead of *Woman's Own* and *Take a Break*.

The doctor gave me a whole uninterrupted hour of his time, which was the least he could do considering his fee. A series of tests and questions and the medical history of me and my family... he didn't even try to stem my flow when I tried to put my old mood swings into words.

'Some days I can feel wonderfully happy, yet other days I feel like my body is made of lead and the prospect of facing the day ahead is unbearable. My life can go from the most amazing buzz to feeling totally helpless. Suddenly, nothing makes sense and you want to solve the world's problems as well as your own, but you haven't really got the time and you can't figure out why the hell you're here. On those down days, I have to drag myself out of bed, do my daily chores as if I'm on auto-pilot. I feel hardly aware of my surroundings, and my only comfort is to walk, and walk, in no particular direction, as if this walk is going to deliver me to a hidden Utopia and my sense of being will return. I'm yet to find the place.

For all I know it could be somewhere north of Pease Pottage Services on the M23 or in a hedonist holiday resort in Jamaica…'.

Ramble, ramble. Then I brought myself up to date, where mood swings would be preferable to the pit I seemed stuck in. I don't think I stopped weeping from the moment I set foot in his office.

The doctor took his time before saying, 'I believe you are what is called bi-polar,' he announced. 'It used to be called manic depression. It's a complex condition, and often goes undiagnosed.'

You're telling me.

'But you show the typical symptoms of an underlying clinical depression, with fluctuating moods.'

'And the post-natal depression wouldn't have exactly helped, would it?' I asked.

He smiled. 'I don't imagine so. I think you should come off the antidepressants you were prescribed, and try a course of Prozac. It's been shown to help people with your condition, as long as you follow the directions exactly.'

He gave me an information sheet. I skimmed over it until I noticed something interesting – some studies have made a link between bi-polarity and creativity. I'd like to think of myself as creative. Who wouldn't? And other studies have claimed that people who are susceptible tend to be driven personalities, very hard working and goal-oriented. Well, that's me to a T. Not all bad, then. But most of all, I wasn't a solitary crazy person – there are lots of bi-polar bears, as I call us, out there.

There was a sense of relief in having a diagnosis. I was kind of mad but I had a label! I skipped off into my manic world with a prescription for Prozac to help me along the way.

It took a couple of weeks for the Prozac to kick in and I did seem to feel a bit more stable. I know people have many different views regarding antidepressants and there can be alternative solutions, but ultimately it was my choice and it seemed to work. In fact Prozac seemed to be my best friend for a while – but then wasn't as good a friend as when I was first introduced to it. The effect began to wear off. A little bit more then I would be better. And right enough, I was – just a wee increase and I was back on the happy trail. Just what the doctor ordered when you're working your arse off and your marriage is disintegrating.

I got through the rest of that year somehow, and resolved that things would change in 2005. I'd sort everything out. I'd take things in hand, starting with myself. I should give up the Prozac, I thought. I've been taking more and more, and I don't want to become dependent; I can handle things by myself. So I did stop, just like that. And before I knew it, the treadmill turned into a spiral staircase, taking me down and down into madness. I must have been mad, to do what I did.

I've gone over in my mind what happened that day, time and time again. Each time I'm appalled, feeling the deepest despair. And each time I'm overjoyed, relief flooding through me, so thankful I survived.

Whatever had been happening in my life, I'd never wanted to end it. I've always loved life. Besides, I'm not a quitter. I'm not. But I was tired, bone-crushingly tired. It was a short rest I wanted, not an eternal one.

I remember that Tuesday in March as the weirdest day in my life. As usual I'd slept badly the previous night, tormented by nightmares that were so vivid it was a relief to wake up, tired as I was. I went through my morning routine to get ready for the day, then woke Honey. We were alone in the house as Dan was staying at his girl-friend's, and James was away working in Monaco. I gave Honey her breakfast and got her bathed and dressed as if I was on auto-pilot. I heard her chattering, but could barely reply. Then it was time for nursery. We walked hand-in-hand down our long quiet road, into the main road with the station and the shops and the noisy traffic. On we went to the little school, and I waved my daughter goodbye.

All the time I felt curiously numb, as if my body wasn't my own. I felt nothing, absolutely nothing. It was like moving in a daydream, but not the pleasant kind. Then on the way home, feel-ings of panic and paranoia began to seep into my consciousness, making my heart pound. Was my mind leaving my body? How could I face the world today?

I remember opening the front door with a sigh of relief. At last I was safe in my haven. I stepped into the hall, closed the door and walked into the living room. I didn't even wonder where Missy was. I sat on the big squashy sofa very still, staring at the opposite wall. Tired, so tired. Beyond exhaustion. I wanted to sleep for a very long time.

What will make me sleep? Pills. I got up, walked to the bath-room and grabbed a bottle out of the cabinet. Then to the kitchen for a bottle of vodka, cold from the fridge, the way I like it.

I turned on the telly. My brother always says there's nothing like daytime TV talk shows if you want to feel normal! And I so wanted to feel normal. Then I poured a large glass of vodka, and lay propped up on the sofa. I take the pills one by one, washing them down with the vodka. One by one. I lost count. How many have I taken? Better a couple more, to be on the safe side. I want a proper sleep...

Then I started to feel terribly unwell, my head swimming and my stomach lurching. The sound of the telly drummed in my ears.

What had I done? How many pills had I taken? I looked at the bottle through swimming eyes. A lot seemed to have gone.

I panicked. I've overdone it! I wouldn't feel this bad if I hadn't, would I? Have I taken too many? Help!

I tumbled off the sofa and crawled around looking for my mobile. I quick-dialled my doctor's number, and gabbled to the receptionist. Then it was Dan's turn – if I was ill someone had to pick up Honey, and his girlfriend lived nearby. Thank God he answered, and again I burbled into the phone, probably incoherent by now.

That's the last I remember till I woke up in hospital under that glaring fluorescent light.

I learnt later that Dan had acted immediately, for which I'm profoundly grateful. He'd managed to decipher my rambling and rushed to the house. He still had his keys and was letting himself in when the doctor arrived. After a quick examination, the doctor called an ambulance, and I was off to get my stomach pumped and generally brought back to functioning life.

As I lay on that hospital bed, it gradually dawned on me what I'd done. And what I could have done. Just a few more pills, maybe, and I could really have overdone it, gone past the point of recall.

But I wasn't a would-be suicide! The notice on my bed might say 'suicide watch' but everything in me cried out against the very idea. I never wanted to die, I never wanted to leave this life where I had so much. Where I loved so much. What would Honey do without me? And my mum and the rest of my family and my friends would be devastated. I wouldn't ever have wished that.

I made a mistake. I cocked up, big time. I was mad, I must have been. That's what I figured out. Deranged – let's hope temporarily. I could only take so much, and I'd taken it. Time for heavyweight reassessment.

Right. Review and reassess. Good intentions – the best, in fact.

Learn to relax. No more obsessing. Patch things up with Dan. Not getting back together, of course – that was never gonna work. But be more civilised. Dignity. Respect. Not so much of the angst. Focus on Honey, her needs. She has a mum and dad who love her to bits, so at least they have that in common.

Get work in proportion. Talk to the agent and the accountant. Sort stuff out. Don't say yes to anything and everything just because it'll bring in the dosh. In the words of the late, great Douglas Adams: Don't Panic!

Well, it might have worked, I don't know. When I was trying, really trying, to get my life in order, something happened that shouldn't be significant in the great scheme of things. But it did matter, and I can't pretend it didn't.

All my hair fell out.

# * 17 *

# Hair Trigger

I found out what had catapulted me into that disastrous state of mind where I'd lost any sense of reality.

'You came off the Prozac too quickly,' I was told.

Apparently you should never suddenly stop it, but wean yourself off Prozac gradually. Sudden withdrawal leads to…well, close on catastrophe for me. Though I daresay that even if I'd been given that warning, I'd have ignored it. Would I never learn? I lay on that hospital bed, going hot and cold as I thought through what might have happened. My heart felt like it was bursting, when I wasn't being sick as a dog. I almost welcomed the sickness – it showed I was still alive.

When I was able to think a bit more clearly, I immediately thought – Honey! I asked for a phone and rang Dan.

'Of course I picked her up,' he said. 'I'm staying with her. I've just told her you're away working and she's fine.'

Then he told me how I came to be in the hospital. I could

tell by the tone of his voice he wasn't exactly brimming over with sympathy. Which was natural, I suppose. I'd done such a stupid thing.

I'd been told I'd have to be kept in overnight, so I asked Dan to bring me some pyjamas that afternoon. Then I phoned James.

'What the hell have you done now!' he said. He might just as well have said, 'Oh God, this girl's a nightmare!' I was learning that anger and exasperation are typical reactions, at least at first.

'I'll see you when I get back,' James said, and hung up.

For the rest of the day and into the night, I lay on that hospital bed attached to a drip, watched continually as a suicide risk. Though the thought of it shocked me rigid, I suppose it was a reasonable assumption. Nobody could have known what was in my mind. So a nurse accompanied me even when I went to the loo. I felt such a fool.

Next morning I phoned Dan, asking him to bring clothes I could wear to go home. I still felt pretty groggy, but couldn't wait to get out of here.

When Dan arrived, he told me he'd been speaking to the doctors.

'They think it'd be a good idea if you went to the Priory,' he said.

'What? What do you mean, the Priory?'

'It's that rehab place—'

'I know what it is,' I snapped. 'Why should I want to go there?'

'The doctors think it'd be for the best,' said Dan. 'You obviously need help.'

'Not that sort,' I retorted. 'They charge a bloody fortune – five hundred quid a night, is it? Or five thousand a week. Bollocks to that. I'd rather spend the money on a holiday. That'd set me up better than any rehab clinic.'

Dan shook his head. 'I think you should give it a try. You've given everyone a scare.'

'But I want to go home and see Honey,' I said. 'Who's looking after her?'

'She's fine,' said Dan. 'I dropped her off at school, and I'll be picking her up. Just listen to what the doctors say.'

And with that he left.

Me at the Priory? I don't need that stuff – but then I felt another surge of nausea, and sat back on the bed shaking and sweating.

One of the doctors came up to my bed.

'Look,' he said reasonably. 'You're not well; you need help. You'll get specialised care at the Priory.'

'No chance,' I said.

He persisted. 'At least give it a try.'

After more along these lines, I gave in. 'OK then,' I said. 'But if I don't like it I'm not staying.'

'Fine.'

After a few hours, I was driven to the clinic in an ambulance car. I can't remember much about the journey – I think it was the north London branch I was taken to, not the posh mansion in Roehampton. Though the building did look a bit like a stately home, I remember. The ambulance man escorted me into the reception, where I waited. I felt an instinctive revulsion. The air was too warm, muggy. A faint smell of institutionalised cooking. People walking around like zombies, most of them furiously smoking fags, adding to the choking atmosphere.

Someone took me to what was going to be my bedroom. It was shit. A single bed, a single wardrobe and a bedside cabinet, all from the bargain bin of some low-budget self-assembly kit. It was more like a prison cell, as if I was being punished for what I'd done. Was I?

I sat and waited, and felt fidgety. The longer I waited, the more pointless the exercise seemed. This wasn't the place for me; I'm not a rock star with a crack cocaine habit.

Then the door opened and a woman in a white coat came in. Next thing I know, she's saying something like I'm a car and my engine isn't working and it needs to be fixed.

'Here's the acceptance form,' she said, handing me a sheet of paper, 'and our scale of charges.'

How much? That settled it. I gave the paper back to her, and I think I remember saying, 'Fuck off.'

Anyhow, she looked startled, and I said, as firmly as I could, 'Please book me a cab.'

'Oh no,' she protested. 'You have to stay here.'

'No I don't,' I said forcefully. 'I'm not gonna stop here and talk to somebody like a bloody idiot going blah blah blah. I'd rather spend the money on a holiday – I know what I like.'

Before long I was sitting in a minicab going home.


I don't know what I expected. I was still feeling sick, but buoyed up by the thought of seeing Honey. I expected to find Dan there, looking after her.

When I opened the front door, I heard voices in the kitchen. Going through the hall, I wondered who was here with Dan.

He was sitting at the table with his girlfriend, drinking wine. They looked up startled as I came in, and with a flash of indignation I recognised my Chateau Neuf du Pape. They're sitting here drinking my posh wine when I've been packed off to the Priory. This was out of order.

I broke the silence. 'Where's Honey?'

'In bed,' said Dan. 'She wanted to sleep in your bed.'

'Fine,' I said.

'But what are you doing here?' he asked.

'I told you,' I said, 'no way am I going to spend all that money on my mental health – for all the good it would do anyway. Look,' I added as he started to speak, 'I know I've fucked up, fucked up spectacularly, but it was an accident, I didn't mean it, and you know I'm grateful for your help. But I can manage now. Please go.'

'If you're sure...'

'I'm sure.'

They both put their glasses down, got their coats and left. I was alone in the house with Honey. I looked in on her, sleeping in my bed like an angel, and after a quick shower slid in beside her, cuddling her close. I felt I'd never let her go. What if I'd...I couldn't bear to think of it. All through that long night, I hardly slept. I was going over and over my resolutions. I was going to shape up, I knew it, for Honey's sake if not my own.

It took me quite a while to get over the sickness, but I managed to make things normal for Honey, taking her to nursery, picking her up, getting her meals. She was looking forward to a treat in about a week's time – the premiere of *Valiant*, a kids' film about a heroic pigeon of all things, with me and James and his daughter. James was still a bit wary of me when he came back. In fact he was pretty pissed off.

'You always take things too far,' he said. 'When you're depressed, you cut yourself—'

'Only when Honey's not here,' I hurried to add.

'I know,' he sighed. 'But it's not good, Gail. You're either up in the clouds and manic or down and depressed. Can't you ever just find a middle way?'

Evidently not. But we managed to look like a happy family on the night of the premiere, smiling and waving to photographers. Then next day I got a call from a *Sun* reporter, saying, 'Someone at the Royal Free Hospital told us you tried to commit suicide last week. Is it true?'

'No,' I said, 'of course not.'

I could have saved my breath as the details were all over the tabloids next day. The *Sun* had a big picture of me, James and our daughters with the caption: 'Just five days before this premiere, Gail tried to kill herself.' Whatever happened to patient confidentiality?

When asked later, I took the line that I was crying for help, rather than actually trying to kill myself. Which must have been true.

I tried to project a confident image, but the tabloid coverage was harrowing, just bringing it home to me again what I'd nearly done. I felt the pressure mounting, so asked Dan to look after Honey all day in his girlfriend's place. I locked myself in at home and switched off the phone. I'd checked for messages and there were loads of them, fifty-odd. I listened to a few and it was all

'What the fuck were you thinking of?' 'What do you think you were playing at?' I couldn't bear to listen to any more, so went to bed and stayed there all day, crying my heart out. I might have cut myself, with Honey not there, but somehow I didn't have the will.

It never occurred to me at the time how people would react to my overdose. As I say, it was usually along the lines of shock and anger, a sense of 'You've gone too far this time!' I suppose I shouldn't have looked for sympathy, at least not straight off. People speak in the heat of the moment, as if they're judging you and finding you very much wanting. Suicide, or an attempt at it, is almost like an affront to others.

My mum and dad, and my brother Keith, were no exception. They were furious, disappointed and thought that I was so stupid. After his first outburst – 'What the fuck!' – Keith calmed down, and was soon back to his laidback self, always there for me. I didn't really care what Dad thought, but Mum was a different matter.

'What if they took Honey away from you?' she demanded.

I didn't even want to go there. But she was right, I should have thought about others. I didn't even think about how Mum would feel to lose her daughter. No wonder she was angry. The anger was the kind that makes a parent shout at a child who's stupidly wandered into the road and just avoided being run over. The initial reaction is anger, that the child has been so stupid, mixed with terror, at what might have happened. The relief comes later. If I'd had an accident, or been attacked, that would have been totally different. It was the fact that I'd done this to myself.

I may have been lost in some kind of madness, but it was me who poured out the drink and put the pills in my mouth.

I'd been so selfish. The guilt was heavy in me, and so it should be.

I thought I'd better go back on the Prozac. My GP had been giving me repeat prescriptions after the initial private one, so I still had a stash. I'd be seeing my doctor soon anyway – the hospital had told me they were writing to him.

When I did see him – I can't remember exactly when, a couple of weeks after I came out of hospital – I had a shock.

'Social Services will want to see you,' he told me.

What? Social Services! My mum would die of shame.

'Why?' I asked. 'Do they think I'm a bad mum?'

'It's not that,' he said. 'It's just that in these cases, where a young child is involved, we have an obligation to inform them.'

Oh God, I thought. It's come to this. The authorities have to check me out in case I'm a danger to my daughter.

In the event, Social Services arrived at my home in the shape of a very nice, sympathetic woman. She spent time with Honey, and looked round the house, no doubt checking for signs of neglect in both cases. She was very reassuring.

'There's no doubt that you're a good mum, you absolutely adore your daughter,' she said. 'Honey is obviously healthy and happy and you've made a lovely home for her.'

'I've just been really depressed,' I found myself saying.

'Yes,' she said. 'People often go through really hard times. They have to find a way to get through that doesn't hurt themselves or others.'

She handed me a card. 'Here's our number,' she said. 'If you ever need our help, don't hesitate to call.'

'Thank you,' I said, thinking, I won't need your help. With such a shock to the system, there's no way I'm gonna screw up like that again.

No. I just needed a holiday…


Three months later, in June, James and I went to the Maldives, the beautiful, enchanting Maldives, just for ten days. I felt guilty at leaving Honey behind, then thought, This is the time I sort myself out. No pressures, no distractions, just sort myself out. Honey will be well looked after by Dan and my mum.

The holiday was wonderful. I could feel knots of tension dissolving. I'd never slept so much, and neither had James. We laughed about the fact that we'd booked bed and breakfast and always slept in and missed the breakfast bit. I took half a dozen books with me and read them cover to cover, soaking up the sun at the same time. We went swimming, snorkelling. James even kept a diary of how much we loved each other. It was so good to be alive, in such a beautiful, inspiring place.

Then as the day for leaving approached, I got my usual crying jag. It was going to be so difficult to leave this paradise. Even though Honey was waiting for me, so was a lot of other stuff that was going to turn nasty. Dan and I were not going to have an amicable divorce, he'd made that quite clear. There were all sorts of implications, not just about Honey's well-being (though I knew he'd never jeopardise that), but also the financial matters. I was going to be taken to the cleaners.

Not a good prospect then. And I did what I'd been in the habit of doing when things got too much. I cut myself – though I had never done it when Honey was in the house, never. Only when she was staying with her dad. When she was with me, my whole focus was on her. When I was alone and unhappy, there was no distraction from the pain that would build up in my gut. It was really like a physical pain. I didn't pretend to understand why another kind of pain would relieve it, but it did.

So on the last day of our holiday I sat alone in our room, while James was out doing something, and took out a tool I'd acquired. It was a Leatherman, a kind of big Swiss Army knife. Handy – you never know when you'll need pliers, scissors, bottle opener, blades of all kinds, in one compact package. I meant to use one of the penknife-like blades, but got confused. There were a lot of implements. I drew what I thought was the blade across my arm, pressing deeply, but instead of a sharp clean cut there was a kind of carnage. I'd used one of the miniature saws by mistake, and it had mashed my arm up. Blood was pouring out and there was other stuff too – shreds of skin and muscle, I suppose.

I'd fucked up here all right. In a panic, I grabbed a nearby T-shirt and tried to staunch the blood. I was still sitting doubled up, clutching my arm, when James walked in. 'What the —'

In an instant he realised what had happened, and was on the phone to reception – 'Get a doctor here!'

He helped me control the flow of blood till the doctor arrived. The doctor made disapproving noises before cleaning me up, giving me a jab and putting in about ten stitches.

James was furious. 'You've done it again!' he said. 'What the hell are you thinking? You could have lost your arm – is that what you want?'

My mind flashed back to some years earlier. When I was really low after I left Keith Flint, I'd cut myself – not very heavily, I thought. But the blade must have been dirty, and next day my arm ballooned up. I got an emergency appointment at the doctor's, and was pumped full of antibiotics. I had septicaemia, blood poisoning. I was scheduled to do a trailer for a show I was working on at the time, *Pulling Power*, and I remember I had to do my jaunty piece to camera with one elephantine arm behind my back. That took a clever camera angle.

The doctor's voice had rung in my ears: 'You're lucky not to have got gangrene – you could have lost your arm.'

Why didn't that sink in? Gangrene and amputation – a heavy price to pay for a momentary relief, surely. But I was evidently very slow at learning lessons.

The next couple of months were an endurance test. Dan was still partly living in the house, and when Honey was out we had some bitter words. I held myself together for Honey, making sure that everything was normal as far as she was concerned, but I was sinking into my old ways. Skipping meals and, when Honey was staying over with Dan at his girlfriend's place, drinking too much.

Apart from the prospect of missing Honey, it was a relief to go back to the States in August for another stint of *Dead Famous*. Especially as I'd be working with James. He'd stopped going on at me for ripping my arm up, and I was hoping to just enjoy being with him. By now, as far as I was concerned, it was Love. As far as he was concerned – well, as someone once said, 'Love – whatever that means…'


We were in Vegas, on the trail of Frank Sinatra. What a crazy town – it's like it's designed to keep you captive. There are no clocks anywhere, every hotel has a casino with no natural light, and every hotel is themed. You could be in Paris, New York, Venice. The whole town is an illusion. One American tourist actually said to me, 'Us Americans are so lucky. We don't need to travel, it's all here in Vegas.' At that I could have thrown myself off a pastiche Eiffel Tower.

The team was staying in a local hotel, one of the low-rent ones (the budget was tight, believe me). Even so, it boasted its very own rollercoaster ride on the roof, and a revolving restaurant with a panoramic view of Vegas. That's what I like, refined good taste. One morning I was in the room James and I were sharing, brushing my hair, and to my shock whole clumps came out in the brush. Not again!

'Look at this!' I wailed to James. 'My hair's coming out again.'

'Oh, don't worry,' he said, 'it'll probably be all right, like it was before. Eventually.'

Yeah, eventually. I tried to put it to the back of my mind and we went out to work. The following morning it was James complaining.

'When I woke up there were strands of your hair in my mouth,' he said. And they were all over the pillow too.

Oh God, more screwed-up follicles, or alopecia to give it its proper name. Can't be pregnancy hormonal stuff this time – it must be stress-related. I'd just have to wait until the baby hair starting growing back. Meanwhile, it'd be a case of cunning make-up and/or the comb-over!

I remember my last evening as a woman with (almost) a full head of hair. We'd worked hard that day, looking for ghosts, talking to colourful characters, and what we wanted was fun.

After dinner in the hotel, James, our director Bernie and I descended to the 'Lookie-likies night'. There was a lookie-likie Madonna, a Michael Jackson and even a Tiffany. Though when I say lookie-likie, that's pushing it a bit. But the worst entertainment often gives you the best night. We drank some very dubious lookie-likie champagne and danced like our dads! At one point, a girl from a band shouted over the microphone that she liked my cardigan and in true, rather tipsy, Gail style, I gave it to her. 'Have it! I mean it!'

That's one of my peculiarities that all my friends have become familiar with. I will literally give you the coat from my back if you wanted it and I was drunk enough. I can't recall how many pieces of jewellery, items of clothing or shoes I've handed out in my inebriated states. As James puts it, I am an expensive drunk! Harmless, though.

After our drunken theme-styled evening we retired to bed. That's actually a polite term for staggering about, getting into the wrong elevators, forgetting our room number, and deciding to gamble 'just one more time'. *Then* we went to bed.

The morning after the night before...at least there was a

window in the room to let in real daylight to bathe our throbbing heads. James got up first, looking at me lovingly. I wondered why he made a kind of sweeping movement with his hand near my pillow. I didn't know he was giving me ten minutes' grace, the time he took to get ready in the bathroom. Then it was my turn, stumbling into the room, rubbing my eyes. Using the loo and heading for the sink to wash my hands. Catching sight of my head in the mirror – and seeing a strange thing looking back at me. The thing was me. I didn't even recognise myself. I'd gone to bed with shoulder-length, glossy, flowing hair, even if there was the odd bald patch. The creature in front of me had a mullet. A wispy mullet. The crown of my head was almost completely bare, while longer wisps straggled down the sides and back.

'Oh my God!' I screamed.

'I know, darling,' came James's sympathetic voice.

That's why he made that sweeping movement. Whole chunks of my hair had fallen out during the night and he didn't want me to see them straight away. My immediate thought wasn't oh, that was amazingly tactful of him. It was oh my God, he's gonna leave me, I'm a freak.

Reeling from the shock, I somehow got ready to face the day. James and I had to go to work. But I wasn't prepared to go public yet – the shock was too much for me, let alone anyone else. I popped on a baseball cap for filming. Not a great idea, as it casts a shadow over your face. Bernie asked me to remove it more than once and I obstinately refused. I was just thankful that James was the cameraman and could make allowances.

Then during the day I suddenly remembered that tomorrow I was filming a commercial for our show to be screened in the States. I panicked – couldn't get away with a baseball cap there! Then I thought of something. Luckily I had the number of the make-up and stylist girl in my call sheet, and I dialled her number.

'Hi,' I said, 'it's Gail Porter. I'm filming a commercial with you tomorrow evening for *Dead Famous*.'

'Oh hi, sweetie,' replied a cheerful voice. 'I was just going to call you. Do you have any preferences with your hair and make-up?'

'Well, I would prefer to have some hair, to tell you the truth.'

'Huh?'

'Well, the reason I was calling is that, well, can you bring head-scarves or hats?'

'Sure thing. Is there a problem?' she asked.

'Kind of – my hair is falling out. Do you have clippers?'

'Now you're confusing me.'

'Do you know what, just bring headgear and clippers and I'll see you tomorrow.'

Conversation over. I had decided in my mind that after the commercial shoot, the mullet had to go.

I struggled through the day. Why me? Had I not had enough? Anorexia, depression, divorce…Would I go entirely bald? What shape is my head? Would James leave me?

James and I had a quiet evening in the hotel. Well, actually, quiet and Vegas don't go together. We sat in a diner as waiters and waitresses took it in turn to 'Step up to the mike' and perform renditions of various Motown songs. It was quiet in the sense that we didn't go out with the crew.

'What am I gonna do?' I shouted at James over a very loud 'I Heard It Through the Grapevine' being slaughtered. I'd drawn up what hair I had into a thin ponytail on top of my head, disguising the baldness with a wide hairband.

'Get rid of it,' he shouted back. 'I think it's the best thing to do. You'll just get more and more stressed with it as it is now, so it makes sense.'

'Will you still love me?'

'Of course, darling, you'll just be a lot less hairy.'

He wasn't joking. When we got back to our room I took a bath. As I lay soaking I noticed a few things.

'James!' I screamed. 'My body is absolutely hairless! No leg hair, no underarm hair and no pubes!'

'Result!' came the reply.

I suppose it was a result. No more leg waxing, no more Brazilians, no more underarm shaving. I guess things weren't so bad. I could almost convince myself.

Bald Day arrived. We worked all day filming ghost-hunters in Vegas. I love ghost-hunters. Most of them wear very large T-shirts announcing the fact that they are ghost-hunters and they have a vast array of ghost-hunting equipment. I filmed *Dead Famous* for three years and the equipment they came armed with never ceased to amaze me. Electronic gadgets to pick up ghostly whispers and detect inexplicable heat, special cameras to capture spectral entities...these guys come prepared for anything.

After a fun-filled ghost-hunting day, my co-host Chris Fleming and I headed off to a graveyard in Vegas to film the commercial. I actually had my own trailer, where the make-up girl was waiting for me. I perched myself on the stool in front of the mirror and popped off my hat.

'There you go, love,' I announced to the girl.

'Wow, you really are losing your hair!'

'I am indeed. Are we in shit or can we work with it?' I asked.

Luckily she had brought a great selection of headgear. We decided on a cute black flat cap. That was the great thing about filming that show, I got to wear black. Most shows encourage you to brighten up your wardrobe but ghost-hunters don't have that pressure!

The stylist twiddled with what little hair I had poking out from beneath the cap. I felt good. My comb-over was hidden and my make-up was lovely. I was a fraud but it felt OK.

They filmed Chris and me walking through the graveyard with a dry-ice machine pumping spectral clouds at us. We delivered our script in our spooky way, quite a few times, and eventually wrapped the shoot just before midnight.

Then it was time. I went back to the trailer, took off my hat and got ready for the unveiling of my head. 'Let's get on with it.'

I was terrified but I couldn't go on with what little hair I had left.

As the make-up girl shaved my head, Chris took great delight in filming the entire process. I covered my eyes until the deed was done.

'OK, you can look now.'

I opened my eyes and there I was. Bald. Not even when I was born was I totally bald!

'Wow!' was all I could manage.

'I think you look really funky,' said the hair shaver. Kind girl.

'You actually suit it,' announced Chris judiciously.

Coming from Chris that was a huge compliment. I wasn't convinced, though.

'Can I take my hair home?' I asked. What a souvenir.

'Sure, honey.'

'Thanks.'

It was going to take a lot of getting used to. Next step, I had to meet James at a club. Chris and I drove back to the Strip. He kept looking at me.

'Stop bloody staring,' I complained.

'Man, you are totally bald!'

'I know, and thank you for reminding me.'

'Totally bald.'

'I totally know.'

We pulled up at the club that James was waiting in. I felt sick with nerves. I had found my soulmate, or thought I had. What if he couldn't stand it? I couldn't endure the nerves much longer. I marched in, with my coat over my head, and sat down beside him.

'Show me then, sweetheart.'

'I can't. What if you hate it? What if you leave me? What if...'

'Stop with the what ifs. I love you.'

I quickly pulled the coat off my head and stared at James.

'Wow!' was his first response. Got a theme going here...

Then he hugged me. 'I think it rocks!' he declared.

'Really?'

'It's really cute and you have a nice-shaped head.'

I didn't care if he meant it or not – he said the right things!

We headed off to join the eclectic Vegas crowd chilling in the lounge bar. We drank champagne to celebrate my newfound baldness. Champagne makes most things better, I find.

'Hey, dude,' came a voice, 'are you in a band?'

One of the party people obviously thought I was making a fashion statement.

'No...actually, yes I am. I'm in a band called The Alopecians – you should check us out on MySpace, dude.'

Yes, as I informed all and sundry, this baldness lark was going to be interesting. I couldn't predict just how interesting.

# * 18 *

# To Baldly Go

Might as well get the jokes in before anyone else does. Baldness Be My Friend. Hair Today, Gone Tomorrow. Shorn in the USA. Some-hair over the Rainbow...At my first public appearance I'd managed a semblance of bravado, but I can't pretend I was anything but deeply shocked and upset. Something you've taken for granted all your life suddenly isn't there – and it's a fact that hair is a big deal for most women. I thought wryly how irritated I used to get with my thick mane – can't do a thing with it! Now I don't have the thing to do anything with.

Of course men can get away with it – young, middle-aged or old, no one spares a second look. But complete baldness in women is very unusual. As I realised on the plane home, a day later, I had to decide pretty quickly how I was going to handle it. Out and proud? Or covered and conventional?

My instinct is always to be open. Other people may well choose to be private, deal with whatever it is away from the public eye, and good luck to them. But I figure: I have this thing, does anybody else? I don't like the feeling of being alone, I like to pool ideas, experiences. I don't want pity – God forbid, that's the last thing I want. But I do want understanding, appreciation, empathy. It's not a shameful thing – why hide away? It's not that I thought of myself as any kind of figurehead, so to speak, but I was in the public eye. Perhaps I could use that exposure to help deal with it, open up discussion. Though what about work? Would anybody want to employ a bald female TV presenter? Thank God I still had the contract for *Dead Famous*.

More immediately, though, what would Honey think?

I didn't have the nerve to travel home bare-headed from the airport, so I'd pulled on a hat. Once back with Honey, I tried to break the news gently.

Kneeling beside her, I said, 'Something's happened to Mummy's hair.'

'What?' asked Honey.

'It fell out,' I said. 'It's all gone.'

And I pulled the hat off.

Honey gazed at me with wide clear blue eyes, her mouth open. Then she grinned and reached out a hand to stroke my scalp.

'Funny Mummy!' she laughed.

Taking it in her stride – good. Though it gutted me that Honey probably would never remember me with hair. She was barely three. At least when she picked up head lice at school she couldn't catch them back off me!

I laid low for a while, trying to get up the nerve to appear in public. I had a bash in London the next month, so I thought I might come out then, so to speak. In the next few weeks some hair did start growing back along the top of my head, and so did my eyebrows and lashes – a good sign, surely? Or would it grow only to fall out again?

Whatever, I thought I'd make the most of it, and dyed the strip on my head bright red, gelling it up into a miniature Mohican. If you've got it, flaunt it.

Stepping out of the cab, I held my head high, looking straight ahead, determined to look nonchalant. But I could hear muttered exclamations – 'What's she done to her hair?' – and see heads turning in my direction. The attention was almost overpowering. People just stared and goggled – shows how unusual it is for a woman, especially a TV presenter, to appear without her crowning glory. People couldn't believe it – thought I'd shaved it off for a stunt. If anybody asked, I told them what had happened, and next day the papers were full of it – 'TV's Gail has alopecia', along with helpful articles explaining what it meant. It's an auto-immune condition where the body's defence system goes wrong and instead of attacking infection turns on itself, on the hair follicles in the case of alopecia. I don't think alopecia had had such a lot of publicity since – oh, the last person in the public eye to go suddenly bald.

Again, my public face was upbeat, but I was still horribly upset. I'd gone to my doctor and been given an appointment with a specialist at the Royal Free Hospital, in about six months' time. I couldn't afford private now, but I was happy to wait for NHS treatment. It may be a time coming, but I reckon when it does come it can't be beaten.

Meanwhile, though, I actually considered talking to a counsellor. I'd regretted not dealing with other problems earlier, so thought I'd give it a try. I phoned one place specialising in alopecia and they said, 'We've got a cancellation for two o'clock this afternoon.'

'But I'm working,' I said. I was just off for a voiceover. 'I'm free next Wednesday,' I said, and they replied, 'Well, we're not.'

That was it, I was off the idea. I know it's my mental health, but with my job I can't ever just drop everything. I'd soldier on by myself.

It was the strangest thing, though. I myself hadn't changed – well, just adding alopecia to my bundle of worries – but people started looking at me in a different way. It was as if along with my blonde hair I'd lost any association with dizzy TV bimbo, and had somehow acquired a new seriousness, even – what a thought – gravitas. Some papers even started calling me 'brave' for appearing in public. That was absurd. Brave be buggered. My hair had fallen out, and I wasn't wearing a wig. Not exactly George Cross material.

It was as if my newly bald head acted as a kind of lightning rod for all kinds of theories and opinions, specifically about me and my problems or as applied to other people suffering the same condition. OK, fine by me. I've never been one for keeping things secret – this was the latest event in my life I was prepared to talk about if other people were ready to listen.

And with all the publicity, I was more in demand by charities. In fact I urged them to capitalise on my novelty value. The whole point is first to raise awareness of a bad situation, and then encourage fund-raising. If I got more column inches as a baldie than I ever would as the old Gail, then the charities would benefit.

I'd always been involved in charity work of one kind or another, especially those helping children or to do with human rights. One of the things impressed on me by my mum was don't live in a bubble, look out for other people. You're in a fortunate position, so you're not being Lady Muck, you're helping people who need the help. So when ActionAid asked me to go out to India that September, to raise awareness of the upcoming Lick Child Poverty Day, I was more than happy. Well, not altogether, as I'd be leaving Honey again and I'd only been back from the States for a few weeks. But I explained to her that I was going to help other children, children who were very poor, and she understood that.

For quite a while I'd been sponsoring an Indian child called Ganga through World Vision. Or more specifically it's his village, but I write to him, send him photos of Honey, and he writes back telling me about his life – his family, his friends, his school. I wish I could send him all sorts of presents, but that's not allowed as it would single him out. It's better to help the village as a whole. I'd always talked to Honey about Ganga and his hard life, and shown her his letters. Now she asked, 'Will you see Ganga?'

'I don't think so,' I said. 'I'll be going to another place. But I'll be seeing lots of kids like him.'

Though I knew something of the poor conditions of India, outside the rich enclaves, nothing could have prepared me for the actuality of the 'rubbish-dump' children of Delhi. That's just what they are. A whole army of them pick away at the city's garbage dumps, looking for anything – the tiniest trifle – that they might be able to sell for a few rupees.

It would break your heart. These young kids, up to their knees in stinking, rotting piles of filth. They're skinny, sickly, haggard – what else could they be? Some of them we met had been working for all of five years, and were now only ten. They should be like the more fortunate kids in the world, going to school, playing out with their mates, not condemned to this life of unending struggle.

You'd expect them all to be crushed under their burdens, but a lot of the kids we met somehow had kept some hope alive, could be cheerful. We even heard some singing as they went about their filthy work. ActionAid has been setting up learning centres to give something of a way out for some of the kids. Inspiring work – I would have done anything to help. It makes your blood boil to see such deprivation in what's going to be a superpower of the twenty-first century.

The problems are so vast you think that nothing you could do would make a difference, but it does. I'll put on my campaigning hat now and say, 'Make a donation! Sponsor a child!'

After that enlightening experience, it was back to the wealthy West for more mundane things, earning the dosh. A few weeks later I said bye-bye yet again to Honey, and flew off to the States. I think she'd become philosophical with my comings and goings. Our way was to make the most of our precious time together. Indoors we'd play with her toys, or read books or watch DVDs sprawled together on the big sofa in the living room. Honey would get out her cute little china tea-set with real metal minia-ture cutlery and serve me an imaginary meal in her playhouse in the garden. We'd walk Missy in the park together, and stop for a picnic under the trees. I'd take her to meetings and parties and premieres that were suitable for children. I love the fact she's so confident, so articulate – much more so than I was at her age. She seems to get the most out of whatever she's doing, and I wanted her to have as many happy memories of us together as possible. When I left her with my mum, or Dan, or a combination of both, I'd ring her as often as I could. And of course she'd always know I was coming back.

So there I was for the umpteenth time at Heathrow Terminal 2, waiting for a flight to New York for the next series of *Dead Famous*. I'd shaved off the last of the Mohicans and was now completely bald. I had a bit of a confidence boost when a nice girl at the duty-free counter had done my make-up, and I looked pretty good, face-wise at least. I've got big eyes, and when they're made up I hope they'll divert attention from my bare scalp. My eyebrows and eyelashes were once again following the rest of my body hair and fading fast, but the girl managed to make the most of what I'd got. I could do with it, as over the past month or so it had been really sinking in how alopecia was affecting me.

Now here's something you probably don't want to know, women's nasal hair not being a common talking point – but that was going too! The whole experience was as if I was being rubbed out.

I'd been wearing a headscarf in the airport at first, but my head heats up so fast and it was uncomfortable, so I took it off. And got the kind of reaction I was getting used to. Stares, of course, some a sideways look, but others full on. What is it with some people? They're supposed to be grown-up but goggle at someone with no hair. So rude! I wouldn't dream of staring at anybody, whatever their condition.

I also encountered another common reaction – the assumption that my baldness must be the result of chemotherapy. A pleasant young man got chatting to me, telling me all about the charity walk he was going to do in Canada to raise funds for leukaemia research. I'm sure he thought I was a 'victim' myself. Bless!

Then there was the other kind of approach, up-front, almost aggressive. 'What have you done to your hair?' a fellow traveller demanded. To which I replied, 'I have alopecia. What have you done to your face?' Bit of a cheap shot, but he was asking for it. At least when a close neighbour had commented on my new look she'd tried to be nice. 'You don't need hair,' she said. 'You're beautiful anyway.' Then she added, 'You look like Andre Agassi' – which rather spoilt the effect. In fact I'd heard a lot of references to Duncan Goodhew, Matt Lucas, Patrick Stewart, Sinead O'Connor and the like. Baldies, full-time or part-time, of the world unite.

This trip was going to be rather testing as far as James and I were concerned – the first time we were spending a lot of time together with me bald. For all his protestations of love and his compliments, at heart I wasn't convinced that things were the same. While I could put on a show, my confidence had hit rock bottom. And, such is the way, I would interpret any little comment I'd normally shrug off as a mortal insult. If James wasn't particularly attentive, it wasn't because he was tired, or just not in the mood, it was because I was ugly and repellent. It was as if I'd lost a layer of skin along with my hair, I was so touchy. And being touchy doesn't exactly encourage harmony.

By the second night I was convinced that James couldn't bear the sight of me. I tried to talk, to explain how insecure I felt, but he just seemed to get more prickly himself. When I was alone I could-n't stop crying. I thought, All I want is just love and cuddles and happiness, and what have I been blessed with? Depression, baldness and insecurities. It was me. I was expecting too much of James.

Then the emotional weathervane would turn and we'd be close again – breakfast in bed, cuddles and kisses. That's my kind of morning.

So it seemed my life would be as much a rollercoaster as ever. Highs and lows. For all my resolutions after the overdose, the old patterns were repeating themselves.

There was one particular time during filming that encapsulated what I'd like in life. I wish I could have bottled it. In January 2006 we were on the trail of Billy the Kid, a trail that took us to Lincoln in New Mexico. We drove through spectacular mountain scenery, and arrived just as the sun was setting in a gorgeous display of colour. Lincoln is one of those Wild West-type towns consisting of just one street of clapboard buildings in the middle of nowhere, complete with rails to tie horses to. We were staying in the Ellis Store County Inn, a wonderfully old-fashioned place, quiet and cosy. James and I could see the mountains from our bedroom window.

I slept well for once and woke feeling refreshed. It was a day off for me, so while James and the rest of the team were out setting up shots and talking to local people, I was left to my own devices. I sat with my feet up on the tranquil porch all morning, reading one of the books I'd brought with me. I always make a habit of taking a travelling library – I never seem to have enough time to catch up on my reading. This time, I remember, it was a choice of Julian Barnes's *Arthur and George*, Lionel Shriver's *We Need to Talk about Kevin*, Patrick Süskind's *Perfume*, John Kennedy Toole's *A Confederacy of Dunces* and Augusten Burroughs's *Running with Scissors*. Desert island choice? *Perfume*, every time.

I joined the boys at lunch, in the company of a cool local cowboy who kept a wolf as a pet. He told us many stirring stories of coyotes, guns and horses. After lunch it was back to peace and reading for me, soaking in the atmosphere, then dinner in the main house in the evening. The inn was run by a delightful couple, Ginny and David, who were great company too. Then more drinks, more chat and finally bed for a deep, deep sleep.

There it is. Peace, perfect peace. Sunshine and wide skies, with a dramatic mountainous backdrop. Pure fresh air. No hassles. Time to read and just chill out. Good moods all round, good company, good food and drink.

That'll do me! I could even swear by the end of the day that my eyebrows were beginning to grow back. If there's a direct link between stress and alopecia, then it may work both ways. Anyhow, that day was a lovely oasis to keep in my mind when the weather changed, moods went sour, tempers snapped and hangovers were mean – and that wasn't just me.

\*

I'd been very relieved that I didn't have to hide my baldness for this series. I'd worried what the network, Living TV, would say, whether they'd make me wear a wig. But the exec, Richard Woolfe, just said, 'You can still walk and talk, can't you?'

It was weird filming myself, though, in black-and-white night vision as we explored creaky old buildings. My whole head seemed to glow. One time we were in a theatre, and when I looked in the viewfinder I realised one of my fake sets of eyelashes had dropped off. I looked like Malcolm McDowell in *A Clockwork Orange*. Inevitably, the eyelashes were found on the sole of somebody's shoe. 'Thought it was a spider,' he said predictably.

It was while we were on this trip that we had the closest I ever came to a supernatural experience. We were all staying in another hotel in the backwoods, and James and I were asleep in our room. At about four a.m. I suddenly awoke, convinced I could hear something. A rustling, a scurrying. I nudged James.

'Wake up,' I whispered. 'There's something in the room.'

He grunted and I nudged him again.

'Well, you're the martial arts expert,' he muttered, 'you go and see to it.'

I turned on the bedside lamp, and got out of bed. After more prodding, James joined me. The sound came again – we looked in that direction and saw a snack-food packet moving purposefully over the floor. For an instant James and I froze.

'There's something in that packet,' I breathed.

'I hope so,' said James. 'Open the door.'

He edged up to the moving packet and gingerly picked it up, with an expression of disgust. With one quick movement he flung it outside and shut the door.

'What did it feel like?' I wanted to know.

'Small and wriggling,' he said.

We hoped it was a mouse – too substantial for ectoplasm! Still, even with a rational explanation it was spooky, and I didn't sleep well for the rest of that night.

During that trip I lost track of the ups and downs James and I had. One moment drawn together, the next driven apart. And each time I felt rejected, I was convinced it was because of my baldness. At the end of filming I flounced off and flew alone to New York. I was on even more of a downer as I'd lost my passport, and the replacement had to have a photo of the new me. Passport photos are usually hideous anyway, and I looked like an alien with bulging eyes and a bulbous shiny head.

After checking in to the Meridien Hotel, I went straight to the gym and had a massage. Lovely. Then I hit the shops. Bought myself an iPod, laptop and camera. I retired to my room – chilled out and watched movies, trying to convince myself that I didn't miss James. But my public face crumbled and I couldn't stop crying. I felt lost and unsettled. Would my life never get on track?

I hadn't lost hope of change. I decided to mark that hope, in a tangible way. I'd have a tattoo – which works as well as anything as a symbol. It was my first one ever, a little star inside the top of my left arm. It made me think of my real little star, Honey.

I'd got the idea from Carlos, my make-up artist. When I first lost my hair I said to him, 'I could have something tattooed on my head' – I was joking, but Carlos was serious. 'Your head is sacred,' he said. 'Never touch your head.'

He himself is absolutely covered with tattoos, except for his head of course. I'd seen his little star and thought it was really cute. Since then I've accumulated quite a few more designs on my travels, though never a name. That would be just asking to have it lasered off when you and whoever fell out. I'm happy with my little star, a couple of others on my back, elegant scrollwork on my ankles and feet, a dragon inside my arm, and the Balinese god of comedy just above my bum, which seems appropriate. I think I'm on my way to being the Illustrated Woman.

That third series of *Dead Famous* was my last. Any trepidation I might have felt about more work was soon dispelled – I had more offers than ever, and they took me in a direction I could never have anticipated.

# ✳ 19 ✳

# A New Hope

I started my first chapter with *Star Wars*, so here seems a good time to call a chapter after Episode IV. You can't have too much hope – and my life, or at least part of it, seemed to be looking up.

To my surprise, some months previously Madonna Benjamin, a Maverick TV executive producer, had approached me about making a documentary on my alopecia, which would be part of the BBC's *One Life* strand. Nothing sensational, but a serious look at what it is, what it means, and how you deal with what I had come to understand is actually not an uncommon condition. Well, that was fine by me. As I've said, other people may choose privacy to get through an ordeal, and good luck to them. But me, I have to talk to people. If I've got alopecia, so have others. Let's talk about it, get things out in the open. I like to be in the thick of things, having a conversation. It's interaction, pooling knowledge.

So for several months a very sensitive, sympathetic crew followed me around, in London and Edinburgh, at home and at work.

The film started with me in a taxi, talking about the strange dreams I'd just been having – all to do with hair. It was the first time since I'd gone bald that I'd dreamed about my hair. I talked about forgetting I was bald, till catching sight of myself in a mirror. I think I'm used to it and then I'm brought up short all over again.

I made a point of spelling out just why I was dealing with the alopecia openly. I did try wigs, courtesy of a lovely woman I was introduced to, Michelle Chapman, who'd been bald since she was a kid. Michelle is all warmth and a big heart. She's been a huge comfort and encouragement, and understood what I was going through. We've become great friends – an unexpected bonus from the film.

Michelle herself chooses to wear a wig, at least most of the time, and has a wonderful collection to suit every mood, but I realised I just couldn't do it. It was like having something alien on top of my head – and I was sure it would blow away, or be crooked, and make me look even odder. It made me realise that if I didn't feel confident inside myself, no amount of wiggery jiggery pokery was going to help.

I tried to be honest about everything. I didn't want to tell viewers that it was no big deal, I'd got over it, as that wasn't true. As James pointed out in the film, I was more insecure than before – you never know how much you take something for granted until you lose it. It reminded me of that other documentary I'd worked on years earlier, about simulated blindness. Not that I'm comparing baldness with lack of sight: that would be ridiculously out of proportion. But there is a sliding scale of loss.

As I say, James featured in the film too, and I spoke honestly about my anxiety over our relationship. For all his support, I couldn't bring myself to believe that he wasn't affected by my baldness.

'Don't talk to any women with hair!' I'd say if he was going out without me. 'Not unless they've got beards.'

The film also showed me going back to Edinburgh with Honey and meeting my mum and my brother for the first time since I became completely bald. The cameras may have made them feel a bit self-conscious, but after the first shock (and my brother's inevitable comments – 'You look weird!'), they seemed to adapt to it. Though nothing quenches my mum's optimism – 'Surely the hair will grow back? She won't be without hair for the rest of her life, will she?' And she's a great advocate of wigs, my mum. She'd accept and support me if I grew another head, but still there's a wistful hope that I'll go out looking normal.

It was important to show the medical side, so the cameras followed me into the consulting room of Dr Ed Seaton, the dermatologist at the Royal Free Hospital. I think he was trying to break things to me gently, but when he said I had a 'disease', that shocked me. For some reason I hadn't thought of alopecia as an actual disease. Why that should make it feel worse, I don't know.

Dr Seaton explained that there are various types of alopecia, depending on the extent of hair loss and the duration. Because it's all quite mysterious, he couldn't give me a definite prognosis, but the upshot for me was that the chances of getting my hair back were quite low. Result: one crushed Gail, grateful for a crummy NHS tissue. Not the first time I've cried on camera, and not the last.

At least the doctor recognised that it's an emotive and distressing condition, and suggested counselling as a way of coming to terms with it. Did I take up the counselling? Did I bollocks. As ever, I'd try to cope my own way.

Not that I'd ever want to discourage anybody with alopecia to go it alone, or to think their prognosis was as disheartening as mine. There's some hope even for me – as Dr Seaton said, it would be fantastic if my hair grew back (and I could hear the unspoken 'Don't hold your breath'). Many other people get all their hair back eventually, or at least some of it.

The doctor did make a good point about 'alternative' therapies. All the masses of gels and ointments and creams on the market might make your scalp smell nice, but probably won't make the slightest difference otherwise. I tried a course of laser treatment myself, all a bit New Age, and I can't say that was conclusive.

To wrap up the documentary, I had to come to some kind of conclusion, and it was honest. In the end, I was going to have to come to terms with it. It was the old chestnut about hoping for the best, preparing for the worst. Of course I want my hair back, but if I cling to that and nothing happens, I'll always be disappointed. And a perpetual state of disappointment is no way to lead your life. Though I must confess, I'm not looking forward to getting older. I can just see myself with a head like a wrinkled wee prune…


The *One Life* documentary covered a charity bash to support Fairtrade Fortnight, an exhibition of photos at London's Oxo Tower. I'm a huge fan of Fairtrade – I'd always looked for

Fairtrade coffee and bananas – but this exhibition opened my eyes to all the other ways we can use our power as consumers to help the people, the farmers and workers, who actually produce what we consume. I was on a photoshoot to promote it, and as a gimmick, and for a laugh, I piled a lot of Fairtrade cotton on my bald head. The resulting photo was used on the official invites – one of my less conventional poses, and all in a thoroughly good cause. I met Maria Malan from South Africa who was totally inspiring. She manages a Fairtrade wine cooperative, where the workers now share in the profit of the farm. With the extra money, they've improved sanitation and brought in electricity. Sanitation and electricity – unglamorous maybe, but lifesavers. What we take for granted in this country!

The documentary was broadcast at the end of May, and got quite a good press. Viewers seemed to appreciate the point behind it – not just another telly ego-trip but an attempt to illustrate what effect a distressing condition can have. I was especially chuffed to hear from a nursing tutor, who said, 'We've started using your programme when we're talking to our student nurses about alopecia. It's good for them to know what it actually means to the patient.'

It was good to be taken seriously, to be allowed to deal with real issues. I never could have predicted this development, but it was opening up all kinds of possibilities.

I think it was the publicity surrounding the documentary that brought me to the attention of V Good Films. They asked me to go to Cambodia, for an investigation called *On the Baby Trail* – again, to raise public consciousness about an important issue, this time the trend for international adoption. And for me, it was an overwhelming experience.

I didn't know much about Cambodia's history before I went there, but soon learned about the terrible genocide in the seventies, when Pol Pot was leader of the Khmer Rouge and embarked on mass murder to 'purify' the country. When he eventually fled, he left devastation behind him, and thirty years on the people are still picking up the pieces. I was mainly in Phnom Penh, the capital, though still a place of dirt streets and rubble and stink. As I visited orphanages and talked to local people, I began to feel a connection, a solidarity. You might think I'm being fanciful, but I sensed a fighting spirit that reminded me of my homeland. 'No one's gonna keep us down – we're gonna get on with it!' They've got a long way to go to shake off that awful legacy, get out of poverty and get rid of corruption, but if anyone can make it, these people can.

And as for the children themselves, I absolutely fell in love with them. They're adorable. Like the street kids in Delhi, they manage to be cheerful and make the best of what they've got – and I'm not being schmaltzy here. They're an inspiration. I was in one orphanage that was looking after children who had HIV/AIDS or cerebral palsy, and struck a special chord with a little girl called Kanya. She was HIV positive, but still showed such spirit. She'd cut all her hair off as she wanted to be a boy. Why? Because girls have to do that graceful dance with the sinuous arm movements, while boys do the monkey dance – hands tucked in armpits, jumping around, going 'Ook Ook!' That was Kanya's idea of fun.

She loved me as I had no hair at all. 'We are cool,' she said, and I thought my heart would break.

I could have taken her – all of them – on the next plane home, but of course that's not the thing to do. What you do is help the fantastic people who are hard at work making a difference in the community. People like Father John, who with just twenty helpers looks after four hundred children, giving them a chance of a decent life. Or the rich businessman I heard about, who gave all his wealth to a charity called Friends. Here, they pick up children from the streets and teach them a trade – mechanics, carpentry, whatever will get them a job so they can support themselves. The charity also seeks out the wider family of children whose parents have died. Rather than fostering the orphans, it looks for grandparents, aunts and uncles, and helps them look after children who are not only bereaved but have suffered violence and abuse on the streets.

When I think of the contrast…I know there are needy children in Britain, and that's a disgrace in such a rich country, but there is the welfare state – not perfect but it does help. The children in Cambodia, and other parts of the under-developed world, have to rely on charities and committed individuals. I tried to remember these good people when others sidled up to me in orphanages and whispered, 'You wanna baby? Hundred dollars.'

Now I'm getting on my soapbox for a rant. Those rich celebrities who fly into a poor country and pick out a baby or two to take home are doing something disgraceful. They're taking children away from their own community, their own culture, even if the child still has relatives around who might be able to help. Rather than adding to their so-called rainbow families, those celebrities would be doing a real service if they set up foundations in the country that would help a lot of children. Name them after themselves if they want to flatter their egos. As it is, as far as I'm concerned, they're utterly bloody wrong-headed and selfish.

Right, back off the soapbox…Cambodia got to me. If ever I have a complete change of life, I can see myself coming here and working for one of those charities. What a fulfilling life…and just to show I'm nothing like a saint, wonderful landscapes and hot sun are part of the attraction.

I'd love to take Honey there one day. I fantasised about upping sticks and going on a kind of hippy trail with her, rucksacks on our backs, a big one for me, a little one for her. What an education for Honey – different people, different cultures, real life. With her enthusiasm, her curiosity, her willingness to make friends, she'd make the most of it. I could teach her the book learning…

Only a fantasy, of course, at least till she's grown up. If I whisked her away, I think her dad would have something to say about it. When I happened to mention that I'd quite like to live in Richmond – the Surrey one – he objected as it was too far away from where he lived. So Cambodia might be stretching it.

On a lower note, the divorce did get messy. Of course we agreed about Honey. Honey would live with me and Dan would have full reasonable contact. Honey loves us both, so that's the thing to do, no question. We came to a settlement. I don't want to talk about it but sufficient to say it wasn't one of the happiest days of my life, but the outcome has made me more determined to provide for my daughter.

Our divorce was finalised in October 2006, and we've managed to remain reasonably friendly, bar the odd friction. The arrangement suits Honey, she's used to it, so that's the main thing.

I had a huge party to celebrate the divorce. I hired the Soho Revue Bar – it used to be called Raymond's Revue Bar, famous for its showgirls and burlesque, and we did that tradition proud. We had pole dancers, trannies, drag queens…and I wore a huge red Afro wig. It was a hell of a way to mark the end of a marriage.

After the Cambodia trip, I was asked to take part in a new TV reality show. It was another one with a serious intention, like the 'blind' documentary. I certainly seemed to have shaken off any connection with the fluffier kind of show, and no one was happier than me. Who would have thought that losing my hair would open these doors! The idea here was to highlight the work of nurses in the NHS. Three media types – Janet Street-Porter, Sean Hughes and me – would work for two weeks as auxiliary nurses in Barnsley General Hospital. After basic training, we'd be assigned to specialist wards, all under supervision of course. The title said it all: *So You Think You Can Nurse?*

Well, actually, I thought I might be able to. I've always fancied myself as a nurse, helping people, and this was a chance to pick up useful skills. I'd wear a sensible uniform and needn't worry about make-up. I'd do a proper job for a change.

I was assigned to A&E, where the head nurse was Kev, a great bloke who kept all the nursing plates spinning. Margaret, a very experienced nurse who'd worked at the hospital for over twenty years, showed me the ropes – where the equipment was kept, how to clean stuff, all that kind of thing. Like Kev, she's from Barnsley, very down to earth and laid back. Quite a character, Margaret – with her bright red hair she's known all over the hospital, and she was brilliant to me, a real mentor.

The job was hard work, but how couldn't it be? I can cope with physical work – 'Gail, will you go and clean up that shit?' or 'Will you wipe up that blood? – no problem. What I wasn't expecting was the emotional toll it took. Every day I felt my heart could break. Seeing patients, often frail and elderly, who can't speak, who can't control their natural functions, or people badly hurt in accidents.

Of course the real nurses can't afford the luxury of tears, they have to get on with their jobs. Which isn't to say they lack compassion, far from it, but they have to keep a certain distance. Even so, there was a great feeling of warmth and good humour on the wards. One thing I loved unreservedly was the camaraderie – if any place needs teamwork, it's a hospital. It reminded me of being a runner, only with a rather more worthwhile purpose.

Amid all with work and pressure we could even have a laugh.

I remember one time when Margaret said to me in her strong Barnsley accent, 'Gail, fetch brufen fr'm kabnit.' Well, that's how it sounded.

'What was that?' I asked.

'Fetch brufen fr'm kabnit,' this time more loudly, and she bustled away.

Kabnit? Ah – must be cabinet. Fine. But brufen?

'Excuse me,' I asked sundry people, 'what's brufen?'

Turned out to be ibuprofen. My ignorance became a running joke. 'Gail, fetch brufen!'

I was staying in the nurses' home – and let me say straight away that they deserve better. This was not exactly high-end accommodation, but I suppose lack of money affects everything. I was sharing a flat with Sean Hughes, who'd also been in the 'blind' documentary. It was great to work with him again: he's a really nice, funny guy. We had a bedroom each, naturally, and shared a living room, where we'd sit on a battered old leather sofa after our shifts staring at the telly. That was all we had the energy for. We made a point of watching *Casualty*, criticising like the instant experts we were: 'Did you see that? She didn't wash her hands.' And, 'He's not putting that tube in right.' All the way through the programme.

We were like the Odd Couple, Sean and I, or Terry and June on drugs – no, not really. Unless you count tobacco. Sean is a chainsmoker and the whole place reeked of Benson and Hedges. But we got on fine, as long as he didn't expect me to do all the cooking and washing up.

The three-part programme was broadcast in the new year, and got quite a favourable response. I must say it was one of my favourite jobs ever. I loved it. I'll never forget my time there, and the friends I made. We've stayed in touch, I'm happy to say – in fact for my last birthday Margaret, Kev and the team sent me a card with the message: 'Hope you don't need too much brufen after your party!'

\*

Meanwhile, Fairtrade had asked me to go to Uganda to highlight its work with coffee farmers. This is a cause close to my heart, especially after the exhibition I'd attended the previous year. I went to the Mbale district in the east of the country, to look at a project called Gumutindo, which links a local co-op with a UK trading association that sources coffee for retail outlets, Twin Trading.

My God, it was hot. Baking. Even this sun-lover was wilting. I tried picking some of the beans myself, and realised just what bloody hard work it is in that heat. You sweat buckets, get filthy. I never mind that – I'm not one of those so-called celebrities swanning round the developing world wearing fancy clothes, long nails and make-up (soapbox alert!). When in Rome, live as the Romans do. Whenever I'm abroad with ActionAid or other charities, I rarely stay in hotels. What a waste of money. It's usually B&B or in someone's home. The streets may be dirt and rubble, the roofs corrugated iron and there's an all-pervading smell of sewage – but how better to get to know the people in a community?

The people who work hard, like the coffee growers, deserve a bigger share of the proceeds – it's a disgrace that the workers get so little. That's what Fairtrade is all about, of course, changing this balance for the better.

Back to tub-thumping – buy stuff with the Fairtrade label on it! Such a small act for us, but with huge implications for workers in developing countries.


When I got home again, life seemed to be settling down into something resembling a routine. James was now living with me and Honey in Belsize Park, and I must say he was brilliant with her; she adored him. I was still being asked to do charity work, though one day with a difference. I'd been working for the Children's Trust, and was invited to a reception held in its honour by Cherie Blair at 10 Downing Street. I must be getting posh. When I told Mum, she said, 'What about Trident?'

'For goodness' sake, Mum,' I said, 'I'm there to talk about the charity, not politics. I'm not gonna march in and say, "Hey, everyone, isn't the Iraq war a good idea?"' It's just a useful way to raise the charity's profile.

Paid work included voiceovers and corporate stuff (where I gave talks on anything from Successful Women to Childbirth) but was mainly on radio. I was co-presenting *The A List* on Sundays for Heart FM, which needed quite a lot of background work during the week – seeing new movies, recording interviews with the stars. That puts you on a kind of conveyor belt: 'You have four minutes with Mr Stallone!' Or 'You have four and a half minutes with Mr di Caprio!' The interviews are that tight.

You'd always bump into other presenters on the circuit of screenings and mini-interviews, and one day I'd sat through a particularly dull movie next to Zoë Hanson, who at the time was presenting Capital Radio's breakfast show. Afterwards I said to her, 'God, that was boring – fancy a glass of wine?' I was a bit more confident by now about being seen in public. In fact I blush to remember this time I actually made a show of being bald.

'Lovely,' Zoë said. 'Just the one, though.'

'Right,' I said. 'We'll have one glass of wine and then we'll go home.'

One glass led to another. I hadn't eaten much, and was getting tipsy. Some people sitting at another table recognised me – 'You're Gail Porter, aren't you?'

'Yeah,' I said, 'I think I am. I look like her anyway – same hair.'

Ha ha. My usual schtick.

We got chatting and it turned out they worked on the Sci-Fi Channel.

'Sci-Fi!' I squeaked. 'I've got a brilliant idea!'

Zoë was sitting there shaking her head. 'Oh Gail,' she said. 'Please don't say anything. After two large glasses of wine your brilliant ideas are so not brilliant.'

Undeterred, I explained my brilliant idea. 'I could be the new face of sci-fi!'

Silence round the table.

'Well,' I said, beaming round on all and sundry, 'I look like someone from *Star Trek*, don't I? I could be Patrick Stewart's Mini-Me!'

One of the guys said, 'Right, well, thanks, here's our card...'

Sorry, guys. But I still think it's a brilliant idea. And of course it took wine to bring on that show of bravado. In vino bollocks. At heart I was very far from being reconciled to my baldness. Against any expectation, it had given a new direction to my professional life, one that I loved, and that augured well for the future. On the personal front, though, I had to admit I was more insecure than ever. The rational part of me could say all it wanted about keeping a sense of perspective, that I was the same person, I've got the same face and body and mind, that I was lucky to have a beautiful daughter and could afford to live comfortably. Along with the new hope there were the same old worries – but now I'm bald and ugly with it!

It didn't take long for at least one of my worries to be justified.

# * 20 *

# Altered States

For some time now, I'd been taking a cocktail of drugs every day to control my thyroid and the bipolar condition. I'd grudgingly accepted that I couldn't heal myself. My doctor had taken me off Prozac and prescribed another antidepressant, which I suppose stopped the worst of the mood swings. Certainly I was able to keep up that fairly demanding schedule of work.

Gradually, though, I began to feel more and more wound-up. Not crashingly down, but very tense. I might be able to control myself when I was awake, but my dreams revealed my true state. They were more nightmarish than ever, so vivid that sometimes I felt I could see through my eyelids – a whole complicated mini-series where people were trying to get at Honey and I was hiding her, then there was a whole race of people who were bleeding and I had to save them...God, if a dream recorder is ever invented, I could give Hammer Horror a run for its money.

So much for recharging your batteries at night. I'd wake up in a cold sweat, muttering to myself and twitching my feet, and be afraid to go back to sleep again.

'I know when you're awake, even when you're not moving,' James told me. 'You're so rigid, I can feel the tension in you.'

One day I felt the need to relax so much that I booked a session at a beauty shop, for a facial and a soothing shoulder massage. Sure enough, I dozed off on the couch, though as the beautician told me later, my legs were still twitching. Suddenly I sat up straight, saying, 'Where am I? What's happening? Where's Honey?' A child had started to cry somewhere in the shop – 'Mummy! Mummy!' and I must have subliminally heard it.

'Don't worry,' said the girl. 'It's not yours – lie down and relax.'

Yeah, right.

The bad nights meant I'd often wake up feeling terrible, wanting just to pull the duvet back over my head and cry. But if it was a school day, I had to get up and get Honey ready. More than once, when I was by myself and everything got to me, I phoned Michelle, my fellow alopecian, crying hysterically. 'I can't leave the house!' She's wonderfully encouraging and understanding, and I always felt better afterwards. One time she said, 'Why don't you have eyebrows tattooed on?'

Ouch. No, not on the head, thank you. Some people have their eyelashes tattooed in too – now that would make me nervous. Mind you, permanent ink didn't seem such a bad idea one afternoon when I was shopping in Selfridges and caught sight of myself in a mirror. I'd forgotten to draw in my eyebrows! That makes me look odder than ever. Keeping my head down, I whizzed over to the make-up counter where a kind girl drew them in. I was mortified.

My first thought when I went bald was how James would react – my biggest fear was still how it would affect our relationship. For all his insistence that it made no difference, I found that hard to believe. I'm sure he felt hounded by my constant badgering: 'Do you love me? Do you still fancy me?' One day he must have been driven to distraction, as he snapped back, 'No!' Cue for hysterical weeping on my part. The sane part of my brain might have warned me that I was being somewhat counter-productive here.

'You were being mad,' James told me by way of explanation. 'I couldn't believe you still had to ask.'

I knew I was difficult to live with at the best of times – Dan had often told me so. One thing I do irritated the hell out of both of them. I can't leave a party or a dinner without thanking everyone concerned. I'd always say, 'It's the way my mum brought me up. You don't just say yeah, great, bye. It doesn't matter if it's three o'clock in the morning. You have to thank people properly, otherwise you're rude.' So for my most recent birthday bash, which I had in a nightclub, I had to thank the bar staff, the waiters, the man who painted my face with a dramatic geometric pattern – everyone. It took about an hour and James was seething.

'But they pulled out all the stops,' I said on the way home. 'They did a brilliant job. I couldn't have just walked out.'

James was not impressed. But I felt I couldn't change that part of my personality and still be me, any more than he could change himself and still be James. The conflict was a symptom. Now he was living with me, it was becoming increasingly obvious that we wanted different things. We were having too many phone conversations along the lines of:

Me: I thought you said you'd be home for dinner.
James: Something came up.
Me: What?
James: Oh, just something.
Me: Why couldn't you ring and let me know…

Or it might be:

James: I'm going away on Tuesday.
Me: Where?
James: Oh, just away.
Me: When will you be back?
James: Dunno – see how it goes…

I got the impression he wanted life on his terms, free to come and go as he pleased. Fair enough. I on the other hand had a child to look after, a house to run and bills to pay. I would have loved to piss off into the wide blue yonder just to hang out and chill, but that wasn't gonna happen.

I suppose I shouldn't have been too surprised when James left me a few weeks after my birthday.

Well, there you go. Shit happens, as I have so often said to myself. And hadn't I been expecting it? How could he bear to stay with a woman who was not only flaky but bald? And evidently turning into a nag. But James will always mean so much to me. I'd known him first as a friend, and for the past two years as a lover, a soulmate.

My heart was broken, of course it was. I missed him so much, it was a physical pain of loss. I was tempted to relieve it by cutting myself, for the first time in ages. One morning shortly after James left and when Honey was at school, I sat in the bathroom with my razor and sliced across my arm. There it was again, a sharp pain, a flow of blood…but this time with no relief. Just self-inflicted pain. I sat there dazed, feeling sick. What had happened to my quick fix? Why wasn't it working? I always knew with the sane part of my mind that it was a stupid, dangerous thing to do – it looked like the rest of my mind was finally catching up.

Looking back now, I think, Such melodrama! That's so me, wallowing in emotion at full throttle. But not for very long. I actually have a kind of defence mechanism, something to do with Scottish pragmatism maybe. When something bad happens I won't brood on it for too long. As the initial pain and shock start to subside, you have to get on with life. Never think what might have been. What's the point? I don't understand people who say, 'I wish I'd done that, I wish I'd done this, if only I hadn't gone there last Tuesday…' It's a waste of energy. I hate it when people ask me, 'Would you change one thing in your career?' Apart from the fact that I'm not a Time Lord, why would I change something that's brought me to where I am now? If something bad hadn't happened, there's no guarantee that something good would have happened in its place. You might have been run over by a bus.

I knew what my mum would say when I told her James had left: 'You can always get another boyfriend.'

To which at the time I could only say, 'I love him, I'm heart-broken, I don't want anyone else.'

Pause.

Then Mum said brightly, 'You know, I think you should treat yourself this week, do something really nice for yourself.'

'That's a good idea,' I said. 'I'll get a facial or something…'

'Och no, I thought mebbe you could get yourself a wee wig.'

She doesn't give up, my mum. In any case, recently I'd been a bit worried about her for a change. She'd been complaining of breathlessness and tiredness for some months, and it's not like her to complain about anything. At the end of last year she was finally persuaded to go to the doctor, reluctant as she was, and he prescribed inhalers. But her condition didn't seem to be improving.

So now I said to her, 'Why don't you go back to the doctor?'

'Och, I'll go when I'm ready. Don't worry about me – you just get yourself sorted.'

We both knew I would get myself sorted at some point. I'd already got through enough bad stuff. I should be used to it by now. And the fact I had got through showed I must have some kind of inner resilience.

I have a great friend, one of the bohemian survivors from old Soho, who always quotes that saying by Nietzsche when he sees me. Standing there, dapper in his venerable velvet suit, leaning on his walking stick with a crystal ball on the top, Mr Christopher Webb (I call him 'Mr' to Honey, and she calls him 'Spider') purrs at me in his mellow, modulated voice: 'Ah, my darling Gail, once again I shall remind you. What doesn't kill you makes you stronger!' He should know. He got up to all sorts himself in the old days, accumulating more wives than he can remember, and only had to stop partying when he had a stroke. I love those eccentric old characters – their stories are the best.

Recently I'd taken to rephrasing that old quote. As I'd tell Mr Webb, 'In my case, what doesn't kill me makes me...mental.' Though another great friend, Tiffany, showed her faith in me when she gave me a silver dragon pendant for my birthday. 'The dragon is a symbol of strength,' she said. 'And you're strong as a dragon.'

Well, something has helped me survive my life, and I don't just mean the overdose. The anorexia could have killed me, if it had gone on any longer. I dread Honey getting a distorted image of her body, getting caught up in that crazy fashion for size zero models. She's still so young, but I know girls – and boys – can develop eating disorders very early in life. Whatever caused mine, whether it was depression or anxiety or perfectionism or a controlling dad or any other of the commonly recognised factors, I've brought Honey up with what I hope is a balanced attitude to food. And to everything, in fact. I so hope that when she encounters upsets in life, she doesn't make my mistakes and try to cope by drinking too much and hurting herself.

In fact I intended to finish this last chapter with my hopes for Honey. I'd started writing the book to see just how I got to that awful place where I could have accidentally killed myself, and how I should face up to the future. I'd learn from my mistakes and celebrate my successes, then I'd draw some neat conclusions and wrap up my story – looking ahead, as ever hoping for the best, preparing for the worst.

Then something happened that blew everything apart. That made my worries over alopecia and relationships and work and money and everything else but Honey shrink into insignificance.

It was a Thursday afternoon. I'd finished an interview for an upcoming charity run, and had met a friend to go to lunch in Marylebone. Just as we were going into the restaurant, my mobile rang. I saw it was my brother Keith calling. Good, I thought. I always love hearing his voice.

'Hi,' I said brightly.

'Gail,' he said – and by his tone I knew something was wrong.

'What is it?' I asked. 'Tell me.'

'Mum,' he said, his voice choked.

'What?' I screamed.

'She's got cancer.'

# *Epilogue*
## *Mum*

'What are you saying? What do you mean? How can she have cancer? Why did the doctor just give her inhalers? Where's the cancer? How long has she had it? What—'

My questions tumbled out. I was shocked beyond measure.

Keith broke in. 'Gail,' he said. 'I haven't got any more to tell you right now. We just know that Mum's got cancer, of the lung.'

'The lung! What? Mum doesn't smoke!'

Keith just said, 'Aye, I know.' I could tell he was upset by having to break the news to me, so I tried to calm down, think clearly.

'Right, when shall I come up?' I asked.

'Not yet,' he said. 'If you come all the way up now, Mum's only gonna think she's on her death bed. And she's not. She's got a fighting chance – and you know what a fighter she is. I'll ring you when there's any more news.'

Let's leave it there, then. Thank God Keith was still living near Mum, sharing a flat in the city with his girlfriend.

By now I was crying uncontrollably, leaning against a wall. My friend was watching me anxiously.

'Please just get me a taxi,' I asked her. 'I've got to go home.'

Thank goodness Honey was at her dad's that afternoon; she wouldn't see me in this state. I sat down on a wooden chair in the kitchen, sobbing my heart out. My mum was suddenly so ill, so dangerously ill. But Keith was right, she is a fighter. She has an indomitable spirit. A wave of guilt rushed over me as I thought of all the fuss I'd been making about my own troubles. They were nothing. How could I have gone on about them to her? To think I'd been deliberately hurting myself, and all the time she was being hurt by something out of her control. This fucking, fucking cancer in her body...

'It's not fair!' I cried out to the empty kitchen. 'It's just not fair!'

Why should Mum get a smoker's cancer when she'd only puffed on a few fags when she was young, and that was to look trendy? It was Dad who was the chain smoker. Why hadn't the bloody doctor been more thorough in the first place? Her lung had collapsed, or was collapsing, and he'd given her inhalers. No one's a bigger advocate of the NHS than me, but was he really so overworked that he couldn't have spent more time, tried thinking outside the box? All that time – five months – lost.

It's not fair! All her life Mum's never done anything but look after everybody, she's the most selfless woman in the world. She even took care of Dad years after he moved out, when he'd been living with his girlfriend and his life had got tangled. She's so forgiving. There's no justice – why do bad things happen to good people?

There's no answer.


I tried to think rationally, to get things in order, so I'd be ready to leave when I had to. I phoned my agent, Debi, who's brilliant – she said she'd let people know. Keith phoned again later that day.

'Mum has an appointment with the specialist in hospital on Tuesday,' he said. 'They'll have all the test results by then. Till then she'll be at home.'

I had to work on Sunday, on my radio show, so there was Friday and Saturday to get through somehow. I was on tenterhooks and the days dragged. Honey and I flew up to Edinburgh immediately after the show.

When we arrived, Mum seemed her old self: 'Hello, darling!' Her boyfriend Derek was with her. For all the years they'd known each other, they'd kept their separate houses, which are only about three minutes' walk apart, but now he'd moved into Mum's home to help out. He's a grand man, like a big, cuddly teddy bear, a teddy bear with a beard, and he's got the Scottish work ethic in spades. Works all hours as a mechanic, when he's not with Mum. I love him to bits, he's wonderful. When we arrived, I could tell he was trying to put a brave face on it, but he was in a state. His first wife had died of cancer.

I remembered when he and Mum had first got together. Sometimes I'd ring Mum at night and there was no answer. 'Where were you?' I'd ask next day. 'I stayed at Derek's,' she'd say, giggling like a schoolgirl. I felt like saying, 'It's all right, Mum, you're old enough now.'

Mum's sister Susan, who lives on the outskirts of Edinburgh, had driven over to be with Mum, and Keith was there too. We were her support group.

In the middle of our mutual greetings, there was a piercing shriek from the other room.

'What the hell's that?' I asked.

'It's the cockatoo,' explained Mum, leading the way to the other room, where a brightly coloured bird was sitting on a perch inside a cage. I'm sure it had an evil look in its eye.

'Where did you get that from?' I asked. 'And more to the point, why?'

Apparently one of Susan's neighbours had died, leaving this cockatoo and a dog alone in the house. Someone had taken the dog, so Mum was giving the cockatoo a home. People, lame ducks, cockatoos...anyone or anything in need of help. The bird made a hell of a racket, though. Not my idea of a house pet.

On Monday we stayed with Mum, keeping her company, and trying to ignore the shrieking cockatoo. She's not even particularly fond of birds as pets, but Derek loves it. The next day we went with Mum to the hospital, all of us – Keith, Susan, Derek and me – travelling mob-handed like the mafia. We went en masse into the consulting room, and the cancer specialist broke the news.

It wasn't good.

The tumour was in a very difficult position to reach, right on a valve where the air goes in, or something. I couldn't quite understand the details. This meant Mum couldn't have an operation to remove it – it would be too dangerous.

'What's the alternative?' we all immediately wanted to know.

'Chemotherapy and radiotherapy,' said the specialist. 'Three days of chemotherapy every three weeks for three months. And ten minutes of radiotherapy every day.'

'What are my chances?' said Mum, upfront as usual.

The specialist replied. 'To be honest, a reasonable estimate is that you have a forty per cent chance of making it through.'

Only forty? That's sixty against! The rest of us sat winded, trying to take it all in. But Mum said, 'That's not so bad then.'

Right.

Then I said, 'When does the treatment start?'

'As soon as possible,' the specialist said. 'There'll be a bed ready this afternoon.'

So soon! We all trooped out, reeling. Mum seemed the most upbeat of all of us. 'Let's go home and have some lunch,' she said.

We had a bite to eat – not that anybody had much appetite – and helped Mum pack her stuff. Then we went back to the hospital, all except Derek, who had to work. Mum was signed in and I went with her to the cubicle where she was weighed and measured and had her blood pressure taken.

'Let's see,' said the nurse, adjusting the height bar. 'You'll be about five foot three, I'm thinking.'

'No,' said Mum immediately. 'Five foot five and a half, that's me.'

'Five foot three,' repeated the nurse, checking the bar. Mum looked crestfallen. 'Must have shrunk,' she said.

It's funny, but I used to have a similar illusion about my height. 'Five foot four,' I'd announce, if anybody asked. When I was measured at the doctor's, I'm more like five foot two. Mum and I must both think we punch above our weight – or rather height.

Now it was time for Mum to make her way to the ward. She must have looked like a celebrity, with all her minders. We were greeted by a nice, rather elderly nurse.

'Welcome to the ward, Mrs Porter,' she said pleasantly. 'Your bed's just along here, my dear.'

And she took my arm.

'It's not me!' I squawked, sounding for a minute like the cockatoo. 'I lost my hair, but I don't have cancer.'

'That'll be me,' said Mum, grinning.

The nurse was chagrined, but Mum laughed it off. 'Anybody can make a mistake,' she said comfortably. In fact she thought it was funny. It reminded me of the time we were in Monte Carlo and I wasn't let into the casino as I looked too young – and Mum thought it was a great laugh and just sailed in on her own.

I don't know how many other people could have a laugh in such circumstances.

As she was getting settled, Mum said to me, 'Right, you mind the house now.'

''Course I will,' I said. 'It'll still be there when you get back.' Adding under my breath, 'Which is more than can be said for that bird if I have my way.'

'What did you say?' she asked.

'Oh, nothing...'

\*

I made my way back to the house, and tried to feel settled in my old childhood home. I wandered about, looking at all the photos and articles about me Mum had plastered on the walls. Blimey, I thought, it's like a shrine.

One thing I had to decide was what to say to Honey. She wanted to know why Grandma hadn't come back with us. What could, or should, I say to a child who's only four and three-quarters? I'd always tried to be honest with Honey, answering all her questions in terms she could understand. That had worked when her dad and I had split. I decided not to hide the truth, but to explain it in the simplest, unfrightening way.

'Grandma has got a bad bug in her chest. It's called cancer. She has to stay in hospital because she needs special medicine. She can only get the medicine in hospital.'

'And the medicine makes her better?'

'That's right.'

'Then she can some home?'

'Yes.'


I was having to go back home the next morning, for work. I felt guilty leaving Mum, but everybody said it was good that I'd at least been with her now. That evening I cooked Derek a meal, and tidied up the house. There'd been a constant stream of flowers and cakes from friends and neighbours, who hadn't known where else to leave their offerings. The house looked like a cross between a bakery and a florist's. And I fielded all the phone calls, people wanting to know how she was doing. All of them spoke so warmly, so fondly, about her, her kindness, her generosity, her good humour. I'm not making my mum out to be some kind of secular saint. She's just an amazing, wonderful woman and I love and appreciate her more than I can say.

There was a touch of light relief when my old friend Charlie phoned. She used to live across the road from my mum, but had moved away. She always keeps in touch, though. She didn't have a chance to say much before the cockatoo let rip at full throttle.

'What the hell's that noise?' she asked.

I explained, and without hesitation Charlie said, 'I have only two words for you. Window. Open.'

Tempting, but Mum would kill me.

The damn thing showed its appreciation of me, though. When I was putting food in its bowl it had the nerve to peck my finger – drew blood. By the time I got home next day, my finger had swelled horribly, throbbing away. Did I get sympathy from one old friend who dropped round? No I did not. He just said, 'That finger's seen a cockatoo,' and laughed himself silly.


How can I even be thinking of jokes? I must get it from Mum. She's the first to play things down. She's always done it, always one for a laugh. But cancer is serious – you can't exactly laugh that away. Though as we know, Mum's a fighter, so there's a good chance. She shows the rest of us how to cope, with her optimism, her conviction she's going to beat this. She does have a gruelling road ahead of her, no question, but all of us who love her are with her every step of the way.

Thinking over my life, I've realised more and more just what a crucial part my mum has played in it, and still does. Loving and supportive, not afraid to criticise my madder antics but eternally forgiving, a true friend, never asking for anything in return. I get my strength from her, my resilience, my concern for others. The best bits, you might say. I've had a good role model. I want to pass on to Honey the values I learned from Mum, so she's well equipped to go out into the world when it's her time.

Meanwhile, I go on juggling home life and work. On the professional front, I'm up for almost anything like I always have been, happy to have new challenges. I do hope, though, that I'll have a chance to work on more documentaries. I love being involved with real issues, something that makes a difference in people's lives. I'll never stop taking an interest in what's going on – and will always jump at the chance to sound off about it! I'm still gobsmacked that this change of direction in my working life was sparked off by alopecia. Talk about unforeseen consequences...

If my hair ever grows back – and yes, at heart I hope it does – I don't think the process will work in reverse. No chance of ever being mistaken again for a manic TV presenter! I'm trying to come to terms with my baldness, just as I've come through the anorexia, depression and self-harm. I know some of the effects will always be with me, and I'll be on pills for ever. But I've learnt a lot from my rollercoaster of a life, and feel better equipped to cope with the downs – and make the most of the highs! Maybe even romance will be on the cards again (and there I definitely would be more confident with a full head of hair). But like everybody else I never know what the future holds.

As long as the present has Mum and Honey in it, that's enough for me.

# Acknowledgements

Thank you to everyone – you know who you are.